PUBLIC ASSEMBLY VENUE MANAGEMENT:

SPORTS, ENTERTAINMENT, MEETING, AND CONVENTION VENUES

PUBLIC ASSEMBLY VENUE MANAGEMENT:
SPORTS, ENTERTAINMENT, MEETING, AND CONVENTION VENUES

KIMBERLY MAHONEY, PhD
LEE A. ESCKILSEN, CFE, CHE
ADONIS "SPORTY" JERALDS, CFE
STEVE CAMP, CFE

International Association of
Venue Managers, Inc.

BROWN BOOKS
PUBLISHING GROUP

© 2015 Kimberly Mahoney, PhD, Lee A. Esckilsen, CFE, CHE, Adonis "Sporty" Jeralds, CFE, and Steve Camp, CFE

Public Assembly Venue Management
Sports, Entertainment, Meeting, and Convention Venues

Brown Books Publishing Group
16250 Knoll Trail Drive, Suite 205
Dallas, Texas 75248
www.BrownBooks.com
(972) 381-0009
A New Era in Publishing™

ISBN 978-1-61254-206-5
LCCN 2015943513

Printed in the United States
10 9 8 7 6 5 4 3 2 1

For more information or to contact the authors, please go to
www.IAVM.org

International Association
of Venue Managers

PUBLIC ASSEMBLY VENUE MANAGEMENT:

SPORTS, ENTERTAINMENT, MEETING, AND CONVENTION VENUES

PREFACE

Those who manage public assembly venues are continually challenged to operate them in ways that bring success to venue ownership while meeting the needs of those who utilize them. Accomplishing this daunting task is neither simple, nor is it consistent from venue to venue. Venues vary in mission based upon type, location, and goals set by those in leadership. In order to achieve the established goals, management must continually fine-tune their venue management skills and keep abreast of ever-changing social and economic trends in our society.

The one-time chairman of Chrysler, Lee Iacocca, once said, "In a completely rational society, the best of us would aspire to be teachers and the rest of us would have to settle for something less, because passing civilization along from one generation to the next ought to be the highest honor and the highest responsibility anyone could have."

The International Association of Venue Managers (IAVM) recognizes the importance of providing both educational resources and continuing professional development to those learning and practicing the intricacies of public assembly venue management. Since 1999, IAVM has supported its commitment to education through the creation of a Body of Knowledge Task Force that created "core competencies" for public assembly venue management. IAVM has previously published two editions of a textbook on the topic (2004 and 2009). For this new textbook, *Public Assembly Venue Management: Sports, Entertainment, Meeting, and Convention Venues*, we have endeavored to assemble as much new information as possible and organize it in a way that takes public assembly venue management education and professional development to a new level.

Scope of the Book

The objective of this book is to introduce the reader to the business of public assembly venue management. Such venues are found throughout the world, and, while their purposes and goals may be different, the management, principles, and practices are fundamentally alike. The reader should be able to glean relevant information that applies to venues of all types, large and small, local and international.

Organization

This book is organized in a logical sequence that takes the reader through the history and role of public assembly venues, followed by the other significant areas of venue management including venue ownership and management, business and financial management, booking the venue, marketing and sales, ticketing and access management, event and ancillary revenue sources, venue operations and services, event management and services, and safety and security. These chapters not only address the functions common to all venues but also illustrate how different disciplines apply to venue management. The appendices include numerous industry examples and supplemental information to support the learning process.

Benefits of the Book

Public Assembly Venue Management is intended for students preparing to enter the industry, as well as practitioners already working in the industry. It provides a strong conceptual and practical basis for understanding venue management.

Students

The textbook was written for both undergraduate and graduate students within sports management, event management, hospitality management, and other related disciplines. Venue management is an important topic for all students regardless of their career plans. Even if a student plans to be a general manager of a baseball team or work in corporate event planning, he/she needs to have an understanding of public assembly venues and how they operate. Therefore, the authors hope this book can serve as a continuing resource for students as they graduate and begin their careers.

Professors

This textbook was written to assist faculty in teaching the important theoretical and conceptual issues within the context of public assembly venue management. Recognizing the practical nature of this discipline, the authors have worked to incorporate their extensive experience and background into the text and companion materials. As a supplement to this book, the authors have developed an extensive collection of companion material to complement and support the educational process for which this book was intended. We recognize this text will be used for both undergraduate and graduate classes, and, therefore, the companion materials were compiled to address the varying needs of faculty members and their students.

Current Industry Professionals

This book has also been developed to serve as a resource for entry-level venue management professionals and to support IAVM and its professional development programs. It may also serve as a resource for those interested in learning about other departments within their venue or other types of venues and, therefore, enhancing their career prospects.

The authors of *Public Assembly Venue Management: Sports, Entertainment, Meeting, and Convention Venues* wish to thank all those in venue management around the world who have been willing to share their experience and knowledge to ensure this new textbook effectively addresses the core competences that cultivate effective public assembly venue management. We dedicate this book to the multitude of professionals who work passionately within this industry. They spend long hours away from their families so that the public they serve has the opportunity to see great sporting events, experience the very best musical concerts, gather in the very best meeting and conventions venues, and enjoy the arts at their favorite theaters. Our goal was to create a book that embodies the spirit of public assembly venue management's efforts to make every guest's event experience enjoyable and memorable.

ACKNOWLEDGMENTS

The authors would like to thank the staff of the International Association of Venue Managers, including Vicki Harwarden, Margot Angles, and Greg Wolfe, for the opportunity to undertake this project and their support during the writing process. We would also specifically like to acknowledge Dr. Rodney Williams for his support and guidance during the early phases of the project.

In addition, the authors would like to thank the following individuals for their assistance in reviewing content, providing industry examples, and responding to our many inquiries.

Lindsey Arell	Bob Johnson	Craig Ricks
Steve Bagwell	Jane Kleinberger	Bill Rhoda
Chris Bigelow	Chris Kibler	Frank Roach
Steve Brown	Leslie Lane	Frank Russo, Jr.
Chuck Cusick	Ted Lewis	Brett Scarbrough
Scott Dickson	Steve Luquire	Cait Schumann
Erik Esckilsen	Denny Magruder	Russ Simons
Adina Erwin	Brad Mayne	Carolyn Speicher
Mike Gatto	Norbert Mongeon	Robert Stewart
Johnny Harris	Michael Norton	Todd Stewart
Lance Hatfield	Joe Odoguardi	Mack Stone
George Hite	Wendy Oglesby	Mike Tanda
Aundrai Holloman	Jill Pepper	Carole Thompson
Lamont Holman	Steve Peters	Colin Thompson
Andrew Horne	Bill Powell	William Traurig
Peyton Jeter	Dave Redelberger	Kyle Trenthem

Hampton Inn & Suites Charlotte/South Park at Phillips Place

The authors would also like to thank their families for their support and encouragement, as well as their understanding of the many hours spent away from home while working on this project.

Left to right: Steve Camp, Sporty Jeralds, and Lee Esckilsen
Seated: Kim Mahoney

ABOUT THE AUTHORS

KIMBERLY MAHONEY, PhD

Dr. Mahoney is currently an assistant professor in sport management at the University of New Haven College of Business, teaching primarily in the areas of event and venue management. She previously served on the faculty of the University of South Carolina and The Ohio State University. Dr. Mahoney also has over twenty years of experience in various segments of the sports and entertainment industry and continues to do consulting work on a variety of special projects. She began her career at the Georgia Dome while in graduate school and then worked as an intern at the Charlotte Coliseum. Since that time she has been involved with the industry as a contractor, a client, and venue management. Dr. Mahoney has been involved in the opening of three new venues, including a convention center, a football stadium, and an arena. Her work as a regional manager with Show Pros Entertainment Services, Inc., provided opportunities to work in range of venues including stadiums, arenas, speedways, and amphitheaters. Dr. Mahoney previously served as an assistant commissioner with the Ohio High School Athletic Association (OHSAA) and as executive director of the OHSAA Foundation. Most recently, she served as the director of communications and program development with Columbus Arena Sports & Entertainment (CASE), which oversees the day-to-day operation of Nationwide Arena and the Jerome Schottenstein Center. Dr. Mahoney received her BA in communications from the University of Kentucky, her MEd in sport and facility management from the University of Georgia, and her PhD in sport management from The Ohio State University. Dr. Mahoney and her husband, Mike, reside in Connecticut.

LEE A. ESCKILSEN, CFE, CHE

Mr. Esckilsen is currently an associate professor at Johnson & Wales University in Providence, RI, teaching in the Center for Sports, Entertainment and Event Management. He stays active in entertainment and sports, venues and events, and development and management through his consulting company, ESVenues. During his thirty-year career, Esckilsen has been involved in the development and management of public assembly venues in both the United States and Great Britain. He has served as the executive director of six arenas, notably the pre-opening and management of the Mullins Center (UMass-Amherst) and the Manchester Arena (NYNEX-UK). He has generated more than $150 million in revenue and has booked and successfully managed more than 1,500 sports and entertainment events in his career. Esckilsen is a Certified Facilities Executive (CFE) awarded by the International Association of Venue Managers (IAVM). He is also a Trained Crowd Manager, certified by IAVM, and a Certified Hospitality Educator (CHE), certified by the American Hotel & Lodging Educational Institute, Washington, DC. Esckilsen was a co-author of *Public Assembly Facility Management: Principles and Practices*, 2nd ed., 2009, published by IAVM. Esckilsen serves as a chair emeritus for the Professional Golf Association Deutsche Bank Championship, played at the Tournament Players Championship Course in Norton, MA. He received his AS in recreational leadership from Dean College, his BS in recreation administration from Bowling Green State University, and his MS in recreational sports management from Indiana University. Mr. Esckilsen and Victoria Warnock live in New England.

ADONIS "SPORTY" JERALDS, CFE

Adonis "Sporty" Jeralds is currently a full-time clinical instructor at the University of South Carolina and also works in community relations with the NBA Charlotte Hornets. Mr. Jeralds is a native of Fayetteville, North Carolina, and graduated with a degree in criminal justice from Guilford College. He has an MA in public administration from UNC Chapel Hill and an MS in sport management from the University of Massachusetts. Mr. Jeralds began his career in public assembly venue management at the Hampton Virginia Coliseum and then accepted a position at the Charlotte Coliseum as assistant manager. In 1990, he became manager of the Charlotte Coliseum, a position he held for fifteen years. In that position Mr. Jeralds oversaw day-to-day operations and managed a $12 million operating budget and a staff of over sixty full-time and six hundred part-time employees. Mr. Jeralds is certified by the International Association of Venue Managers (IAVM) as a Certified Facilities Executive (CFE), a designation currently awarded to approximately 300 executives worldwide. During his career, Mr. Jeralds has helped coordinate such internationally recognized events as the NCAA Men's and Women's Final Four, the NBA All-Star Weekend, a visit by Mother Teresa, and a variety of major concerts and sports events. Mr. Jeralds is the author of three successful books, *The Champion in You* (2004), *Let Your Light Shine* (2010), and *Follow the Bouncing Ball* (2014), and in 2006, he was awarded the Harold J. VanderZwaag Distinguished Alumnus Award from the Sports Management Department at the University of Massachusetts-Amherst. Mr. Jeralds and his wife Teresa are the proud parents of Jazmine and Jacob.

STEVE CAMP, CFE

Steve Camp retired after a rewarding thirty-four year career in public assembly venue management, destination marketing, organizational management, and sports-related event management. Mr. Camp has been certified by the International Association of Venue Managers as a Certified Facilities Executive (CFE) and has distinguished himself as one of the industry's leading professionals in the Southeast. Mr. Camp has been involved with four major public assembly building projects in North and South Carolina and has successfully established organizations to manage and operate those venues. Mr. Camp learned his trade at the Charlotte Coliseum under the legendary Paul Buck and honed his experience at the Dean E. Smith Student Activities Center at UNC Chapel Hill, and he then returned to open the new Charlotte Coliseum. In 1989, Appalachian State University designated Mr. Camp as a Distinguished Alumnus. Mr. Camp served as managing director of Charlotte's Auditorium/Coliseum/Convention Center Authority from 1989 to 1997, overseeing the operation of four venues with an operating budget of approximately $23 million, and a full-time staff of over two hundred. While in this position, Mr. Camp also oversaw the construction and staffing of the new Charlotte Convention Center. Beginning in 2001, Mr. Camp served as president and CEO of the Midlands Authority for Conventions, Sports & Tourism, overseeing the construction and staffing of the new Columbia Metropolitan Convention Center in South Carolina, which opened in 2004. During his career, Mr. Camp has managed venues that have hosted the very best in the sports, entertainment, and meeting and convention industries. Those events include the 1994 NCAA Final Four, ACC basketball tournaments, major musical concerts, Broadway plays, and a variety of other high-profile events. Mr. Camp and his wife, Jackie, live in Charlotte, North Carolina.

CHAPTER 1

HISTORY AND ROLE OF PUBLIC ASSEMBLY VENUES

INTRODUCTION

HISTORY OF PUBLIC ASSEMBLY VENUES

TYPES OF PUBLIC ASSEMBLY VENUES

ROLE OF A PUBLIC ASSEMBLY VENUE IN THE COMMUNITY

FUNCTIONS COMMON TO PUBLIC ASSEMBLY VENUES

- Administration/Management
- Business and Financial Management
- Booking the Venue
- Marketing and Sales
- Ticketing and Access Management
- Management of Event and Ancillary Revenue Sources
- Venue Operations Management
- Event Management
- Safety and Security

COMPETITION AND FLEXIBILITY

SUMMARY

INTRODUCTION

Public assembly venues could be considered a modern-day reflection of the hippodromes, stadiums, or theaters of ancient Greece and Rome or the European cathedrals of the Middle Ages. Through the centuries, people have had the opportunity and the desire to congregate in a central place to watch some form of athletic contest, live entertainment, religious rite, political ceremony, or other compelling event. Today, communities continue to construct venues for these purposes, making them focal points of their communities because, as in earlier times, there are still powerful urges for people to assemble. The development and operation of venues, of which there are numerous types, requires a specific set of skills and abilities. These skills and abilities are necessary if a community wishes to construct wisely and operate successfully. As the cost of constructing venues has risen, it has become a difficult decision, often causing local debate, as to whether or not the community should invest resources in these venues or whether those resources are best directed to other more fundamental services provided within the community.

Whether or not the substantial investment of public funds required to construct such venues can be justified financially, many governmental and civic leaders feel they are an asset necessary to remain competitive with their rival cities and towns. They believe they are necessary to attract or retain one or more professional sports franchises, major touring concerts, conventions, meetings, trade shows, and performing arts events. Community leaders consider these venues to be necessary components that can put or keep their city on the competitive map. In addition, they view these venues as opportunities to enhance the community's quality of life by attracting businesses that could stimulate the local economy. No matter what reasons are presented for opposing the development of public assembly venues, they continue to be built, despite the ever-increasing costs, to take advantage of their value-added status in the community or region.

Public assembly venues, such as amphitheaters, arenas, complexes, conference centers, congress centers, convention/civic/expo/trade centers, theaters, special event sites, and stadiums have been developed in response to the needs of social communities to build permanent structures for public assembly. These assemblies can be for political and commercial activities, religious gatherings, sports spectacles, artistic exhibitions, musical or theatrical performances, or educational opportunities. On any given day, literally thousands of public assembly venues worldwide are open and serving the public because their community and business leaders have responded to the need or desire to have such an asset.

With all the positive reasons justifying why a public assembly venue is necessary, or at least desirable, it should be noted that very few of these venues operate profitably, especially when accounting for debt service, the principal, and interest payments on the cost of construction. Many, if not most, require some level of operating subsidy. Given the often staggering cost to build and operate modern-day public assembly venues, it is little wonder that public rather than private financing is most often necessary to get these venues built and operational.

HISTORY OF PUBLIC ASSEMBLY VENUES

Since the first public assembly venues of ancient Greece and Rome were built, more than 2,000 years ago, the transformation of the venues themselves has been constant. By all accounts, the Roman Colosseum was unique and versatile. It hosted a variety of spectator events including circuses, athletic events, and gladiatorial contests, and it incorporated sophisticated architectural and mechanical innovations. This open-air stadium accommodated approximately 50,000 people, while most other early venues were smaller in size and contained only basic amenities (Beck, 2001). Since the construction of those early venues, history records a steady process of making public assembly venues more accommodating to both patrons and users.

Roman Colosseum - Rome, Italy

As the development of public assembly venues progressed, the initial focus seemed to be on capacity. In the last fifty years, the idea has been to build your community's venue just a little larger than your competitor's venue. It seemed logical that having a larger capacity was fundamental in attracting the larger and more desirable events. The larger venues required a new focus by management on marketing and advertising, and they struggled if their market couldn't successfully fill the venue in question.

It was not until the 1920s that public assembly venues began to appear as serious contributors to the process of hosting events and the resulting economic development in North America.

By 1924, following the end of World War I, the United States had experienced five years of prosperity and a high rate of employment. People were moving off farms and into cities and lifestyles were changing. Commercial radio prospered, enhancing the citizens' appetites for entertainment. As a result of this changing focus by the populace, venues like the Rose Bowl and Hollywood Bowl in California, Yankee Stadium in New York, Soldier Field in Chicago, the Forum in Montreal, and the Warner Theater in Washington, DC, were built. Managing these venues became a significant business requiring special skills (Beck, 2001).

Rose Bowl - Pasadena, CA

In addition to the entertainment and athletic requirements, the desire for groups and associations to come together on an annual basis led to the development of venues designed to handle larger conferences and trade shows. The 1920s also saw the birth of convention and meeting venues to accommodate that growing need. The Great Depression slowed the development process somewhat, but as the nation emerged from that downturn, the Work Project Administration (WPA) built approximately thirty venues that included auditoriums, arenas, and coliseums (Beck, 2001).

In the 1940s, the number of entertainment events exceeded the number of sporting events. The desire to attract both types of events led cities to look to the public assembly venue as an avenue to gain both regional and national recognition for their community and at the same time tap into the resulting economic benefits. The development of the touring ice shows and the fact that circuses moved indoors in the 1950s established the public assembly venue as a major force in the quality of life options for a community. The popularity of rock-n-roll was also a major contributor to the rise of the public assembly venue and was an additional force in the 1950s and 1960s. The combination of large venues, new technology, over-the-top visual effects, and costumes gave birth to a venues-only genre known as arena rock (Beck, 2001).

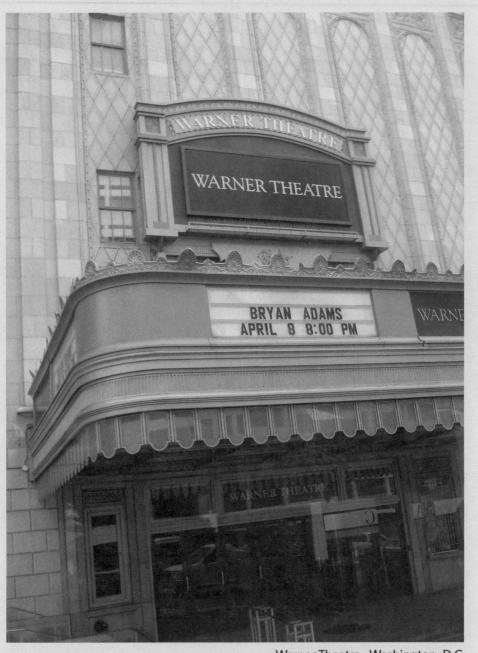

Warner Theatre - Washington, D.C.

Hollywood Bowl - Los Angeles, CA

As the public assembly venue industry entered the 1950s and 1960s, arena capacities, at least in North America, were nearing the 10,000-seat level. The Charlotte Coliseum, in Charlotte, NC, opened in October of 1955 and, according to *Look* Magazine, was the largest unsupported domed venue in the country, with a seating capacity of just over ten thousand (*Look*, 1956). During that period, outdoor stadiums were built to accommodate 30,000 to 80,000 spectators. Two of the most iconic venues include the Houston Astrodome, the first domed stadium, which opened in 1965, and the New Orleans Superdome, which opened in 1975 (Beck, 2001). During the 1950s and 1960s, convention and civic centers grew to between 50,000 and 250,000 square feet of meeting and exhibit space.

During this same period, auditoriums and performing arts centers began to emerge in the industry with capacities in the range of 1,500 to 2,500 seats. As competition increased among communities wanting to be in the sports, entertainment, meeting and convention business, the capacities and square footage limits continued to increase.

By the 1980s, it was not unusual to find arena seating capacities in the 20,000-seat range, stadiums expanding to between 60,000 and 100,000 seats, and convention and meeting venues measuring 1,000,000 square feet. Today, the largest venue is McCormick Place in Chicago, with over 2.7 million square feet of prime exhibit space.

Beginning in the late 1980s and early 1990s, the focus turned from capacity and square footage to amenities and opportunities for revenue generation. The increasing costs of construction combined with the cost of operating sports franchises compelled management to concentrate on revenue-producing options to carry both operating costs as well as debt service requirements. Special **premium seating** emerged, better and healthier food selections were offered, sponsorship opportunities increased, and business entertainment options began to drive the public assembly venue industry.

Charlotte Coliseum (Original) - Charlotte, NC

Today, the public assembly venue has taken on a new look and a new purpose. It remains both an opportunity for a community to improve its overall quality of life, while at the same time, because of the costs involved, it often becomes a point of contention among community leaders. These leaders are often faced with covering both construction and operating costs associated with the venues while continuing to meet the cost of providing basic community services to the citizens they serve. The balancing act continues, and while development of new or improved venues often slows during difficult economic times, there remains eagerness among community leaders to be active participants in the game of attracting events that generate positive economic benefits and increase the community experience.

There is little doubt that the competition among venues of every type is as intense today as ever, and there is no reason to believe that will change in the foreseeable future. For that reason, the public assembly venue industry requires knowledgeable and dedicated individuals. The study of *Public Assembly Venue Management: Sports, Entertainment, Meeting, and Convention Venues* is intended to satisfy that need and to develop the expertise necessary to ensure success for the industry in the years ahead.

Houston Astrodome - Houston, TX

Mercedes-Benz Superdome - New Orleans, LA

TYPES OF PUBLIC ASSEMBLY VENUES

Public assembly venues come in a variety of styles and functionalities. Therefore, in the information that follows, the term public assembly venue (venues) will refer to *all public and private structures designed to accommodate people who assemble for a common purpose.* The term public assembly venues will include, but is not necessarily limited to, amphitheaters, arenas, auditoriums, conference centers, congress centers, expo centers, convention centers, civic centers, complexes, exhibition halls, performing arts centers, theaters, stadiums, and special events venues. Public assembly venue forms may be defined as follows:

- **AMPHITHEATER**
  An open-air venue, which usually includes a permanent stage. Seating configurations may include fixed permanent seating and/or lawn seating. Typical Events: concerts, stage presentations, and community events

- **ARENA/COLISEUM**
  An indoor venue, with fixed and/or portable seats surrounding an open floor area. The floor area can be set with different event configurations. It may have a permanent stage, but most use a portable stage when required. Typical Events: basketball, hockey, other sports, concerts, ice shows, circuses, and other family shows. These venues may also have occasional conventions, trade shows, and meetings, but they are not primarily convention and exhibition centers.

INTRUST Bank Arena - Wichita, KS

- **AUDITORIUM**
  An auditorium is a multi-purpose venue that may have a flat floor, a stage at one end, and a balcony on one or both ends. Some auditoriums may have a sloped floor similar to a theater. Typical Events: small concerts, community events, religious meetings, small sporting events, and stage presentations.

- **COMPLEX**
  A combination of two or more venue types, presenting typical events as indicated. Typically, a complex operates under a single management structure and has combined financial reporting.

- **CONFERENCE CENTER**
  Primarily designed for small-scale meetings and conferences. They typically provide state-of-the-art educational meeting rooms and may also provide sleeping rooms.

- **CONVENTION/EXHIBITION/TRADE SHOW CENTER**
  An indoor venue with large exhibit areas, supplemented by various sized meeting rooms. Internationally, convention centers may be referred to as congress centers. Typical Events: conventions, trade shows, consumer shows (e.g., boat, home, auto), banquets, receptions, meetings, and major local events. Exhibition halls are most often part of a convention center and may contain up to 1,000,000 or more square feet of contiguous flat-floor space and ceilings 25 to 35 feet in height. However, the vast majority are more likely to have floor space in the 60,000 to 200,000-square-foot range.

Trade Show Floor

- **PERFORMING ARTS VENUE—CONCERT HALL/THEATER**
  An indoor performing arts venue or concert hall, usually with some type of permanent stage and permanent seats on a raked (sloped) floor, or possibly a center or thrust stage with permanent and/or portable seating. Typical Events: concerts, symphony, drama, dance, touring Broadway shows, ballet, opera, stage presentations, and other community events. These venues may also have conventions and meetings, but they are not primarily convention and exhibition centers.

- **SPECIAL EVENT VENUE**
  An indoor or outdoor venue designed to accommodate a specific activity or event, such as tennis stadiums, velodromes, curling rinks, natatoriums, horse and dog racetracks, and motor speedways. These venues, like most public assembly venues, are on occasion used to host activities or events not related to their primary purpose.

- **STADIUM**
  A large venue, either open-aired or domed, with fixed seats and/or bleachers surrounding a field area. Typical Events: baseball, football, soccer, major concerts, spectacles, and major civic events. A large domed venue with full-field football/ soccer capability is considered a stadium even though its event schedule may include exhibits, basketball, family shows, and other arena-type events.

Lucas Oil Stadium - Indianapolis, IN

ROLE OF A PUBLIC ASSEMBLY VENUE IN THE COMMUNITY

Considering the substantial economic investment a community makes in its public assembly venue, the role that venue takes in the overall quality of life in that particular community is extremely important. How it is managed, the events it is able to host, the financial viability of the venue, and the overall perception of that venue by the local citizenry is of the utmost importance. Since the community has invested so much public money, it is always advisable and particularly helpful if those who have invested local taxes can see, or at least have a good feeling about their community's investment, and believe that the investment is paying dividends for both the local economy and to them as taxpayers.

FUNCTIONS COMMON TO PUBLIC ASSEMBLY VENUES

Exactly how a venue is organized is determined by factors such as ownership, purpose and mission, and venue type. Nonetheless, all venue managers face certain common tasks. For example, the manager of an arena and the manager of a performing arts center are both concerned with **crowd management** and **risk management.** Some of the commonalities date back to ancient history. Many of the operational areas considered vital by the manager of the Roman Colosseum when staging gladiator contests are also considered vital by the manager responsible for staging a rock concert in a modern amphitheater or other type of public assembly venue.

Public assembly venues usually operate within the scope of a written statement of purpose or a **mission statement**. They formulate these mission statements to help governing boards, management, and staff maintain focus on central goals and objectives. Mission statements often identify the purpose of the venue and provide a basis for making policy decisions regarding issues of scheduling, booking priorities, tenant oversight, reporting, and budget development.

COLUMBIA METROPOLITAN CONVENTION CENTER – Columbia, SC

To provide superior operations management, marketing, and facility maintenance for the successful implementation of events related to meetings, conventions, trade shows, sports, entertainment, and other special occasions. Designed to blend in with the existing architectural fabric of the historic Vista, the primary objective of the facility is to stimulate economic growth to the Columbia Riverbanks Region as a preferred venue for a diverse range of both public and private events.

FOX THEATRE – Atlanta, GA

We are dedicated to preserving and sharing the Fox Theatre.

HONG KONG CONVENTION AND EXHIBITION CENTRE – Wanchai, Hong Kong

To consistently deliver superb customer care through the provision of world-class facilities and services with a responsive and enthusiastic team of professionals guided by a high level of integrity, pride, passion, and industry knowledge.

JEROME SCHOTTENSTEIN CENTER – Columbus, OH

The Schottenstein Center is committed to being an industry leader, nationally recognized as the finest facility of its kind. We strive to provide the best in service to clients and guests. We will provide students with educational, leadership, and employment opportunities as we reach out to the campus and central Ohio community through the presentation of world-class athletic, entertainment, and other related events. We will operate in a fiscally responsible manner and strive to achieve the highest ethical standards. We celebrate uniqueness through the presentation of diverse events and programming, while providing a safe and welcoming environment for staff, guests, and participants. We will support the mission of The Ohio State University and the Department of Athletics. We will work together as a team to achieve excellence beyond expectation.

SEGERSTROM CENTER OF THE ARTS – Costa Mesa, CA

Segerstrom Center for the Arts exists to present a wide variety of the most significant national and international productions of music, dance, and theater to the people of Southern California. We believe that experiencing the best in the performing arts adds meaningfully to the quality of life in our community and are committed to providing an unsurpassed attendance experience. In conjunction with its artistic mission, Segerstrom Center is also entrusted with stewardship of its world-class facilities, which provide the performance base for its resident companies.

By 2025, the world's finest artists and companies will seek to perform first on our stages because we have cultivated the nation's most enthusiastic, loyal, and knowledgeable audiences for important music, dance, and theater. The caliber of our presentations will be second to none, complemented by innovative programs of community education and engagement. By bringing together existing and new audiences to experience programs that excite the creative tension between tradition and innovation, the Center will be recognized by everyone as the dynamic cultural and civic center of our community. Infused with an engaging energy and welcoming to all, the Center will stand as a national model for an artistically ambitious, financially sustainable performing arts center.

Figure 1-1 : **Sample Mission Statements**

Rarely does a public assembly venue operate in a single purpose environment. Twenty-first-century governing bodies and managers, therefore, need a comprehensive knowledge of how these operating dynamics affect their venues as well as understanding the effects they have on those with whom they compete.

Successful venue oversight demands diligence and creativity. Publicly owned venues, especially those constructed with a **feasibility study** that projects increased tourism revenue, usually require special taxes placed on the hospitality industry for assistance in covering projected operating deficits. Recognizing the financial impact that public assembly venues provide, some communities create special taxes or taxing districts to subsidize operating budgets of public assembly venues. An example of such an approach is the hotel/motel "bed" tax or **transient occupancy tax (TOT)** assessed to out-of-town visitors, thus saving local citizens from the need for any additional tax. Other options include an entertainment district tax assessed much like a sales tax or designation of a surrounding area as a **Tax Increment Financing District (TIF)**, where local businesses that directly benefit from the events in the venue are assessed special taxes (Peterson, 2001). Regardless of the method, these supplemental funding approaches reflect recognition by the community that there are other far-reaching quality-of-life values that the venue provides to community residents.

Public assembly venue managers and their governing bodies must be willing to consider a reasonable risk based on their risk tolerance level and legal requirements. Thus, like other entrepreneurs, the venue manager might be allowed to organize, operate, and assume the risks inherent to in-house promoted events. Since the success of the public assembly venue hinges on the business and political savvy of its manager, it is imperative for the owner and governing body to employ managerial personnel who possess business skills and political insight. The owner, through the **governing body**, must then cultivate and nurture an appropriate entrepreneurial environment that will enable the manager to exercise those business and political skills.

The public assembly venue manager, regardless of the type of venue, is responsible for nine core functions that are common to all venues. Those core functions are:

1. Administration/management
2. Business and financial management
3. Booking the venue
4. Marketing and sales
5. Ticketing and access management
6. Management of event and ancillary revenue sources
7. Venue operations management
8. Event management
9. Safety and security

While different public assembly venue configurations may have unique characteristics, these nine functions are vital to any operation. Additionally, the manager must act as a leader to ensure that each functional area is properly staffed and performs at the level necessary for the venue to achieve its performance objectives.

ADMINISTRATION
- Prepare reports / presentations for owners
- Monitor the operating budget
- Oversee daily building activities
- Service contracts & tenant leasing issues
- Staff recruitment & training
- Performance evaluations
- Enforce employment policies & procedures
- Recordkeeping
- Negotiating labor agreements
- Negotiation & oversight of 3rd party vendor agreements

FINANCIAL
- Prepare/monitor operating & capital budgets
- Financial reporting
- Internal audits
- Inventory control / records
- Bookkeeping & accounts payable / receivable
- Tax payments / reporting
- Purchasing
- Payroll
- Human resources
- Risk management & insurance
- Cash handling policies / procedures
- Event settlement
- Manage automated teller machines (ATMs)

BOOKING
- Rental rate schedules
- Developing user priorities
- Negotiating tenant leases
- Negotiating individual event leases
- Booking events
- Promoting & co-promoting events

TICKETING
- Ticket inventory & distribution issues
- Occupancy & seating configuration
- Financial accounting & controls
- Staffing, training & supervision
- Ticketing policies & procedures
- Tax collection & remittance
- Secondary market issues

MARKETING & SALES
- Market venue to prospective tenants
- Market venue to promoters & prospective events
- Market venue to general public & businesses
- Marketing of events
- In-house advertising agency
- Advertising signage sales
- Group ticket sales
- Sponsorships
- Promotions
- Public relations
- Media relations

ANCILLARY SERVICES / REVENUE
- Food & beverage service / concessions
- Catering sales
- Merchandise sales
- Parking
- In-house business revenue
- Equipment rental
- Premium services
- Customer service issues
- Inventory controls

OPERATIONS & EVENT MANAGEMENT
- Physical plant repair & maintenance
- Venue equipment maintenance
- Housekeeping
- Utility management & control
- Event management
- Conversions / changeovers
- Sustainability initiatives
- Staging, light & sound
- Information technology
- Capital improvements
- Shipping & receiving

SAFETY & SECURITY
- Crowd management
- Event safety & security
- Building safety & security
- Customer / employee safety & security
- Emergency preparedness

Figure 1-2 : **Outline of Daily Operational Areas Pertinent to All Types of Public Assembly Venues**

Simply stated, the successful venue manager must make a significant commitment to focus on these nine core functions and to establish in each a clear understanding of their collective importance to the ultimate goal of producing an effective, efficient, and visibly satisfying operation for the owner, management, and community. A description of these nine core functions follows.

Administration/Management

Regardless of venue ownership, the on-site management personnel are typically under the supervision of a general manager, who may also be known as executive director, managing director, vice president, or some similar title. This individual must wear a multitude of hats and be a conduit between the venue and the community, a liaison between the governing body and the venue's staff, and an administrative supervisor, mentor, and leader. Although balancing available resources to achieve the venue's mission is the general manager's primary responsibility, a successful manager must also become the governing body's prime resource, the user's partner, the staff's leader, and the guest's advocate and sympathetic ear.

A successful general manager not only directs the day-to-day operations of the venue, but must also devise a realistic but ambitious goal for the future of the venue and its staff. The manager must have the ability to convey this vision of the future to the venue's ownership and to its entire organization. Without this vision and the skills to communicate it, the venue risks lagging behind industry trends and losing both its competitive edge in the marketplace and its leaders who depart for opportunities with more progressive organizations.

In most instances, the venue manager must ensure all policies and procedures that govern the business activities of the venue are followed, including state and federal regulations. In addition to effectively managing personnel, a venue manager needs a working knowledge of sound business practices, strong negotiating skills, effective communication abilities, and political savvy. Venue managers must also have a passion for the industry and a desire to contribute to the quality of life in the community.

Business and Financial Management

Every venue has a business dynamic that includes budgeting, financial accounting, fiscal management, **accounts payable, accounts receivable**, payroll, human resources, purchasing, asset management, and inventory and audit control. These functions may be under a department called the business office, finance/accounting department, or some other similar name. The accounting and auditing aspects of revenue-generating activities normally come under the direct supervision of the business office. Business offices often provide accounting and auditing services to the public assembly venue's ticketing activities, especially if financial transactions with the tenant are tied to ticket sales and event settlements. The fiscal management function of a public assembly venue must focus on the financial performance of the venue as a business, just like any other business.

Public assembly venues, regardless of type, should have a business office, or at least one designated individual available and prepared to handle large amounts of cash. Collecting and accounting for cash, checks, and credit card receipts from sales transactions involving the venue's revenue sources (e.g., ticket sales, concessions, merchandise, and parking), making bank deposits, executing wire transfers, reconciling bank statements, and completing post-event financial settlements with event **promoters** are typical activities performed by business offices or the venue's designated individual responsible for financial matters. While far from an ideal situation, the designated individual might be the ticket office manager, the food and beverage manager, the merchandise manager, or the parking manager, whose responsibilities include the financial accounting of each of those respective revenue-generating functions. Other business office responsibilities may include the preparation, distribution, collection, and reconciliation of cash boxes used in the concessions and other revenue-generating operations. Alternatively, these tasks may be handled directly by the involved department manager. The final responsibility for implementing financial controls lies with the venue's business manager or finance director, who ultimately reports to the owner or governing authority through the general manager or executive director.

Historically, cash was the most frequent form of payment by patrons of public assembly venues for tickets, concessions, parking, and merchandise. Ticket sales, however, have moved steadily toward electronic (online) and credit purchases. The consuming public's prolific use of credit cards to pay for telephone, online, and on-site purchases has resulted in the majority of revenues being generated through credit card transactions in most public assembly venues. One new trend in ticket sales involving credit card transactions can be described as up-selling or bundling, wherein customers are encouraged to pre-pay for parking, concessions, and/or merchandise at the time they order event tickets. This is an example of generating additional ancillary revenues by providing convenience to the customers attending events in public assembly venues.

Booking the Venue

Booking is a process designed to maximize yet safeguard the venue's two most important commodities: time and space. Efficient management of these elements is vital to expanding the number of event bookings and the number of potential revenue streams. Booking is the process that results in the programming of a venue's master calendar and should take into consideration the venue's mission statement along with the needs of its primary tenants and those of the entire community.

When done in a creative yet disciplined manner, the task of booking will yield a diverse program of events that meets the needs of the entire community, including the venue's stakeholders, served by the public assembly venue. Booking involves managing the venue calendar with uncompromising integrity, establishing booking priorities, sequencing events into the calendar to yield the maximum number of event days, working closely with the local convention and visitors bureau (CVB), avoiding booking errors, and respecting the right to freedom of speech of artists and event producers as defined in the First Amendment to the US Constitution.

Marketing and Sales

Depending on the venue type, profitable enterprises may include the selling of venue assets such as advertising signage, sponsorships, and space and time. Regardless of the type of public assembly venue, the effective use of marketing, advertising, and promotion is crucial in order to present the venue favorably to potential users and customers. Though marketing can be defined in many ways, within the context of public assembly venue management, it can be interpreted to include the process of searching out and identifying potential business for the venue. Marketing also might include involvement in the process of negotiating an agreement for booking an event.

There are two basic areas addressed by marketing in the public assembly venue industry. First, the venue must be marketed to the industry in order to secure a diverse schedule of events. Marketing of the venue, as well as the marketplace it serves, is directed at potential users, such as event promoters, nonprofit community organizations, and meeting planners who provide the supply of events to the public assembly venue industry. The second area is the marketing of the events to the community, which consists of potential ticket buyers, fans, and event attendees. This latter marketing effort is directed toward target audiences and advertises the specific activity, time, place, date, and price.

In addition, it is very important to market the venue and its programs internally to staff, the governing body, owners, tenants, and other major stakeholders. These various individuals and groups need to understand the vision, mission, goals, and objectives of venue management and how they apply to the specific venue. The operating and event staffs are the individuals on the front line interacting with the guests. They can make or break the venue's image, program, and ultimate success. Prudent venue managers ensure that the venue's staff, governing body, owners, tenants, and major stakeholders clearly understand the overall objectives of the venue's programming and marketing strategies.

Ticketing and Access Management

Ticketing services and ticket office management have evolved greatly throughout the history of public assembly venue management. This evolution has seen the use of color-coded and/ or numbered pottery shards, specially minted coins, pre-written or pre-printed hard tickets, and computerized electronic tickets utilizing bar code technology. Regardless of the phase of evolution, the public assembly venue manager uses the ticketing services for financial accounting and inventory control. Issuing tickets helps the public assembly venue manager address issues common to virtually every venue type. These issues include managing and controlling admission to the venue while providing a level of financial accountability for the parties involved with presenting and managing the event.

When used to control access to the public assembly venue, tickets provide for the safe, efficient movement of people while communicating venue and event-specific information directly to the customer and, in some cases, providing a source of revenue to the venue through advertising opportunities. When used in connection with the process of financial accounting, ticketing services provide management with an accurate accounting of the revenue generated for each ticketed event held in the venue, as well as an accounting of all taxes collected on behalf of a local or state authority and any ancillary revenues generated through service charges, venue fees, or surcharges on behalf of the venue.

The venue ticket office manager works closely with event promoters and tenants to establish the ticket price of the various seating locations within the venue. This is described as valuing a seat location and usually involves a process referred to as **scaling the house**.

Ticket office managers also work closely with those same clients and the venue's operations manager to ensure all seating in the public assembly venue is in compliance with the Americans with Disabilities Act (ADA) in the United States, or similar laws in other countries. Providing appropriate signage, appropriate numbers of seats in each price category, making seats accessible via elevators and ramps, having assisted-hearing devices available, designating seating locations for visually impaired guests, providing spaces for wheelchairs— with seating for companions of guests with disabilities—and having seats with lifting armrests, or no armrests at all, are but some of the accommodations required by the ADA which can be addressed through effective ticketing services.

The Internet and computerization of ticket distribution transformed the manner in which ticketing services are provided to customers of public assembly venues. Today's customer expects direct access to the ticketing system twenty-four hours a day, seven days a week. They have the ability to shop for tickets, select seat locations, and download those selections to their personal electronic device. The trend of vending tickets at higher than face value through the **secondary resale market** is common and forces venue managers, event promoters, and sports teams to reconsider their ticketing prices, as well as their ticket distribution systems.

As stated previously, the future of ticketing services involves generating ancillary revenues through the sale of products and services at the time of the ticket transaction. Ticketing services will continue to be impacted by advancements in technology and the consumer's demand for newer, more advanced conveniences.

Management of Event and Ancillary Revenue Sources

The public assembly venue, like all retail businesses, faces the challenge of attracting customers with discretionary time and income to maximize sales of **ancillary services**, thus generating revenues. Creating product demand and repetitive sales for the special commodities available at public assembly venues requires a unique type of salesmanship and entrepreneurship. Meeting and exceeding the customer's expectations whenever possible is one of the goals for every venue manager in providing ancillary event services. Often, these services are delivered through a third-party contractor using part-time temporary labor, which adds an additional dimension to the responsibilities of the venue manager. Whether these ancillary services are provided to the venue's customers through in-house staff or through a third-party contractor, the goals should be to deliver a value-added experience through the venue's ancillary services.

The most common ancillary services offered to event attendees include food and beverage services, merchandise/novelty sales, and parking services. Each of these ancillary services generates revenue for the venue.

Some public assembly venues may have a wide variety of ancillary services available to their tenants in addition to their event customers. Services such as equipment rental, freight handling, utility services, telephone and Internet connections, decorating services, event marketing, and advertising are offered to assist the tenant in successfully presenting their event while providing the venue manager an opportunity to generate additional revenue.

The scope and number of possible ancillary services are very broad and many contribute significantly to the venue's overall revenues. Creative entrepreneurship coupled with consistent quality customer service will ensure that the venue's ancillary resources enhance the guests' and tenants' event experience while elevating the bottom line of the public assembly venue's overall budget.

Venue Operations Management

The venue's operations department is responsible for general maintenance, housekeeping, engineering, heating, ventilation, and air conditioning (HVAC), utility usage management, and safety and security, as well as **event production** requirements. For most touring attractions, it is not economical to bring their own production personnel, such as loaders, riggers, **stagehands**, deckhands, and forklift operators to the venue, to say nothing of potential difficulties with local unions. Consequently, venues are expected to provide these skilled personnel to meet the production needs of those events requiring such services.

Thus, the venue's operations department is critical to ensuring that "The show must go on!" In busy venues with frequent **changeovers** of multiple types of events (e.g., basketball, hockey, concerts, rodeo, wrestling, motor sports, and **exhibitions**), a skilled and motivated operations department carries enormous responsibilities in meeting the venue's contractual obligations and providing competent, quality customer service in a timely and efficient manner.

Event Management

How successful venues carry out the events they schedule is often the determining factor in the level of success the venue is able to attain. Event management becomes a very important process that the venue manager and staff must address, and accomplishing that process takes ample time and strategic planning. Simply hosting high-profile events in the venue is not enough to ensure success, especially if those attending do not perceive the events to be well planned and smoothly executed. Customers today pay substantial ticket prices to attend events, and they expect the experience will be on a level equal to the price they paid for access.

For a venue to succeed at event management, all elements of the venue's operation must work together to make sure every detail is handled as if it were the most important to the overall success of the event. Operations must make sure that the event's set-up is as planned and at the same time meets all codes and regulations required. Ticketing must make sure all seats have good sightlines and capacities are not exceeded. Food and beverage service must make sure ample amounts of all products are available at the right times and locations. All safety and security issues must be addressed and employees advised of any and all concerns about the event and any possible safety or security issues. Parking and traffic security must handle the expected traffic flow and make sure that guests **ingress** and **egress** as quickly and as safely as possible.

All event staff must be trained on how to meet and greet guests, handle seating issues, and understand safety procedures in case of an emergency. Oftentimes, the staff can eliminate real problems by knowing and applying the procedures established by management on issues they are likely to encounter.

The bottom line is that public assembly venues present events. Each event is equally important to the success the venue hopes to attain. If venue management employs proper strategic planning, staff is properly trained, and all other **event operations** are handled correctly, the venue should enjoy the success that results from quality event management.

Safety and Security

As previously discussed, regardless of the type event, a venue's goal is to keep guests, users, and employees safe. Each venue must recognize safety and security issues, train their employees to minimize those risks, and be prepared to execute predetermined plans should safety and security issues arise. In order to achieve this goal within the overall management strategy, venue managers must incorporate complete safety and security planning to guard all assets and personnel. Management must also evaluate the risks and threats associated with venue operations during **event production**. This is an ongoing process within which there is always potential for threats, which may present themselves in a variety of forms and degrees of severity.

The safety and security of patrons, employees, and users is of the utmost importance to the venue's ownership, management, and community where the venue is located. In today's world, the venue manager must take every precaution, consider every possibility, and prepare for a variety of different challenges that often occur when large numbers of people gather in one place. Effective safety and security procedures, while often transparent, are important to the venue's success.

COMPETITION AND FLEXIBILITY

The public assembly venue industry has grown and continues to expand and diversify at a significant rate. A by-product of this growth has been intensified competition for events and customers. The combination of increased growth and intense competition has heightened the need for prudent financial investments in public assembly venues and utilization of efficient management practices in order for the venue to serve its constituents in a financially responsible manner.

It is unlikely that a public assembly venue can be financially successful if its manager is handicapped by governmental policies and procedures that make it difficult, if not impossible, to conduct the venue's business in a competitive, business-like manner. Public assembly venues' governing bodies must strive to free their managers from constraints that inhibit the application of sound and reasonable business practices.

SUMMARY

As with many business occupations, public assembly venue management is both an art and a science. However, venue management is unique due to its complicated need to find a way to blend public ownership and control with the tools needed to operate the enterprise in a competitive manner. The successful venue manager must know how to continuously and effectively navigate this ever-changing landscape. Working hard to help the governing body appreciate the necessity for a business orientation and to provide the atmosphere required to achieve success are some of the manager's most critical responsibilities.

Competition within the public assembly venue business is intense. Success is dependent upon governing bodies allowing the venue manager to operate the enterprise in a business-like manner. Regardless of type, all venues have many common operating dynamics. Managers must possess an understanding of these dynamics and how they affect their venue, as well as the effect they have on their competitors.

Successful governance requires financial diligence and a good measure of creativity. Some communities create special taxes or taxing districts designed to raise money specifically to subsidize public assembly venue operating budgets. Other communities impose an entertainment district tax or surcharge on ticket sales to accomplish the same financial assistance goal.

Each public assembly venue should have a written **mission statement** created and periodically revised by its governing board. This document will clearly identify the purpose of the venue and provide a basis for the governing body when making policy decisions regarding issues of scheduling, booking priorities, tenant oversight, reporting, and budget development.

Therefore, having a venue that is active, locally visible, financially viable, and well managed should not only be the desire of local leadership, it should also be the major focus for venue management. The public assembly venue must strive to become a community or regional asset and claiming that role must be the goal of both ownership and management. Providing the information that can assist in that quest will be addressed and explained in the chapters to follow. Options will be presented on how best to approach the various challenges public assembly venues experience.

The public assembly venue manager is responsible for the organization's nine core functions which address: administration/management, finance, booking, marketing and sales, ticketing, ancillary revenue sources, venue operations, event management, and safety and security. Additionally, the manager must act as a leader to ensure each functional area is properly staffed and operates at the level necessary for the venue to achieve its performance objectives.

Simply put, organizing for success starts at the top of the organization. Public assembly venue managers committed to this principle are well on the way to developing an efficient team of employees and establishing a positive relationship with all of the constituents and communities involved.

CHAPTER 2
VENUE OWNERSHIP AND MANAGEMENT

INTRODUCTION

VENUE OWNERSHIP

- Public Ownership
- Private Ownership
- Public vs. Private Ownership
- Ownership by Academic Institutions
- Ownership by Nonprofit Organizations

VENUE MANAGEMENT

- Management by Government Department
- Management by Authorities, Commissions, or Nonprofit Organizations
- Management by Academic Institutions
- Management by Private Companies
- Public vs. Private Management
- Management by Professional Sports Teams

KEY SKILLS OF A VENUE MANAGER

- Ability to Negotiate
- Ethics
- Managerial Leadership
- Team Building Abilities
- Entrepreneurial Instinct
- Ability to Communicate

PROFESSIONAL ASSOCIATIONS AND CONTINUING EDUCATION

SUMMARY

INTRODUCTION

While ownership is more often in the hands of a public entity, there are examples of private ownership for each type of public assembly venue. Even when a private entity has ownership, it is usually provided with some form of financial assistance from a local public source. Providing infrastructure costs and some form of tax relief or rebate are examples of incentives used by the public entity to assist private ownership and encourage development. It is extremely difficult for private ownership to successfully assume the total cost of the venue and bear the responsibility for expenses of the operation. As a result of the ever-increasing cost associated with building a venue, public revenue streams are frequently tapped to fund much of the construction cost and subsidize at least a portion of the operating costs.

Management of public assembly venues is varied and can be public, private, third-party, or some combination of the three. Whatever method of management is ultimately chosen, it is important to all concerned that the management is of the highest quality possible and that management of the venue be allowed to operate in a business-like manner, giving the venue the best chance to be successful.

The challenge for all public assembly venues is to organize for success. While at first glance this may seem simple, it is easier said than done. This challenge is compounded by the fact that most venue managers are under pressure from a public **governing body** to maximize both event days and revenues generated by those events. In order to accomplish these objectives, the venue manager must juggle variables such as time, space, monetary resources, and staffing, not to mention the demands of the owner and expectations of the general public.

The dynamic nature of the industry makes staffing very difficult because the manager must be able to assemble a workforce which can adjust to the different labor demands associated with each event booked. At the same time, the manager must be able to motivate full-time employees to work extraordinarily long hours, very often during evenings, weekends, and holidays. In addition, to assemble this workforce, the manager must be able to call upon the services of a large number of part-time and contractual service employees who are available on an as-needed basis. All employees, full- and part-time alike, must be trained in their specific job responsibilities and must understand the need to be customer service oriented at all times. Although the hiring, training, and retention of such a work force is challenging, it is necessary if the public assembly venue is to operate at peak performance.

The focus of this chapter is to examine various ownership and management options and identify the strengths and weaknesses of each option. This chapter will also look at the skills necessary to be a successful venue manager and the challenges these managers face.

VENUE OWNERSHIP

Public Ownership

Governmental entities finance, construct, and manage the majority of public assembly venues. The cost of venue construction, combined with infrastructure costs, has made it extremely difficult for private ownership to finance the development expenses without assistance (see Figure 2-1). Governmental entities have access to revenue streams that only they can have or create, as well as the benefit of building tax-exempt venues. They alone can tout the economic benefits realized by the public assembly venue and use those benefits as a logical reason to invest public money in their construction and operation. Management and governance of a public assembly venue varies from city to city, but the venue's management reporting responsibility is usually assigned to a city or county manager, chief administrative officer, or in some cases to the chief elected official, usually the mayor (see Figure 2-2).

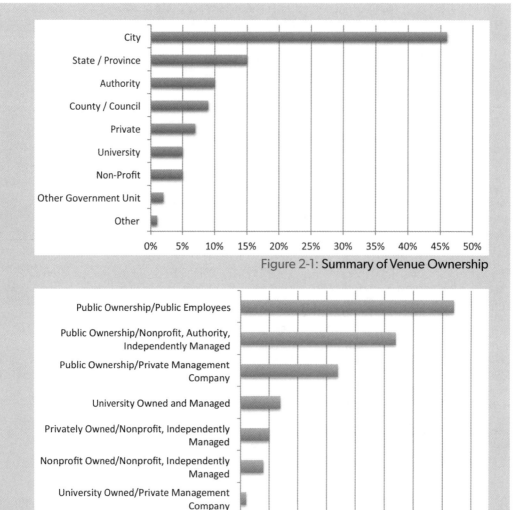

Figure 2-1: **Summary of Venue Ownership**

Figure 2-2: **Summary of Venue Ownership & Management Structure**
(Source: IAVM 2014 Salary Survey and 2014 Operating Expense & Revenue Survey)

Private Ownership

In some cases, public assembly venues are owned by private organizations. In most of these instances, the venue owners also own a professional franchise that is the major tenant. Even when privately owned, these venues often receive some form of financial assistance from local government sources. This assistance may come in the form of reduced tax liabilities, investment of public funds, or infrastructure development. There are also examples of private ownership in venues other than those housing professional sports franchises, and some of these are privately owned without a professional team as a major tenant. Theaters, especially in major cities, also tend to be privately owned.

Public vs. Private Ownership

Whether a venue is privately or publicly owned is not really the important question. Both can support successful operations, and both can result in operations that experience problems that prevent them from being successful. What is important is that the venue, whether public or private, generates the desired results for both its ownership and the local community. While privately owned venues tend to focus more on financial returns—not unusual for any type of private business—they also recognize and understand the importance of their effect on the economics of the community. Likewise, publically owned venues strive not only to meet their financial requirements, but at the same time make it clear that their existence is important to the community as a quality-of-life enhancement and an economic generator.

Ownership by Academic Institutions

Academic institutions such as colleges and universities, whether public or private, own and operate on-campus venues such as performing arts centers, stadiums, arenas, and conference centers. Although administrative responsibility of specific venues may be aligned under applicable departments (e.g., student affairs, auxiliary services, business and finance, or athletics), governance of collegiate venues may also be delegated to an advisory committee comprised of elected and/or appointed representatives of the venue, administration, and student body. Ultimately, however, governance authority rests in the hands of the university's president and governing board.

Ownership by Nonprofit Organizations

Some public assembly venues, particularly performing arts centers, may be owned and operated by private nonprofit organizations. With this type of ownership, management is determined by the organization's membership. It is important to remember that the nonprofit designation is only a tax status. The true nature of many venue nonprofit organizations is to serve as an organization dedicated to presenting cultural entertainment as a part of the overall quality of life in a community. Symphonies, opera and dance companies, chamber orchestras, and other such entertainment, including Broadway dramas and musicals, do not always enjoy mass appeal, and yet they are critical elements in the intellectual and spiritual life of our society and must be allowed to find audiences. Nonprofit organizations find ways to close the financial gap by generating revenue through donations and sponsorships.

VENUE MANAGEMENT

There are a number of variables that will determine the success or failure of a public assembly venue. Quality management should be rated highest on the list. Aggressive marketing of the venue can influence the number of events that a venue hosts, but it is only through efficient and effective management that contracted services with tenants, event producers, and patrons can be delivered in a manner that meets or exceeds each group's expectations.

As previously stated, all public assembly venues and their governing boards should have a well-thought-out, concise, and clearly written mission statement. A venue's **mission statement** should be a result of a collaborative process involving the venue's owner, governing body, and its manager and staff. If the professional staff is not included, the mission statement is being developed without the input and knowledge required to ultimately implement the plan. By engaging in a collaborative group process, vital information is gained and shared relevant to the different perspectives of those involved. Subsequently, the probability of identifying and eliminating inaccurate or unrealistic expectations is significantly enhanced.

The ultimate goal of developing a mission statement is to produce an accurate and complete description of the venue's reasons for being. Often, the venue's public purpose can be found in legislation written to enable the funding and construction of a public assembly venue. Regardless of how the venue's public purpose is formulated, the resulting mission statement/ public purpose document also provides a basis for the governing body when making policy decisions regarding issues of booking priorities, tenant oversight, reporting structure, budget development, and competitive marketing strategies.

A clearly defined venue mission statement and accompanying listing of objectives provides the best foundation for effectively positioning this unique economic driver, the public assembly venue. The addition of effective operating policies and procedures that allow the venue's management team business flexibility to navigate and maneuver within the industry's competitive marketplace is necessary for the venue to reach its maximum potential.

Following the adoption of the public assembly venue's mission statement, it is the governing body's responsibility to create a top management team possessing the insight, intelligence, experience, and energy to bring the venue's mission and objectives to fruition. Building such a management team is often referred to as organizing for success. It is accomplished by first hiring a general manager or executive director. Although the title may vary from venue to venue, the major management functions are quite common.

As explained in chapter 1, there are nine core functions common to all public assembly venues, regardless of size, type, or location. Whether the public assembly venue is a massive convention center located in a major metropolitan location or a performing arts center located on a university campus, management will need to address each of the nine aforementioned functions in order to successfully staff and operate their respective venue.

The type of ownership of a specific public assembly venue will greatly influence the organizational structure of the management team. Publicly owned venues managed by public employees far outnumber any other form of ownership and management. While this form of ownership/management may be more common, there are a number of other organizational structures which, when effectively constructed and implemented, can also successfully serve owners of public assembly venues. Four different organizational models are discussed in the information that follows. It must be stated that while each of these forms of organizational structure is successfully employed in different public assembly venues, the most efficient and effective model for managing a specific venue varies widely. The organizational structure must match the needs of the organization and that of the venue's owner(s).

Regardless of the form of organization, it is essential that all public assembly venue operations are able to identify the actual cost of running the venue and to ensure venue management abides by the governing body's operating procedures. In some arrangements, the venue may be somewhat autonomous, with its own dedicated staff, and have the ability to outsource a variety of support services.

There is no standard, single form of organization within the public assembly venue management industry. What works in one community may not work as well in another community, just as what worked in 2015 may not work for that same venue in 2020. Variables such as market competition, the general economy of the region, and the changing demographics of a community may dictate the need for change from one organizational structure to another.

Figure 2-3 presents a possible organizational chart typically found in a public assembly venue. Additional organizational charts can be found in Appendix A 2-1 representing different venue types, including a theater, stadium, arena, and convention center. Each illustrates the relationship of positions and the reporting lines typically found in a public assembly venue. While all of these functions/tasks must be performed, it is not unusual that individuals may be assigned to more than one of these areas. The functions/tasks may be common to all venue types, but the actual organizational structures vary significantly depending on variables including venue size, location, type of events, form of governance, and the venue's physical aspects. This chart is provided as a sample of how the management team of a public assembly venue may be organized for illustrative and discussion purposes.

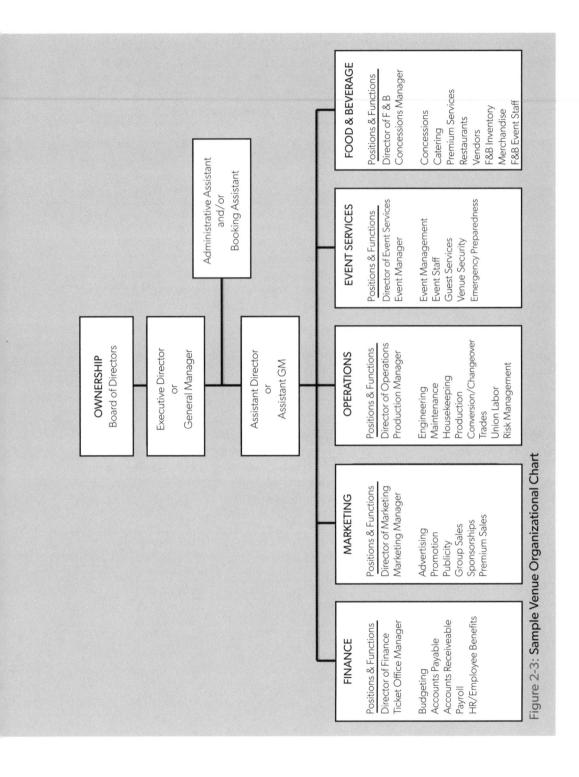

Figure 2-3: Sample Venue Organizational Chart

Management by Government Department

The environment in which a public assembly venue exists will affect the nature of its organization. A publicly owned venue might be organized as a governmental department on a level with city services such as public health, traffic, transportation, or public works. In this organizational context, the venue's general manager might be classified as a public employee who reports directly to another public official. For example, the venue manager may serve as a department head reporting to a city manager or mayor. This reporting structure creates a direct reporting line between the venue manager as a department head and the public official who is either elected by the voters of a civic/municipal jurisdiction or appointed by a public board. The venue manager often has equal rank with most other department heads. The venue manager must rely on other departments within the governmental structure to provide many of the business and operational functions such as purchasing, payroll, recruitment and hiring, and bill paying. There are also a number of venues that operate with this management model on the county level as well.

Support services for a public assembly venue could be provided through various other departments. In such instances, the venue would be subject to the public agency's policies related to human resource management, purchasing, accounting, contracting for outsource services, and other services that often restrict the venue's ability to operate in an entrepreneurial manner. Some municipalities establish departments such as public events, parks and recreation, or facilities administration headed by a general manager and employ civil service personnel to lead the department and operate the venues.

Management by Authorities, Commissions, or Nonprofit Organizations

Many venues are governed by an authority or commission, which is typically created by a city, county, or state government as a result of state legislation. This enables the venue to operate in a more businesslike manner and without the day-to-day bureaucratic policy and procedure limitations that typically restrict government service departments. While they may exist in a variety of forms, common examples of authorities or commissions that operate public assembly venues include:

- **Authority:** An independent board charged with the operation and oversight of a public assembly venue, usually appointed by more than one elected body or appointed officials.

- **Commission:** An independent entity charged with the operation and oversight of a public assembly venue, members of which may be appointed by a single governmental body or official.

- **Nonprofit Organization:** An independent authority established to manage a public assembly venue, usually having an operating agreement with the owner or public body.

Typical responsibilities of these bodies include:

- Hiring and firing the venue manager
- Annual operating and capital budget approval
- Setting booking and usage policies along with rental rates and fee structures
- Approving tenant lease agreements
- Providing direction for overall marketing strategies
- Overseeing risk management programs and insurance coverage
- Approving any inter-agency or inter-jurisdictional mutual aid agreements

A **governing body** usually appoints members of the authority or commission. In publicly owned venues with multiple jurisdictional governing bodies, each constituent jurisdictional governing body will have a proportional number of appointments to an authority or commission. Generally, the authority or commission form of operation is less politicized, and decisions can be achieved in a more expeditious manner than when having to involve other governing councils in the deliberative process. Many cities and counties view an authority or commission structure as a more comfortable alternative than privatizing the venue in order to remain competitive and financially sound.

Management by Academic Institutions

The university itself usually operates university-owned public assembly venues, although there are some that choose privatization in this specialized sector. In the vast majority of cases, the university public assembly venue is organized as a distinct, independent department with its manager enjoying the same rank as other department managers within the institution. The manager will then typically be under the supervision of a Vice President for Administration, a Director of Auxiliary Services or Business Services, Director of Intercollegiate Athletics, or Division of Student Affairs. The venue manager will follow university policies and procedures for all business functions but should be allowed to conduct business as needed to be competitive in attracting events. Often, other university departments may provide services such as accounting, personnel, purchasing, payroll, parking, security, and contracting with outside service providers. In many situations, the university's **physical plant** may provide support services such as utilities, maintenance, and groundskeeping.

Universities own and operate outdoor stadiums for their intercollegiate athletics departments' athletic teams, including football, baseball, soccer, and softball; arenas for their basketball, hockey, and volleyball teams; theaters; concert halls, and performing arts centers for their academic departments of music, dance, and theater, and conference centers for the purpose of providing continuing education and training opportunities for students, faculty, and staff. The management structure for these venues varies as widely as the colleges and universities vary themselves. Regardless of the specific management structure, the wide spectrum of public assembly venues located on college and university campuses in the United States serves not only the students, faculty, staff, and alumni of a specific institution, but the entire population of the communities in which they reside.

A growing number of universities have recently built new arenas on campus that are primarily for university basketball and hockey teams but which are also more open in nature, competing directly for a wide array of events with other similar arenas in their markets. The motivation behind university administrators operating their arenas in a more open or public manner include the following:

- Better venues offering a variety of sports and entertainment events assist in the recruitment and retention of a higher caliber of students and athletes. These venues also provide a greater opportunity to enhance alumni support.

- More diverse audiences enhance the possibility of increased enrollment and more interaction with the business community, which can lead to sponsorships, academic research grants, and student internships and jobs.

- Greater likelihood of attracting events that a somewhat captive student population can enjoy on campus.

- Additional sources of revenue to fund payment of construction costs, bonds, and/or operating expenses to lessen the burden on a university's annual general fund.

- Creating an environment that engages students in on-campus activities.

Management by Private Companies

When achieving operating objectives becomes difficult for public management, the option of using a **private management** company may be a viable option for owners and public officials. The operating objectives for the public assembly venue may be to achieve an actual operating profit, to minimize actual operating losses, and/or provide a more desired schedule of event programming. If the objective cannot be attained with existing management, then private management is an option. The agreement to use a private management company is usually the result of the owner/public entity issuing a **Request for Proposal (RFP)** from qualified management companies. Then, through a selection process, a management company is chosen that best fits the needs of the venue in question. The utilization of private management comes at a cost to the owner/public entity, but the hope and goal is that the cost will be offset by an increase in revenues and decrease in expenses resulting from the expertise available through the selected private company.

The base management fee (cost of private management) and any incentive income the private management company receives are shown as expenses in the venue's operating budget. A private management agreement often includes the potential for earning the incentive income if the company exceeds predetermined financial and operational benchmarks that could include one or more of the following:

- Increasing operating revenue over an agreed dollar amount
- Decreasing operating losses under an agreed dollar amount
- Increasing annual attendance
- Increasing gross concession sales
- Increasing hotel/motel sales tax revenues
- Maintaining the venue in superior condition
- Positive customer satisfaction surveys

If a venue has been financed with tax-exempt bonds, bond counsel should review the private management agreement to be sure there are no violations of IRS provisions.

Whether ownership is public or private, privately managed public assembly venues tend to be organized along the lines of dynamic entrepreneurial operations and are less affected by traditionally restrictive government guidelines. Regardless of ownership, privately managed venues often encounter less resistance to the implementation of competitive business concepts than their publicly managed counterparts. Private management companies tend to be more bottom-lined focused, a main reason they are engaged by the venue's ownership or governing body. Private management companies are merely an agent of the venue owner, though they may be better equipped to balance the community's needs with improved bottom-line financial results (Russo, 1990).

Finally, private management can bring with it a body of intellectual property and combined industry resources that provide advantages over individually operated venues. The fact that private companies usually manage more than one venue allows them the luxury of sharing information and expertise that the single management option does not enjoy. On selected important occasions, private management is also able to call on its staffing from other venues to help ensure the success of a particular special event.

Public vs. Private Management

In the end, there is not an automatic or simple answer regarding how a public assembly venue can best be managed. In some cases, it may be better to be publicly managed, and in others, the private option may prove to be more advantageous. There are a number of variables that must be considered and addressed. The decision is extremely important, and many factors come into play when making the final direction. Each situation is unique and can offer varying options for the community and the venue. The governing body has to make the hard decisions as to what it wants its venues to be and how much control it is willing to delegate to another entity. The public body has to determine if the return for the expenditure necessary to have **private management** for the venue is cost effective in terms of dollars, programming, and fulfilling the venue's public purpose.

Communities that choose to manage their public assembly venue(s) with some form of public management must understand that the operation of the "venue must be run in a businesslike manner and at the least cost possible for the local taxpayer" (Camp, 1990, p.9). Whether management is a department of the local government or by an authority or commission, public management must understand what is necessary to compete successfully in the industry and what is required of the governing body in its selection of a management team. Qualified, knowledgeable, creative, and energetic management is required in both public and private management. Identifying the necessary skills for managers and staff is one of the most important elements in achieving the goal of a successful operation.

There are a number of reasons why government may decide to privatize the management of their venue. The following conditions or issues may prompt consideration of private management:

- Bureaucratic controls over the budget that are contrary to free-market thinking;
- Financial losses caused by local economic problems; intense competition from new venues in the area; difficulties with managing a sales and marketing

enterprise with rules that apply to governmental taxpayer services; customer and tenant dissatisfaction; physical deterioration of the venue and equipment; and burdensome labor agreements;

- The demand for more event activity, especially for venues in secondary and tertiary markets;

- The need for investment dollars for renovation, expansion, and/or equipment purchases;

- The need for experienced, professional direction for new venues from planning, to grand opening, and on to day-to-day operations; and,

- Unwillingness by ownership to undertake the substantial effort required to effectively and successfully manage a public assembly venue.

A concern often voiced about private management is that the owner loses control of the venue operations. If the contract is written correctly, this should not be a major concern. In most private management arrangements, the owner retains control of all major areas of responsibility including at least approval of the following:

- Annual operating and capital budgets
- Venue manager candidate
- Booking and scheduling policies and rental rates
- Long-term and prime tenant leases
- Major contracts
- **Co-promotion** and/or in-house promotions that involve financial risk
- Financial and venue audits

Unlike most public management options, private management companies can risk venture capital in the development or promotion of events and activities that might not otherwise be presented in venues operated by governmental entities. In any case, private management offers government, universities, and sports teams an effective and proven option in the operation of their public assembly venues.

Management by Professional Sports Teams

A growing trend has been for professional sports teams to manage sports arenas and stadiums in which they are the prime tenants. Prior to the 1990s, cities, counties, and state governments frequently built and managed the sports arenas and stadiums in which the major league teams played. Sports teams in city after city have taken over management of the next generation of sports venues. The new venues offer the ancillary revenues from luxury seating, enhanced food and beverage options, advertising and sponsorship opportunities, and other services teams needed to remain competitive and increase revenues for team owners. Even though many professional teams have taken over management of their venues, it is not their primary focus and, therefore, should employ experienced managers to operate the venue. Figure 2-4 summarizes this growing trend.

Owner / Management of Venue	MLB	MLS	NBA/NHL	NFL
Public Owner / Public Management	13%	6%	6%	23%
Team Owner / Team Management	27%	39%	34%	13%
Public Owner / Team Management	50%	44%	44%	45%
Public Owner / Private Management	10%	6%	16%	19%
Other	0%	6%	0%	0%
Total	100%	100%	100%	100%

Figure 2-4: **Trends in Venue Management by Professional Sports Teams**
(CSL International, 2014)

KEY SKILLS OF THE VENUE MANAGER

Regardless of who owns the venue, what method of management is used to oversee the venue, the venue type or location, the capabilities of the venue manager are essential for the venue to meet expectations. The venue manager is the one element that can overcome challenges, grasp opportunities, and direct the operation that can lead the venue to success. If the manager has the necessary abilities, knowledge, desire, tenacity, and stamina to fulfill the mission, then all else is just a process. With that in mind, the following are the key skills a manager should have to manage the venue successfully.

Ability to Negotiate

One of the most important managerial skills that a manager of a public assembly venue must possess is the ability to be an effective negotiator. Negotiation is a part of everyday life for the venue manager. Whether it is a negotiation with an employee on the outcomes of a work project or the artist fee and merchandise commission rate with a talent agent, public assembly venue managers must effectively negotiate with others to achieve results that are in the best interest of the venue and the organization managing the venue.

Every venue manager must be able to skillfully negotiate a contract. Some of the more common types of contracts that venue managers must negotiate include, but are not limited to:

- Venue rental/license agreements
- Contracts with service providers in areas such as ticketing
- Maintenance supplies and landscaping
- Food and beverage services
- Co-promotion talent contracts/artist agreements
- Union labor agreements

The outcomes of negotiations for most contracts have financial implications for the venue manager. It is critical for the venue manager to understand those financial implications and how the other parties, including the venue's governing body and ownership, will view them. More and more, public assembly venue managers are being judged and evaluated on the venue's bottom line.

It must be noted that different venue managers have different levels of authority to negotiate certain contracts. Some managers have no real authority to commit the resources of the organization in a negotiation. Some managers have the ability to negotiate terms of an agreement but must then seek final approval from some form of higher authority. Others have both the ability to negotiate the terms of an agreement and to make the final approval of those terms. In some ways, the effectiveness of some public assembly venue managers is reflective of the amount of authority they have to negotiate contracts.

Ethics

Venue management is a business like any other that provides many opportunities for ethical lapses in judgment. Venues and **promoters** have a long history of successful relationships, but also, at times, those relationships are strained. Entertainment promoters often are small, entrepreneurial companies, and executing profitable events is their sole livelihood. It is extremely important that the venue manager cultivates and maintains a reputation for honesty, forthrightness, and consistency in following standard, acceptable business practices in what can, at times, be a somewhat undefined business environment.

Many venue managers are employees of or have contracted with governmental entities, such as city government or state colleges or universities. Service in government carries another dimension of ethical obligations, with many legal/criminal liabilities for misconduct. The codes of ethics of the International Association of Venue Managers (IAVM) and the International City/County Management Association (ICMA) are shown in Figures 2-5 and 2-6. Note that a theme common to both documents is the duty to refrain from any conflict of interest, that is, any activity that may be in conflict with the interests of the venue manager's employer or owner of the venue. The successful venue manager develops and abides by a personal code of ethics and demands the same from all employees.

The venue manager should:

- Strive for continued improvement in the proficiency and usefulness of service;

- Maintain the highest ideals of honor and integrity in all public and personal relationships;

- Emphasize friendly and courteous service to the public and recognize that the function of the building is at all times to serve the best interest of the public;

- Exercise fair and impartial judgment in all Association and professional business dealings;

- Maintain the principle of fairness to all;

- Have a firm belief in the dignity and worth of service rendered by the building and have aconstructive, creative, and practical attitude; and,

- Refrain from any activity that may be in conflict with the interest of the employer.

Figure 2-5: IAVM Code of Ethics

Certain principles shall govern the conduct of every member of ICMA, who shall:

1. Be dedicated to the concepts of effective and democratic local government by responsible elected officials and believe that professional general management is essential to the achievement of this objective.

2. Affirm the dignity and worth of the services rendered by government and maintain a constructive, creative, and practical attitude toward local government affairs and a deep sense of social responsibility as a trusted public servant.

3. Be dedicated to the highest ideals of honor and integrity in all public and personal relationships in order that the member may merit the respect and confidence of the elected officials, of other officials and employees, and of the public.

4. Recognize that the chief function of local government at all times is to serve the best interests of all people.

5. Submit policy proposals to elected officials; provide them with facts and advice on matters of policy as a basis for making decisions and setting community goals; and uphold and implement local government policies adopted by elected officials.

6. Recognize that elected representatives of the people are entitled to the credit for the establishment of local government policies; responsibility for policy execution rests with the members.

7. Refrain from all political activities that undermine public confidence in professional administrators. Refrain from participation in the election of the members of the employing legislative body.

8. Make it a duty continually to improve the member's professional ability and to develop the competence of associates in the use of management techniques.

9. Keep the community informed on local government affairs; encourage communication between the citizens and all local government officers; emphasize friendly and courteous service to the public; and seek to improve the quality and image of public service.

10. Resist any encroachment on professional responsibilities, believing the member should be free to carry out official policies without interference, and handle each problem without discrimination on the basis of principle and justice.

11. Handle all matters of personnel on the basis of merit so that fairness and impartiality govern a member's decisions, pertaining to appointments, pay adjustments, promotions, and discipline.

12. Seek no favor; believe that personal aggrandizement or profit secured by confidential information or by misuse of public time is dishonest.

Figure 2-6: **ICMA Code of Ethics**
© ICMA. Used by permission.

Managerial Leadership

No matter how the venue's management structure is organized, operating a public assembly venue on a daily basis is very demanding and requires a manager who possesses a unique intelligence combination of a strong IQ (traditional intelligence quotient) and an equally strong EQ (emotional intelligence quotient). These combined forms of intelligence provide the ability to acquire the knowledge base from which the manager can draw upon in order to skillfully manage. Venue managers who are not capable of quickly recognizing and appropriately responding to existing or foreseeable situations, especially when under pressure, will not survive. Good managers tend to be people-oriented, inquisitive, eager to learn and apply new management and business principles, and intensely devoted to fulfilling their job responsibilities. In today's competitive market environment, the successful manager must also be intelligent, responsive, knowledgeable, persistent, flexible, and an excellent motivator and leader.

Successful venue managers possess an extensive understanding of each managerial function associated with the operation of a public assembly venue. They also understand how the venue is organized and how that impacts the operational alternatives. Managers of this stature have acquired their knowledge and experience through varying scenarios. In some cases, a manager may have come up through the ranks, advancing from an entry-level position to higher or different positions within the organizational structure, and then eventually being elevated to venue manager. This form of career development generally ensures that the individual has had personal involvement with many of the venue's operational units and, in all probability, has had the opportunity to work with venue contractual agreements and the process of conducting financial settlements.

Other managers may have developed their careers by starting at mid-level management positions such as venue operations, marketing, or promotions, and then being promoted to venue manager. On-the-job training has proven an effective way to gain information but is not the only method, and may not be the most efficient method, for gaining the requisite knowledge and leadership training. Similar to trial and error, on-the-job training can sometimes be painful and expensive compared to a well-structured training program. It is critical that the venue's management structure be organized in such a way to include strong, consistent, effective training and professional development programs. These programs need to be customized to the job functions, education, and experience levels of the employees involved. Cross-training by moving personnel around the various departments is an excellent way in which to impart and continue institutional knowledge within the staff. However, even though there is an element of on-the-job training in all management career development routes, other education opportunities exist that can impart lifelong learning.

Team Building Abilities

Even with all the skills necessary to be successful, the venue manager must also be able to motivate the staff in a way that encourages all employees to dedicate themselves to the mission, not only to accomplish their respective responsibilities but also to provide support for their fellow employees.

President Harry Truman once said, "It is amazing what people can accomplish, when they have no concern for who receives the credit." Team building is as important as any aspect of the public assembly venue management process. Creating an atmosphere in the workplace that employees enjoy will encourage them to be more dedicated and more involved in the entire process of management. The successful venue manager will recognize the importance of building a successful "team" and will reap the benefits for both management and ownership.

Entrepreneurial Instincts

Even though a venue's mission may not emphasize the creation of new revenue centers or new revenue streams, skilled venue managers will focus energies toward becoming creative and entrepreneurial in seeking out opportunities that serve to maximize the venue's resources and thereby generate additional income. The creative manager knows how to package a public assembly venue in a way that is attractive to businesses, promoters, and customers. The entrepreneurial manager knows how to devise and implement marketing and promotional strategies capable of producing favorable financial results. Increasingly, bottom-line financial data are used to evaluate both the manager's and the venue's success or failure. Consequently, both the manager and the venue run the risk of elimination if they do not achieve the economic expectation and thus become an economic drain on their funding source(s).

Ability to Communicate

Effective communication is a key element in successful venue management. Public assembly venue managers must be able to effectively communicate with distinct groups: the owner(s), governing body, staff, tenants, event presenters, media, attendees, and the community at large. It is the manager's responsibility to develop and maintain direct and efficient two-way lines of verbal and written communication with each of these groups.

The successful manager is a team leader who can work effectively in the present environment while envisioning and preparing for the future, is a consummate advocate of the public assembly venue and its potential, and is aggressive in striving to achieve announced goals. Managers' visions should both inspire and motivate all within the organization. In addition, the successful manager is not only efficient and productive but also skilled in dealing with delegation of responsibilities, discipline, organization, creativity, and, most importantly, leading by example.

PROFESSIONAL ASSOCIATIONS AND CONTINUING EDUCATION

The International Association of Venue Managers (IAVM) is dedicated to continually providing its members with the most up-to-date information on industry trends and challenges. IAVM places a high priority on education of its members, and it has taken great strides in providing opportunities that allow members to share and learn from their peers, as well as offer continuing education options that keep the members on the cutting edge of industry trends.

Appendix D provides a more detailed explanation of these efforts and what programs are available to enhance the opportunities for success for the public assembly venue manager.

SUMMARY

Venues may be owned by the public, private entities, academic institutions, or by nonprofit organizations. All can be successful, and all can experience problems over the course of their operation. Management of these venues can also vary. Venues can be run as a government department, by an authority or commission, by an academic institution, by private management, or by professional sports teams. Once again, the method of management does not by itself determine success. Each management option can be successful and meet its goals and its mission.

The one factor that is extremely important, regardless of ownership or method of management, is a knowledgeable and dedicated manager who exhibits key skills that give that manager the best possible chance to be successful. This manager must not only exhibit certain skills but also be able to use those skills to successfully train employees to handle the many responsibilities and duties required by a venue staff. The successful venue must have a wide range of knowledgeable employees who can both plan for and react correctly to all the different challenges that are inherent in the public assembly venue industry.

Managing a public assembly venue is a complex task that requires the delicate balancing and leveraging of many relationships. Managers of public assembly venues must be effective leaders who are self-motivated and focused. They must be well equipped, through practical knowledge, formal education, and past experience, to accept the challenges presented by new events, new technology, and changing societal practices and standards and use them as vehicles to enhance both the image and productivity of the venue.

The public assembly venue manager understands it is neither safe nor productive to subscribe to the "build it and they will come" theory. While the building may serve as the physical site for accommodating events, it is the quality and efficiency of the personnel employed by the venue that determine the satisfaction level perceived by the venue's various users. This team must be carefully constructed, employing both full-time and part-time personnel, possessing varied skill sets, who understand their role in providing a positive experience for all users.

It is extremely important to understand that personnel employed in the lowest levels on the organizational chart typically have the greatest number of personal contacts with the venue's users. It is often these individuals, many of whom may be part-time employees, who establish through their interaction the basis for an event attendee's positive or negative perception of the public assembly venue and the events it presents.

The public assembly venue manager is responsible for the organization's nine core functions and must act as a leader to ensure that each functional area is properly staffed and performs at the level necessary for the venue to achieve its performance objectives. Simply put, organizing for success starts at the top of the organization. Public assembly venue managers committed to this principle are well on the way to developing an efficient team of employees and to establishing a positive relationship with all of the constituents and communities involved.

CHAPTER 3

BUSINESS AND FINANCIAL MANAGEMENT

INTRODUCTION

It is important to recognize that public assembly venue managers are not in the sports, entertainment, and convention business, but rather manage venues that support the sports, entertainment, and convention business. Therefore, they must study, understand, and apply business skills in all venues regardless of type, size, ownership, or geographical location.

At the core of venue management is the responsibility of fiscal accountability, without which any successful business would cease to exist. Business and finance are simply the method of measurement that determines decisions and evaluates final outcomes. This chapter addresses the fundamental business and financial concepts and principles commonly related to the venue management industry. The successful administration of venues should not only center on sound financial management but begin with an understanding of these basic principles to transforming them into sensible financial leadership applications.

Regardless of size, type, mission, or ownership, there are many common business strategies associated with operating all types of venues. The business and financial management of a small performing arts center is remarkably similar to that of a stadium, arena, or convention center. These general endeavors usually involve:

- Developing and managing the venue's operating budget
- Creating the capital expenditure budget
- Developing and managing annual, monthly, and event financial reports
- Developing venue rental rate and pricing schedules
- Developing pre-event revenue and expense projections
- Administering event settlements
- Negotiating and managing event contracts
- Negotiating and managing labor agreements
- Administering the venue's human resources
- Monitoring the accounts receivable and accounts payable process
- Monitoring and managing ancillary revenue sources
- Managing cash flow and investments
- Managing internal and external audits

Venue management requires the unique ability to forecast revenue and control expenditures for the purpose of accurately projecting the annual financial performance of a venue. This requires creating budgets with projections based on variables over which the venue manager has no control. For example, with sports tenants, the venue manager and their finance staff do not set schedules for their tenants, control personnel decisions, or win games. Consequently, the number of people that attend games is based on the competitive level and success of the team and, therefore, is out of the control of the venue. With traveling shows, the venue manager and staff do not determine who will be touring or the routes of those tours. Likewise, the number of events on a venue's schedule and the number of people attending the events are somewhat out of control of the venue manager and finance staff. The venue manager and finance director have a greater level of control if their governing body allows them to also act as event presenters. Regardless, it is crucial for venue management to track the event and non-event revenues and expenses on a monthly basis and adjust projections accordingly. Accounting for any potential negative variances during the **fiscal year** is important so potential operating changes can be made before any negative variances become a major year-end concern.

The finance department, sometimes referred to as the business office, is a critical component of any successful venue operation. Unlike some types of governmental accounting systems, public assembly venues require a more profit-oriented approach to controlling revenue and expenses typically known as **cost accounting**.

Importance must be placed on event-related budgeting whereby revenues and expenses are tracked primarily by events. The typical annual event-based budget has the following characteristics:

- Estimated number of events by specific event type
- Number of event days/performances for each event type
- Historical average attendance for each type of event
- Ticket sales and average ticket prices
- Estimated gross ticket sales and associated fees
- Estimated venue rental income or **co-promotion** revenue share splits
- Estimated revenue based on per capita spending for concessions and merchandise
- Estimated parking revenues and expenses
- Other revenues based on venue service charges and fees

Logically, all non-event-related salaries and hourly wages, as well as venue non-event operating revenues and expenses, must be viewed in parallel with all anticipated event-related revenues and expenses. The venue manager and staff must understand where they stand financially on a daily and event-by-event basis. This is a critical function of venue management, and the finance department staff requires specialized skills and knowledge of specific accounting procedures.

FINANCE DEPARTMENT

The finance department is the component in the organizational chart that generally deals with most, if not all, of the venue financial matters. While this functional area generally does not produce revenue, it collects and accounts for all non-event and event revenues and expenses. Financial department costs, however, are shown as an expense on the income statement and must be addressed by management. Generally, the finance department and its employees are considered non-event-related expenses.

While the finance department serves as the "financial historian" for the venue, with the proper people and tools, the finance department can provide detailed analysis of the past performance to enhance future strategic planning.

FINANCE DIRECTOR

A finance director usually reports directly to the venue manager and is responsible for gathering, interpreting, and providing venue financial information that enables management to make accurate and timely business and financial decisions. The typical finance director holds at a minimum a bachelor's degree in accounting, finance, or business administration. Many have more extensive educational backgrounds and advanced degrees in accounting, finance, marketing, management, human resources, or similarly related business administration curriculum. Due to the complex nature of the business, many venue managers employ a Certified Public Accountant (CPA) as the chief financial officer. It is also important for the individual in this position to be knowledgeable in all financial aspects of venue management due to the unique manner in which these venues are funded and administered.

While the skills required to be a successful venue finance director are quite similar to those required for similar positions in other organizations, there are certain unique practices in venue management with respect to the finance department. Regardless of the differences, many of the skills required of a venue finance director include an individual's ability to manage the following business functions in compliance with Generally Accepted Accounting Principles (GAAP). Some of the basic business functions include, but are not limited to:

- Budget research, creation, and management
- Preparation and verification of financial statements
- Preparation of pre-event budget estimates
- Reconciliation of event settlements
- Accounts receivable and accounts payable
- Payroll and benefits
- Non-event and event equipment and supplies purchasing
- Internal and external audits
- Establishment and oversight of internal cash controls
- PCI compliance
- Insurance coverage
- Reconciliation of bank accounts
- Ticket office oversight
- Tracking financial aspects of sponsorship and premium seating contracts

In summary, finance directors must be able to view their venue's finances through the eyes of the venue manager. A finance director with a CPA license is valuable and preferable, but, most importantly, a finance director must have an understanding of the venue management business. Their ability to assist and support the venue manager's decisions as they relate to the overall management of the venue and the events they host is crucial to the financial solvency of the overall organization.

OPERATING BUDGET

The annual operating budget identifies anticipated annual operating revenues and expenses, identifies the resources allocated to fund shortfalls, and provides management with a monthly report and analysis of current and year-to-date (YTD) revenue and expenses as compared to the actual budget. Due to the nature of the industry and the challenges in predicting revenues and expenses, the finance director may use a rolling forecast, which is adjusted as new information becomes available. The procedures by which a particular operating budget is developed and managed are ultimately the responsibility of the venue's ownership and administration.

The venue's annual operating budget combines the previous year's financial results with the anticipated revenues and expenses for the coming year. It can be considered a roadmap or game plan for venue management (Hales, 2011). Operational budgets also provide mechanisms to translate organizational goals into financial terms, assign departmental responsibilities and scarce resources, and, most importantly, monitor actual performance (Doupnik & Perera, 2009).

All venues have similar revenue and expense categories. Basic line items include, but are not limited to, the following:

- Revenues
- Venue rent
- Self-promoted event revenue
- Food and beverage
- Contractually obligated income (e.g., naming rights, suites, sponsorships)
- Parking
- Merchandise
- Ticketing fees
- Expenses
- Self-promoted event expenses
- General and administrative expenses
- Management salaries and benefits
- Full-time salaries and benefits
- Part-time wages
- Utilities
- Janitorial and maintenance supplies

Appendix A 3-1 includes a detailed list of common revenue and expense categories for public assembly venues.

An operating budget is divided into revenue and expenses, and the results are categorized as either profits or losses. **Net income**, which is the revenue remaining after expenses have been deducted, may contribute to funding venue operating expenses, be used for capital requirements, or be placed in a reserve fund to cover any future years losses. However, in many instances, the venue's revenue production is not sufficient to cover its general operating expenses. In addition, most venues also have the financial responsibility to repay **debt service,** which is the principal and interest owed on monies borrowed to construct or refinance the venue. The venue may also be obligated to set aside cash reserves for future **capital improvements.** Therefore, whenever an income shortfall occurs, some type of ownership subsidy is required to cover the overall operating deficit, as well as debt service and the **capital reserve fund.**

The annual operating budget, in addition to providing a basis for the financial plan, provides management with a financial projection for a specified period of time expressed in detailed economic terms. A calendar year budget begins on January 1 and concludes December 31. A **fiscal year** (FY) budget may begin on any specified date and conclude twelve months later. Many municipalities operate on a FY budget that begins on July 1 and runs through June 30 of the following year. Numerous venues, such as arenas and stadiums, also use fiscal-year budgets, in order to capture the financial data in one complete season from their primary sports tenants. FY budgets combine months during two calendar years and, therefore, are commonly referred to by those years. For example, a FY budget commencing on July 1, 2018, and concluding on June 30, 2019, would be referred to as the FY 2018-2019 budget.

The budgeting process requires advance research and planning to develop and present financial projections to the **governing body** and ownership. Once the operating budget is completed and approved, it provides management with an ongoing fiscal mechanism for communicating their financial plans and objectives. The development of an operating budget represents one of those unique administrative processes that require managers to communicate both up and down the organization's hierarchy.

The operating budget process usually flows through the following four stages:

1. **Research and Preparation**
   The venue manager and finance director review historical data, project event volume, and estimate revenues and expenses for the upcoming year, based on their industry experience and departmental input.

2. **Presentation**
   The venue manager and/or finance director present and explain the proposed budget to ownership and the governing body.

3. **Approval**
   Ownership and/or the governing board must formally approve the budget. The approval of the operating budget normally occurs prior to the beginning of the new fiscal year.

4. **Execution**
   At the beginning of the fiscal year, venue management implements the newly approved operating budget, which is used as a tool for business decisions.

(Magruder, 2013)

The timing of the budgeting process varies from venue to venue. Research and presentation, though an ongoing process, typically begins up to six months prior to the beginning of the new fiscal year. Presentation and approval normally occurs up to three months prior to the start of the new fiscal year.

Thorough research, preparation, and effective presentation of the proposed annual budget are extremely important to the success of the venue. The budget development process can be complicated as it involves the following:

- Accumulating and organizing historical revenue and expense data related to anticipating the venue's event activity and operations
- Assessing and projecting the venue's position in the current market and economy
- Establishing goals and objectives consistent with the venue's **mission statement**
- Understanding the overall economic and political environment in which the venue exists

A variety of budget formats may be used in public assembly venues. Two of the most common formats include **line item budgeting** and **incremental budgeting.** Regardless of the format used, the operating budget is an important tool for venue management to set goals, track progress, and evaluate results.

CAPITAL IMPROVEMENT BUDGET

In addition to the operating budget, most venues also develop a capital improvement budget that identifies projected major expenditures. Capital budgeting is the process of identifying, evaluating, and selecting projects or equipment that requires the commitment of significant funds and generates benefits stretching well into the future (Doupnik & Perera, 2009).

Capital expenditures refer to the amounts spent for real estate, furniture, fixtures, equipment, and certain major repairs or improvements. Policies vary, but typically capital expenditures are those that exceed a predetermined amount and have a lifespan of three years or more. In a venue, this may include a **Zamboni**, a scoreboard, HVAC replacement, refrigeration equipment, seat replacement, new portable basketball court, and vehicles.

Often, venue management will present to owners a five-year capital expenditure forecast, which is updated annually. Each year of the five-year capital improvement budget is included in the annual business plan. Competent capital expenditure forecasting and budgeting is essential to the operation of a well-maintained venue.

Funding for **capital improvements** may come from excess operating revenues, designated tax funding sources, and appropriations from governmental entities. Planning for capital improvements and replacements is an important responsibility of the venue manager and the finance director and often requires consultation with department managers regarding their needs and recommendations.

FINANCIAL REPORTS

A critical aspect of a venue's financial management system is the creation and use of accurate and timely financial documents necessary for the overall effective management of the venue. Useful financial management tools may include a **Profit and Loss Statement (P&L), a Balance Sheet,** and a **Capital Expenditures Report** (see Appendices A 3-2 and A 3-3 for sample financial reports).

All financial statements and reports prepared by the finance department must be in compliance with generally accepted accounting principles (GAAP) (Bragg, 2012). They include the standards and rules accountants use in recording and summarizing financial transactions and in preparing financial statements. These financial statements, in turn, determine the venue's tax liabilities, if any. An international equivalent to GAAP is the International Financing Reporting Standards (IFRS) issued by the International Accounting Standards Board (IASB) (Doupnik & Perera, 2009).

Profit and Loss Statement (P&L)

The **P&L statement** measures the financial performance of each department within the venue for a given period of time. In a venue, a P&L statement enables mangers to measure specific line item performance and compare the actual monthly operations to the budget projections and to last year's monthly performance (Hales, 2011). The P&L statement may also be known as an Income Statement, or an Income and Expense Statement.

This financial document is designed to report the financial performance of the venue for a specific period of time such as a month, quarter, or year. Venues often include this information both on a current basis (such as this month) and *year-to-date* (YTD) statements and compare to budget for the respective periods.

Balance Sheet

The **balance sheet**, sometimes referred to as the statement of financial position, reports the venue assets, liabilities, and any applicable equity of the organization (Kieso, Weygandt & Warfield, 2012). While the P&L statement reports financial activity for a specific period of time, the balance sheet reports the venue's financial status at a particular point in time. The balance sheet specifically addresses the venue's current financial status and provides information helpful in predicting the amounts, timing, and uncertainty of future cash flows.

Capital Expenditures Report

The **capital expenditure report** shows the financial status of capital improvement projects in progress or completed. This report assists management in tracking capital expenses, thereby helping to ensure management stays within budgeted amounts.

COST ACCOUNTING

It is the responsibility of the finance director to monitor the financial health of the venue and its various activities through a systematic process. One of those processes is referred to as **cost accounting**, which identifies and isolates every venue financial activity and determines the associated costs. Through this process, the finance director is able to produce a thorough and in-depth assessment of the venue's financial status.

An example of how precise and in-depth a financial management and cost accounting system must be is evident by the thorough review needed to determine the price of a simple beverage sold in the venue. One must consider the actual cost to the venue, which includes the following costs:

- Product
- Storage
- Inventory
- Taxes
- Labor
- Paper products
- Spoilage
- Equipment and its depreciation

The same detailed process must be used when determining rental rates, as well as other revenue-producing sources for the venue. The finance director should have the ability to identify event costs and arrange that information in logical and useful format. The venue manager can then use this information as a management tool that will:

- Measure the activities of the venue operation based on current economic terms;
- Assist venue staff with making potential general business decisions; and,
- Justify the need for increased or decreased funding for any part of the venue's business.

The allocation or distribution of costs is an inescapable challenge in nearly every venue. Difficult questions must be addressed, including how the expense of shared services is allocated, how fixed overhead is allocated, and how variable expenses are applied. The answers are not always clearly apparent, and, therefore, venue managers use cost allocation to guide those decisions.

Cost allocation, in a general sense, is the assignment of costs to one or more expense categories. Cost allocation encompasses the assignment of expenses incurred from direct and indirect cost categories. Direct costs are those expense items that can be attributed to a specific event, such as event services labor, **stagehands**, equipment rental, catering, and other expenses that would not have been incurred had the event not been booked. Indirect costs, commonly referred to as **overhead costs**, are expense items that cannot be attributed to a specific event, such as general administration costs, full-time management salaries, insurance, non-event utility usage, and overtime wages not related to a specific event. Indirect costs are those that would be incurred whether you had the specific event or not. They may vary based upon the number of events but cannot be specifically traced to one particular event.

Venue overhead represents expenses allocated proportionally to the venue or specific departments. Overhead is applied to non-event products and services because of management's desire to account for and recover all venue expenses. It is essential to recognize and understand the importance of overhead expenses and how they impact the ultimate cost of goods and services.

When the finance department allocates overhead costs, it is important to categorize them as fixed, variable, or mixed. Fixed costs, such as **debt service**, service contracts, and professional services are constant. Variable costs, such as event labor and supplies, change in proportion to event activity. Mixed costs or semi-variable costs contain both fixed and variable elements, such as an employee who is paid for a forty-hour workweek and then earns overtime pay for additional hours.

FINANCIAL PROCESSES

In addition to implementing and managing the processes that allow for the monitoring of venue revenues and expenses, the finance director is also responsible for the oversight of many of day-to-day financial activities, such as:

- Cash management
- PCI (payment card Industry) compliance
- Inventory control
- Fixed assets management
- Accounts receivable and payable
- Purchasing and procurement
- Event contracts
- Event settlements
- Audits

Cash Management

Every public assembly venue must accurately account for the collection and balance of cash, whether it is derived from ticket sales, rent deposits, parking collections, concession sales, catering sales, or merchandise sales. Cash on hand is a persistent concern in venue management. The following are some of the general issues most venues encounter when their employees are responsible for handling cash.

Typically, finance directors, ticket office managers, accountants, concession managers, and those employees whose everyday work involves the handling of cash are generally covered under embezzlement insurance purchased by the venue. This is often a less expensive form of covering a venue from employee theft. In some instances, venues may forgo the expense of bonding insurance and simply accept the risk (Peters, 2013).

Most venues use cash registers and/or **point-of-sale** systems. This improves the efficiency of the reconciliation of cash drawers and cash on hand at the end of every shift with the cross-reference of a register report. Leaving large amounts of cash in the venue overnight presents serious risks that may be reduced by the use of a night watchman, controlled access, alarm systems, video surveillance equipment, and a secure vault. When possible, daily bank deposits of cash should be arranged with an armored car service. Many banks now offer clients the ability to scan and remotely deposit checks. Where available, this should be done on a daily basis.

Unannounced cash audits, also referred to as spot audits, are strongly recommended. Formal, internal cash audits conducted periodically allow for surveillance of cash management. Cash audits of the box office, or any cash operation, should include validating the amount due against ticket and product sales.

The venue's checking account must also be secure and restricted. All checks should be preprinted and consecutively numbered. Checks in excess of a specific dollar amount should always require two authorized signatures. The venue's bank accounts must be reconciled monthly in order to verify deposits, balances, and withdrawals. Whenever staffing levels allow, an individual who is not responsible for handling deposits or writing checks should perform the bank reconciliations to reduce the risk of theft and fraud.

Another component of venue cash management is the control of petty cash, which is typically used for small, unanticipated expenses, often on event days. The venue should not maintain a petty cash fund larger than needed. Strict procedures should be established concerning the use of the petty cash account, and it should be reconciled regularly. It should be firmly established that without prior authorization and the presentation of purchase receipts, petty cash is not part of the purchasing process. The use of petty cash is becoming far less common with the frequent use of venue-issued debit cards, credit cards, or procurement cards.

In the past, if a venue had a history of generating large amounts of cash from ticket sales, short-term investment of that cash in interest-bearing accounts or certificates of deposit was often an option. Unfortunately, due to low interest rates and high bank fees, this has become a time-consuming practice that yields little revenue and, therefore, is no longer practiced by many venues (Peters, 2013).

Due to the challenges described above, as well as customer spending trends, venues, both domestic and international, have transitioned to debit or credit card systems. The industry is moving toward cashless venues where customers pay for tickets, parking, merchandise, and concessions with the debit or credit card of their choice.

PCI Compliance

All businesses that accept credit cards as a method of payment are responsible for proper management of the information acquired as a result of any transaction. The Payment Card Industry Data Security Standard (PCI DSS) is a set of requirements designed to ensure that *all* companies that process, store, or transmit credit card information maintain a secure environment (PCI Compliance Guide, 2014). Public assembly venues must adhere to these standards or risk severe penalties.

Inventory Control

The finance department must be involved in monitoring the venue's inventory of supplies and equipment. Supplies and equipment must be stored in a secure area with a check-in/check-out system in place and enforced. Such a system will lessen the potential for misappropriation or waste. Unscheduled or spot audits of inventory are recommended. Also, venue supervisors are responsible for maintaining and accounting for expendable products such as housekeeping and general maintenance supplies.

Timely submission of requests for equipment and supplies prevents expensive rush orders. When equipment and supplies are required to go to bid, adherence to established bid procedures may speed the process and reduce administrative costs. When equipment and supplies are received at the venue, they should immediately be verified and recorded to ensure order accuracy. As a general rule, supplies should be inventoried and stored on a first in-first out (FIFO) method, especially perishable items.

Fixed Assets Management

Fixed assets include land, buildings, equipment, and furniture. Fixed assets are tangible items acquired for use in venue operations. They are long term in nature and usually are depreciated over time (Kieso, Weygandt & Warfield, 2012).

Accounts Payable and Receivable

Accounts receivable refers to the billing and collecting for products and/or services. A procedure for dealing with accounts receivable should be established by the venue manager and finance director and strictly followed. All accounts receivable should be frequently reviewed to verify payment. Delinquent accounts should be sent documented notification by mailing registered letters to delinquent account holders. Venues expect to collect current receivables during the current operating cycle (Kieso, Weygandt & Warfield, 2012). If the debt continues to remain unpaid, a reserve may need to be established for what may eventually be declared uncollectable and written off. Each step in this process should be undertaken in a timely manner and carefully documented.

Accounts payable are balances owed to others for goods, supplies, or services purchased. Accounts payable develop because of the lag time between the acceptance of goods or services and the receipt of the corresponding invoice or bill (Kieso, Weygandt & Warfield, 2012). Accounts payable should be managed as diligently and thoroughly as accounts receivable.

Purchasing and Procurement

Many venues are governed by public jurisdictions, which have policies and procedures for purchasing goods and procuring services. Venue managers must adhere to the policies and procedures established by their governing authority. Managers must impress upon their municipal owners and authorities the need to make prompt and prudent fiscal decisions in order to be competitive.

A venue manager's ability to provide effective customer service may be complicated by the fact that purchasing policies may prohibit the timely acquisition of the tools necessary to ensure a positive event experience for guests. For this reason, it becomes extremely important for management to anticipate, when possible, necessary event-related purchases.

As described previously, the use of debit cards has increased dramatically in recent years. Similar to a personal/business credit card, some venue employees or department heads may use this method of payment to purchase goods and services on behalf of the venue or an event. These cards are issued by a lending institution and allocated by the finance director along with specific guidelines for their use.

The venue's finance department should verify all purchases in accordance with the purchasing policies, regardless of the method of payment used to complete the transaction. Since most venues spend hundreds of thousands of dollars in purchasing goods and services each year, this is an extremely important process. In addition, strong relationships should be established with the venue's suppliers, who may be interested in opportunities for sponsorships, signage, and luxury suites and/or club seats.

Event Contracts

An event contract is an agreement between two or more parties to conduct an event and/or activity. In most cases, the event contract exists between the venue and the event **promoter** who is working on behalf of the agency, artist, or **trade show**. A contract creates and sets forth operational obligations and financial responsibilities between the two organizations. In addition, a contract usually includes the following components:

1. Offer and acceptance
2. Intention to create a legal relationship
3. Capacity (authorized representatives of the two organizations)
4. Adequate consideration (what one party gives the other party)
5. Certainty of terms and conditions (if too vague, this may be unenforceable)

The event contract is a rental or lease agreement that allows the venue, or a portion of it, to be rented for a *specific period of time* for a *specific event or activity*. The venue usually receives an agreed-upon financial compensation (rent) from the event **promoter** for use of the venue. In addition to the rental fee, the promoter usually reimburses the venue for expenses such as event staffing (ushers, ticket takers, security, **stagehands**, etc.), ticket expenses, and equipment rental. Rental structures can be composed in many forms, depending on venue and event type. Common rental structures include all-in contracts, flat-rent plus expenses, variable rent based on space used, and percentage of ticket. Figure 3-1 outlines common rental structures.

Contract Type	Description
All-In	A flat rate includes rent and most other expenses.
Flat Rent + Expenses	The flat rent is a set amount, and most other event expenses are line items in the settlement.
Variable Rent Based on Space Used	May be based on square footage of exhibit space and/or meeting rooms used plus expenses.
Percentage of Ticket Sales	Rent is determined based upon a percentage of ticket sales (after applicable taxes, fees, and expenses) plus expenses.
Per Person + Expenses	Rent is determined based upon a fixed amount per person in attendance plus expenses.
Per Person	Rent is determined based upon a fixed amount per person.

Figure 3-1: **Common Rental Structures**

In some instances, the venue itself is the promoter. It negotiates an agreement directly with the event producer, which is generally referred to as "buying" a show or self-promoting an event. While this can be done, in any type of venue, it is most often used in performing arts centers. Performing arts centers that are nonprofits, overseen by a board of directors, or privately owned centers, are the most likely candidates for self-promoted events. Municipalities and educational institutions are more likely to be risk averse.

Due to the large number of contracts issued annually in many venues, it is critical for the venue manager to understand and be able to successfully use many different negotiating principles and strategies. Unlike some contract negotiations, venue managers frequently negotiate different types of contracts with the same party. Consequently, the perceptive venue manager will keep in mind the need to develop and nurture relationships along while trying to negotiate a satisfactory deal for both the venue and promoter. Many successful venue managers describe this as the "win-win" strategy of negotiations. This requires an understanding that the deal has to be good for both parties if a long and mutually beneficial relationship is to occur.

In most venues, the venue manager, with the support of the finance director, conducts contract negotiations. The venue management staff will supply information to the venue manager in the areas of marketing, ticketing, and operations, as well as food and beverage, based on the event **production rider** provided by the promoter. It must be acknowledged that for venues to remain competitive, management must understand the market and how the promoter may use this for leverage when negotiating the contract.

Once the venue staff has reviewed the promoter's event requirements, the finance director will collect all of the information and create a pre-event estimate. The venue manager will use this estimate to negotiate the final event contract with the promoter. The manager may also refer to this document during settlement to help address any issues that may have developed, as well as any last minute requests by the promoter or artist. A thorough event contract leads to a smooth, successful settlement.

Event Settlements

Event settlement is the accounting and distribution process by which the event promoter and venue management divide monies as outlined by the event contract. The process itself is not as unusual as the actual timing of the activity. In most businesses, billing and collection activities occur after the sales transactions have taken place. Bills are issued, and payments are normally made at the end of the month or within thirty days. The settlement process in a venue, however, may take place during the event day and occasionally while the event is still in progress. For example, a concert that generates a million dollars in ticket sales might be settled while the headliner is still on stage. This process allows for the distribution of funds, enabling all parties to pay accumulated bills in a timely manner. Table 3-2 outlines common settlement timing based upon venue and event type. See Appendix A 3-4 for sample event settlement statements based upon various rental structures.

Venue Type	Event Type	Common Timeline
Amphitheater	Concerts	Night of the event
Arena	Venue Tenants	Monthly
	Concerts	Night of the event
	Tournaments	Within one month
Convention Center	Meetings & Conventions	Within one month
	Trade Shows	Within one month
	Banquet Only Events	Within one week
Theater	Local Events	Next business day
	Multi-Day Touring Events	After the final performance
Stadium	Venue Tenants	Monthly
	Concerts	Night of the event
	Bowl Games	Within one month

Figure 3-2: Common Settlement Timing

Representation of the venue at the settlement depends on the structure and timing of the event. For example, a settlement for a traveling theatrical event promoted or presented by a performing arts center will require a representative from the venue who is authorized to issue checks and a representative from the theater company who is often the tour's accountant. Venue staff present at the settlement for a concert will usually be a representative from the venue, the tour's accountant, and a representative for the promoter. Depending on the contract, typical documents needed to successfully complete the settlement may include:

- Ticket office audit statement detailing and certifying tickets distributed and associated revenue
- Invoices for event expenses
  - In-House production including staging, audio/visual, draping, and utilities
  - Event labor such as stagehands, police, ushers, and house security
  - Equipment rented and used specifically for the event
  - Backstage catering and supplies invoices
  - Advertising invoices with back-up materials

At the event settlement, the venue may withhold rent and expenses from ticket receipts or collect an amount equal to the promoter's or the artist's financial obligation to the venue. Venue management works with the promoter or tour accountant to facilitate distribution of the remaining revenue. Promoters who require cash on event day are obligated to inform the venue in advance to ensure availability in requested denominations as long as that amount does not exceed the amount due the promoter. Once both the venue representative and promoter sign the final settlement, funds may be distributed by a venue check but are more commonly remitted through a bank wire transfer.

Audits

An audit is a review of the venue's finances, operations, and management processes and practices. Audits may be conducted internally by the finance staff or externally by an objective third-party accounting firm. Scheduled and unscheduled audits are tools that provide the venue with an overview of the financial health of the organization.

Scheduled external audits are normally an annual occurrence, while internal audits can be scheduled on a regular basis or at any time for a specific need. This audit process includes a review of contracts, advertising agreements, ticket office receipts, **settlement sheets**, payroll documents, and payments to vendors, clients, and customers. Special attention must be given to those charged with conducting the internal audits to ensure that no favoritism or collusion occurs. Although departments may be selected for audit randomly, a system must be in place to ensure all departments are audited within a specified time frame.

Unscheduled external audits are extremely rare and only occur in the instance of a potential impropriety. An unscheduled internal audit may be used when an area of concern has been discovered. Generally, focusing on the area of concern may enable management to identify the issue in question and outline possible solutions.

During external audits, the venue manager is provided a draft of the audit report and given a period of time to investigate, review, and discuss any negative issues that have been exposed by the audit before the report is released to the **governing body** and subsequently becomes public record.

Although potentially stressful and time consuming for venue personnel, the audit process and the subsequent report should be viewed by management and their governing body as an excellent opportunity to review and evaluate the performance of the entire organization.

HUMAN RESOURCES

Human resources is a complicated aspect of venue management. While all departments may share the responsibility for identifying, recruiting, hiring, training, and managing venue employees, the business office often creates employment policies and procedures and provides administrative support. They are likely to process employment paperwork, benefits, workmen's compensation issues, and payroll for all venue employees including full-time, part-time, and event-related staff. Depending on the size of the venue, most employ a relatively small staff of full-time employees while maintaining a large pool of part-time workers who are employed on an event-related basis.

Ultimately, placing employees in positions in which the employee's qualifications and the position's requirements fit best is generally viewed as more art than science. Venue managers in the United States may hire whomever they desire as long as: the positions are properly posted and advertised; the candidate meets the qualifications stated in the job description; the decision to hire is in accord with the requirements of the Equal Employment Opportunity Commission and the Americans with Disabilities Act; and there has been no discrimination on the basis of certain protected characteristics such as age, national origin, gender, sexual orientation, race, color, qualified disabilities, or religion. The following pages will address issues related to full-time staff, part-time staff, sources of part-time labor, and orientation and training.

Full-Time Staff

One of the most important responsibilities of a public assembly venue manager is to select intelligent, experienced, and dedicated individuals to address the needs of the venue and fulfill their roles as part of the organization. A skilled full-time staff is perhaps the most important ingredient to attaining overall success for the venue, its governing body, and the community it serves. An accomplished staff is able to handle daily operational responsibilities independently, allowing the venue manager to focus on a wide array of issues relating to the overall mission of the organization, as well as business and political functions.

The type and volume of events, as well as whether the venue has tenants, generally dictate the size of the venue's full-time staff. Small venues usually have a general manager, a finance director/manager, an operations manager, and/or building superintendent/engineer. Conversely, a large venue may also employ directors, managers, supervisors, and coordinators, as well as support staff for security, marketing, catering, concessions, box office, event coordination, and housekeeping.

Full-time staff can be either salaried employees or hourly employees. Salaried employees are expected to work both normal business hours and additional time as required by the event schedule. Salaried employees receive an annual salary and, therefore, are not eligible for overtime. In some instances, salaried employees may be eligible to receive an annual bonus. Due to the extended hours often worked by salaried employees, the venue manager may allow for some flexibility with comp time to make up for the extra hours.

Most full-time, hourly employees are scheduled to work forty hours a week. These hours may be during normal business hours or, at the discretion of their supervisor, may fall outside the traditional nine-to-five day. The nature of the public assembly venue business requires employees to work when event schedules dictate. These employees receive an hourly rate and may be eligible for overtime pay. This category usually includes some of the operations staff, particularly the union labor personnel. It also may include the food and beverage staff due to the nature of their work.

However, the definition of full-time employees is changing. From a budgetary perspective, venues can now determine the definition of a full-time employee in terms of how many hours they work. This will undoubtedly have a scheduling and budgetary impact on all public assembly venues, as well as our national economy (Peters, 2013).

Part-Time Staff

Part-time staff may include hourly or project-based personnel. Part-time, hourly staff is used to cover duties generated by event requirements or normal venue operations. Project-based personnel may be employed to complete specific tasks as needed, such as plumbing or carpentry projects. Management of public assembly venues is unique relative to other industries because of the large number of part-time, hourly employees required to meet the demands of the event calendar. Consequently, a large portion of time is dedicated to the systematic and thorough recordkeeping for this segment of the venue's labor.

Sources of Part-Time Labor

Regardless of venue type or location, few, if any, can afford to maintain a full-time event staff including ushers, ticket takers, ticket sellers, security guards, and **runners**. It is an essential function of the public assembly venue's human resources representative to assist management with the identification, training, and retention of a capable part-time workforce to ensure successful operation of the venue and its events.

Part-time labor needs can be met through any methods, or a combination thereof, including in-house, contracted, or unions. When managing part-time labor in house, the venue assumes the responsibility for identifying, recruiting, hiring, training, managing, insuring, and paying them. Sources may include local colleges and universities, civic clubs, and hospitality industry professionals, as well as individuals with accommodating schedules, such as teachers and firefighters. One of the most common sources of part-time labor is through word of mouth from existing personnel.

In some instances, venue management may decide to contract out some or all of their part-time labor needs to third parties. Commonly contracted labor and services include landscape companies, maintenance, peer security, and foodservice. In many publicly owned venues, contracting for these services must go through a bid process. Once the bid is awarded, a single provider usually supplies all the required part-time labor called for in the contract. When labor is contracted, the venue typically initiates the labor call, the provider supplies the labor, and the venue is then billed for the personnel and the provider's administrative expenses. In some instances, these expenses may be passed on to venue users. Allowing a subcontracted provider to supply part-time labor not only eliminates the expense of recruiting, training, and insurance, it also eliminates the cost of producing and managing the payroll. The venue manager should obtain proof of insurance from the contractor that names the venue and owner as additional insured.

Where unions exist, venue management may choose to contract a union workforce to cover part-time labor needs or specific event requirements. Event load-in, **rigging**, forklift operation, spotlight operation, and load-out are examples of duties often contracted to union labor. Where unions are strongest, they may supply nearly all event-related personnel.

Each option, including in-house, contracted or union, has its advantages and disadvantages. The determination of which to use should be based on the availability of the labor pool, payroll, skill requirements, available training programs, employment statutes and regulations, the political climate, and other related factors.

Volunteers are unpaid employees who represent yet another labor category. Volunteers are generally found in certain types of venues and/or in certain roles. For example, the entire **front-of-house** staff at nonprofit performing arts centers may be volunteers. Many on-campus venues use volunteers and find the practice both efficient and effective. The venue manager must keep in mind that although volunteers are unpaid, their personal safety is still the responsibility of the venue. Therefore, they need to be protected by the venue's general liability insurance policy and/or worker's compensation program. The venue manager must also remember that volunteers play an important role in the venue and event and, therefore, require appropriate training, proper uniforms, and incentives to motivate them just like paid employees.

In some instances, the **promoter** may request permission to use their own volunteers to work as event staff. While this may reduce expenses, those individuals are not familiar with the venue or the proper procedures to be followed in the event of an emergency. The venue manager must not compromise the event experience or, most importantly, the safety and security of guests, performers, and employees.

Orientation and Training

Orientation of new employees to workplace policies and procedures is a critical part of the overall staff training program. The orientation process should be a well-organized program structured to assist new employees in understanding the venue's overall goals and objectives and their roles in achieving those goals and objectives. A well-organized program may include employee manuals, orientation videos, and face-to-face meetings. The venue may require a background check for certain positions as a condition of employment (Peters, 2013).

Training provides instruction and guidance for the development of new employees. To be successful, the training program should guide the employee through a series of exercises or experiences that explain how to respond to specific requirements of the job. While orientation is normally a one-time activity, training should be an ongoing part of the employee development process. Effective training may include traditional instruction, as well as training videos, guest speakers, online training modules, role-playing, and situation-simulation drills.

Full-Time Employees

New full-time employees receive basic orientation information from the human resources (HR) representative, including an employee manual that addresses details about compensation, benefits, codes of conduct, and organizational policies and procedures. The new employee is often required to sign a document acknowledging receipt of the manual and agreeing to abide by its contents. The HR representative may also share the venue's mission, review the employee's job description, and discuss professional development opportunities.

While most full-time employees have been hired because they already possess the skills and expertise required for the job, additional training may be required to address the unique aspects of the particular venue or the industry. For example, an accounting professional must learn the nuances of the settlement process, and an operations employee must learn the process necessary for efficient **changeovers**. In order for the venue to remain competitive, continued employee training and development is necessary.

Part-Time Employees

Part-time employees often lack experience with public assembly venue operations or events. While orientation is important, the proper training of part-time employees is even more critical for success. Part-time employee orientation is generally conducted by representatives from the respective venue departments and includes information about parking, uniforms, scheduling, pay cycles, disciplinary procedures, basic job expectations, and general venue policies and procedures.

Training for part-time employees is more specific to their individual job requirements and may include topics such as guest services, equipment operation, event communication procedures, event policies and procedures, safety and security issues, and emergency preparedness. Training for part-time employees is challenging, considering the potential number of employees needed and their availability, since many may have full-time jobs. Therefore, training often takes place in the evenings or on weekends, and the employees must be compensated for their time.

Generally, human resources has a more limited involvement with the part-time staff, primarily limited to assisting with the hiring process and payroll, and often coordinating completion of all pre-employment documents.

The venue manager is responsible for determining the most effective and efficient employee training programs for the venue staff to implement. The management and these programs should be aligned with the venue's overall goals and objectives. Venue management staff should document and keep verifiable records for each employee who successfully completes both orientation and training programs.

SUMMARY

The success of a public assembly venue is dependent upon an effective business and financial operation. Venue management is a complex business, and, to be successful, the venue manager will need an effective finance director with a combination of skills enhanced by experience. One of the most important skill sets for this position is the knowledge of industry-accepted principles of financial management. The finance director must be supported by the best possible staff with expertise in addressing the nuances of the venue industry. This staff is responsible for budgeting, cost accounting, financial processes, and human resources.

The venue manager must develop a very cohesive relationship with the director of finance to help create and successfully manage the venue's annual operating budget in the face of many factors that are beyond the control of venue management. The venue manager's role is to understand and react to this environment and, with the assistance and support of the finance director, operate their venue as efficiently and successfully as possible without diluting customer service and safety.

As in most businesses, the manager and staff will not only be evaluated by the processes and systems used to manage revenues and expenses, they will also be judged on how their responsibilities enable other departments to effectively track those revenues and expenses. The venue management business is just that, a business.

CHAPTER 4

BOOKING THE VENUE

INTRODUCTION

Booking is how the venue ultimately generates revenue. Rental charges, leases, **co-promotions**, and in-house promotions are primary revenue sources. The amount of revenue generated by these sources is dependent upon market competition, size and type of venue, and the number of events booked annually. In some instances, revenue generated from venue rental may be exceeded by ancillary revenues, which are addressed later in the book.

Since time and space are the primary commodities of the public assembly venue, it is essential to understand the value of these assets and their perishable nature. Accordingly, the scheduling calendar used to manage the venue's time and space is the most important tool for the booking manager to use in controlling these assets. This instrument and its inventory of dates must be closely managed, with uncompromising integrity and accuracy, to maximize profitability and minimize negative client relations.

In many instances, especially in smaller venues, the venue manager handles the booking responsibilities. Depending on the venue, these responsibilities may fall to an assistant venue manager or a director of sales and marketing, and, in some venues, the volume of events necessitates a full-time employee who serves as a booking manager. For the purposes of this chapter, the term booking manager will refer to whoever is responsible for booking the venue, whether it is the venue manager or another individual.

One of the greatest challenges for any booking manager is to book a full and diverse schedule consistent with the mission and public purpose of the venue and the economic expectations that govern its operations. Competition for viable events in most markets is intense, as is the competition for audiences among organizations that own their venue, such as theater companies and sports teams. So how does one succeed in this area? The booking manager must possess certain qualities, and venue management must support their efforts to create an environment conducive to successfully booking events. The following are essential for success:

- Widespread industry presence and well-established industry relationships
- Honesty and integrity that instill trust with event promoters
- Flexibility in negotiating mutually acceptable deals
- Management of the venue in a way that exceeds expectations
- Support by skilled staff to promote and facilitate events
- A willingness to take some risk as a co-promoter, when permitted

Event activity, the result of successful booking, is important to the communities served by public assembly venues. They are important because they improve the quality of life, generate positive economic impact, and increase local, regional, and national visibility. Ultimately, the key to a venue's success is the ability to effectively identify and book events as expected by venue ownership and desired by the marketplace. In the end, that is why the venue exists.

Events drive all revenue and, therefore, are critical to a venue's success. This chapter examines the principles and practices of booking events, industry relationships, and the processes required to secure event activity.

BOOKING POLICIES AND PROCEDURES

Most venues have booking policies and procedures approved by the **governing body**. These policies and procedures spell out the ideal priorities by which dates are assigned. The booking manager should have flexibility in areas such as rental rates and cost reimbursements, set-up and teardown time, and, if necessary, switching dates to achieve a realistic maximum level of desired event activity.

The venue management industry is one of relationships. There are no formal rules that govern the relationships between booking managers and promoters. Within this relatively closed professional area, a certain level of trust between booking managers and promoters is necessary for the system to work. If a promoter cannot trust a booking manager's word, the promoter may choose to bypass the venue. Conversely, without this relationship, a booking manager may require a non-refundable deposit for a tentative hold date, or dates. As within any select community, word gets around quickly about who is or is not trustworthy.

One of the most important booking responsibilities is management of the venue schedule. Therefore, it is critical for only one or two people to have the authority to enter and remove event dates. Proper booking procedures enable management to avoid double bookings and reduce the risk of losing an event.

THE VENUE SCHEDULE

The ultimate goal of the booking manager is to produce a well-rounded schedule. The venue schedule should provide the best possible mix of events that meet the needs of the community, users, and the venue. A diversified event program, properly scheduled and effectively presented, requires a clear understanding of expectations of the events, the event's consumers, and the venue's governing body, coupled with an understanding of the venue's physical and/or personnel limitations.

Achieving a diversified schedule requires a thorough understanding of the community the venue was built to serve. The timing and content of other events in the market must be considered when booking the venue and may impact the **on-sale date** and marketing efforts. Local, regional, and national holidays, along with vacation patterns of area residents, should also be considered before booking events. In addition, other activities outside the community, but within the region might impact an event's success and must be taken into consideration when developing the public assembly venue's schedule.

For example, scheduling a symphony orchestra performance on the same evening when 80,000 people will be attending a college football game in a nearby stadium may affect, in a number of ways, either or both events. Nonetheless, the core fact is public assembly venues are in the business of selling the perishable commodity of time and space. All activity by the venue manager and the venue's staff is focused on this singular objective. Nothing else happens if this is not accomplished. Once an opportunity has passed, it is gone forever.

Wrigley Field - Chicago, IL

USER PRIORITIES

Like many businesses, venues give priority to their best customers. Priorities given to prime tenants or venue users can help ensure a high level of event activity without giving such users exclusive rights (Marion, 2013). In most cases, priority policies and criteria are clearly defined and written to include time-sensitive benchmarks.

A number of variables, such as the venue purpose and mission, market, social and economic climate, community demographics, availability of events, and venue capabilities, can offer direction and guidance concerning an appropriate event mix and schedule. Attempting to host events considered unsuitable for the venue and community or that might conflict with the venue's prime tenants could produce negative reactions.

The key to establishing a priority policy lies in the designated use of the venue. For example, if a performing arts venue is built to serve the local arts community, including symphony, ballet, and theater groups, then those groups should be given certain priority to reserve space. Priority in a convention center should be given to large conventions as opposed to a consumer show, particularly if funding from hotel accommodations taxes is used to retire the construction debt and to pay operating expenses.

Understanding a venue's purpose or mission can also assist in resolving booking priority conflicts and revenue distribution issues when they arise. A venue manager caught between a popular basketball coach demanding more practice time and a **promoter** with a high-profile concert should be able to rely on the venue's purpose for guidance in establishing and adhering to booking priorities. Figures 4-1 and 4-2 provide examples of booking priorities for two types of venues.

FIRST scheduling priority is given to conventions, trade shows, corporate meetings, and similar activities that use a minimum of 1,500 room nights during the event and that are not normally open to the public.

SECOND scheduling priority is given to conventions, trade shows, consumer or public exhibitions, and corporate meetings using more than 100,000 square feet and less than 1,500 room nights. Second priority will also be given to events which book either the ballroom plus a minimum of 48,000 square feet of exhibit space or the ballroom when accommodating a minimum of a 600 person banquet function.

THIRD scheduling priority is given to smaller consumer or public exhibitions, local corporate meetings, special events, banquets, and other activities that primarily draw from or appeal to the general public and/or local attendees.

Scheduling for second-priority events will not be confirmed more than 18 months in advance. Third-priority events will not be confirmed more than 12 months in advance. Both second- and third-priority events are subject to change to accommodate first priority events unless a rental agreement has already been executed by the venue.

Figure 4-1 : **Sample Booking Priorities for a Convention Center**

Scheduling policy is designed to obtain maximum utilization of the facilities and provide fair and equitable availability to a broad spectrum of sports and entertainment presenters. All events are inclusive of load-in, production, rehearsal, performance, and load-out.

#1 Priority	Multi-week / multi-performance events
#2 Priority	Week-long performance events, 6 or more
#3 Priority	Multiple performance events, 2 or more
#4 Priority	Single performance events

Figure 4-2 : **Sample Booking Priorities for a Theater and Arena Complex**

It is important to note that booking convention center business is slightly more complex because of the number of entities involved in the process. Strategic collaboration among the convention center's general manager, the convention and visitors bureau (CVB), representatives from area hotels, and the local hospitality industry is most important. Typically, the CVB operates as the marketing arm for long-range events and will market the convention center's calendar for scheduling of events eighteen months and beyond while the venue management team will concentrate on short-term bookings. Frequently, CVBs and/or hotels will arrange for group accommodations. This process ensures the necessary housing for attendees is available for specific dates of scheduled conventions, conferences, multi-day meetings, and **trade shows**. Because of the coordination among hotels, CVBs, and convention centers, many major conventions may be booked seven to ten years in advance.

It is paramount that convention center managers, like all venue managers, accept the responsibility for cooperating with other community entities to coordinate their venue's use with the community's long-range goals. At the same time, the venue manager may be committed to traditional annual events for which the venue was built. In most cases, priority is given to the scheduling of dates based on the impact the event has on the number of **hotel room nights** that can be guaranteed by the attendees or delegates that accompany a given convention. These major conventions are actually placed on the venue's calendar before smaller conventions, conferences, multi-day meetings, and trade shows.

Since community needs and tastes are subject to change, a venue manager must continually monitor those changes and adjust the venue's programming accordingly. Thus, as a community's programming interests and social standards evolve, the venue's **mission statement** should be revisited and updated to reflect the needs of the current market. By paying close attention to both the community's evolving needs and available event business, the venue manager can guide the venue's governing body, clients, and consumers toward the formation of a revised mission.

VENUE BOOKING TIMELINES

As previously discussed, there are many types of public assembly venues. Every venue hosts a variety of events. Each event has different requirements in terms of how far in advance they need to be booked to maximize their opportunity for success. Concert tours being booked at large stadiums may need to be confirmed eighteen months in advance, whereas a small luncheon in a convention center meeting room may only need to be booked three weeks in advance.

For those venues with tenants, such as sports teams or resident performing arts companies, their first priority is obviously to make sure those dates are placed on the calendar. After the request for those dates is honored, the booking manager is free to book other events. While there are exceptions, below are the general booking lead times for each venue type:

Amphitheaters	3 months – 2 years
Arenas	3 months – 3 years
Convention centers	3 months – 7 years
Theaters/performing arts	3 months – 2 years
Stadiums	6 months – 2 years

As a result of the length of time required to plan monumental events such as a collegiate national championship, the Olympics, or a national political convention, they may need to be confirmed five or more years in advance.

EVENT BOOKING PROCESS

Booking is the process of identifying desired events or activities appropriate for the venue and the community, contacting event owners or promoters, and engaging in negotiations leading to a contract. From the perspective of both the venue manager and the promoter, determining the when, where, and at what cost are the prime decisions in the booking process.

As stated previously, the responsibility for booking events should be closely monitored. In most cases, one or two members of the organization control entries and deletions in "The Book" that may be a scheduling calendar or a software program. There are several industry-accepted computer programs and systems available to venues. Some, but not all, software programs eliminate duplication and double bookings for the same space. In addition, there are systems that have other time- and cost-saving features that allow for inventory, ticketing, accounting, security, scheduling, and communications. These systems can also provide windows for viewing multiple spaces for concurrent events (Marion, 2013). Regardless of the reservation system used, the old adage about too-many-cooks-in-the-kitchen certainly applies

Greater Tacoma Convention & Trade Center - Tacoma, WA

to venue booking. When more than one individual is involved in the venue booking process, there must be excellent communication and coordination between those individuals.

While only one or two people are involved in the actual booking, an administrative assistant may assist in the booking process by assuming responsibility for some of the following routine functions:

- Offering **avails** (i.e., **available dates**) by phone/e-mail
- Issuing standard rental application forms to prospective clients
- Conducting background reference checks
- Issuing standard rental agreements
- Ensuring executed agreements, required deposits, and certificates of insurance are received as required and on time
- Answering routine questions from prospective clients

The booking manager will often use a Booking Memo, as seen in Figure 4-3, to disseminate pertinent information related to a potential booking.

EVENT _____

Event Date(s): _____   Event Time(s): _____

Event Type / Genre: _____   Schedule: _____

Expected Attendance: _____   Set-Up: _____

TERMS

Lease Start Date: _____   Lease End Date: _____

Rental Rate: _____

Ticket Office Rate

Initial deposit of _____   due by: _____

Second deposit of _____   due by: _____

Additional deposit notes: _____

PROMOTER / AGENT   Signatory: _____

Company: _____

Contact: _____   Address: _____

Phone: _____   _____

E-Mail: _____   Fax: _____

Permit Application: Received / Approved for Use

EVENT TICKETING

Pricing Scales: _____   Ticket Header: _____

_____   _____

_____

Total Capacity Holds: _____   Discounts: _____

Pre-Sale Date: _____

On-Sale Date: _____

Figure 4-3 : Sample Booking Memo

A promoter will not agree to a contract with a venue until first convinced the venue is appropriate, available, and economically viable. In similar fashion, a trade show promoter is not able to attract exhibitors without knowing the specific date(s), location(s), and costs of the show. Producing an event normally includes advertising, ticketing, marketing and promoting, staffing, and rentals considerations. All of these are critical to the success of the event, and the booking process hinges on them. Once the booking process is complete, the production process begins.

The event booking process starts with an up-to-date venue calendar and generally includes the following steps:

1. Promoter's inquiry for venue information
2. Promoter's request for available dates
3. Venue's request for **production rider**
4. Check for competing events
5. Promoter's request for dates to be held
6. Receipt of event rider
7. Qualifying the event
8. Negotiation of rental terms
9. Promoter's confirmation of event date in venue
10. Issuance of rental agreement by venue
11. Selection of **on-sale date** for ticketed events
12. Venue's receipt of the signed rental agreement and certificate of insurance
13. Event goes on sale

This is the ideal sequence of the booking process, but experienced booking managers realize that flexibility is necessary based on the circumstances. For example, there may be a last-minute opportunity to book an event, the event promoter may not be familiar with the booking process, or the promoter might be a frequent user of the venue.

Qualifying the Event

A key step in the event booking process is qualifying the potential event. Whether the venue *promotes* the event itself (contracts for the event to happen and accepts all of the financial risk), *co-promotes* the event (contracts for the event but shares the financial risk with the promoter or event producer), or *leases* the venue (rents space to a tenant/promoter, thereby not incurring any direct financial risk), the venue booking manager must answer several common questions:

- Does the promoter have the necessary experience, authority, and financial resources?
- Is the event consistent with venue mission and expectations?
- Are the date(s), time(s), and space(s) requested available?
- Does the event fit from a scheduling perspective?
- Is the venue able to accommodate the event's space and production requirements?
- Can the venue meet the demands of the event such as staffing, marketing, changeover, etc.?
- Will the event impact a tenant either positively or negatively?

- Are there similar events on the schedule that may confuse the public or potential exhibitor base or fail to serve the best business interests of the venue or event?

It is the booking manager's responsibility to determine if the potential client is legitimate and, in fact, has the authority to deliver the event in question. In the interest of fairness, consistency, and good business practice, venue management should have a rental application process for qualifying all new promoters or prospective tenants/clients. A rental application may not be necessary for previous users of the venue, though it is advisable to verify qualifying information on an annual basis.

Bank and financial verifications, confirmation of previously promoted events, and recommendations from the manager of former contracted venues are several ways to help determine the applicant's qualification to book an event. Requested date(s) can still be held on a tentative basis during this process, but all booking requirement deadlines must be met.

There is a correlation between a venue's success and the processes and procedures by which it accepts business. Experienced, reputable, financially sound promoters are essential to the success of a venue. However, some promoters fail to meet the necessary requirements. Therefore, it is in the best interest of the venue to complete the pre-qualification process efficiently in order to minimize the risk of doing business with promoters or events that are likely to fail. Rental applications are designed to acquire the necessary information (a sample can be found in Appendix A 4-1).

There are a number of reasons why potential promoters or meeting planners will request a hold on a date(s) even though they may lack the authority to actually deliver the attraction. While most of the reasons are legitimate, the public assembly venue manager needs to be prudent about over-committing date inventory carelessly without establishing control processes to protect the venue from fictitious holds.

Booking managers need to evaluate any unusual risks and potential liabilities associated with a proposed event. Is the proposed event one that may cause controversy in the community? Potential controversy, however, should not necessarily result in an automatic rejection. Not allowing an event deemed inappropriate by the venue's governing body might be illegal, based on the laws and regulations of the legal jurisdiction under which the governing body operates. In addition, denying the event may ultimately prove expensive and embarrassing if the promoter seeks relief in the courts. Refusing to book an event solely based on the management's or governing body's perception of its content might be construed as a violation of the promoter's and the event's right to free speech. Court charges, assessed penalties and fines, and a damaged relationship between the venue's manager and the event's promoter frequently result from a decision to disallow the event. Three critical decisions booking managers must make about each inquiry received are:

1. Is the proposed event safe?
2. Does it meet all legal requirements?
3. If not, can it be made safe and/or meet all legal requirements?

If an attraction is safe, meets all legal requirements, and is not in direct violation of the venue's policies and procedures, the booking manager should give the application the same consideration accorded all other inquiries.

Booking the venue actually involves more than simply answering the telephone. Booking the venue is about relationships, trust, and accountability as partners. Booking begins with a promoter contacting the venue's booking manager for venue information and available dates. It is the booking manager's responsibility to ensure future business by cultivating potential promoters. An effective booking manager will seek to create new and/or alternative opportunities to fill the event calendar.

The venue should provide an environment that encourages maximum profit with minimum risk to both the promoter and the venue. Essential elements in nurturing the relationship between an event promoter and the venue's booking manager include maintaining close contact with these individuals and being constantly aware of touring attractions and potential meeting, convention, and trade show clients. In addition, creating a sense of trust and building a strong relationship is essential to a productive, long-term partnership.

Promoters who trust the venue management team and believe their best interests will be served will book more events. Reputation and personal relationships become paramount to ongoing booking success. Unscrupulous promoters will often promise and advertise one act or attraction and deliver another, less popular act. Therefore, it is critical that booking managers require confirmation of artists scheduled to perform, which may necessitate that the booking manager contact a tour manager or agency directly to verify the legitimacy of the promoter requesting the dates.

Prime Tenants and Annual Events

Many venues must develop their annual and long-term schedule of events around one or more prime tenants, such as:

- Ballet company
- College/university team(s)
- Family shows
- Opera
- Sports franchises
- Symphony orchestra
- Annual trade and consumer shows

The prime tenant typically requests date holds, which likely will be more than the final number of dates actually needed. Once the prime tenant's dates are confirmed, the venue can begin booking other events. If not managed properly, this process can result in dates being released too late for the venue to book other events.

For arenas and some stadiums with sports franchises, the process gets more difficult and often very frustrating due to the requirement to block out possible post-season playoff dates. Often, if a team is not mathematically eliminated from the playoffs until late in the regular season, there may not be enough time to use those dates for other events, much less conduct an effective promotion and marketing campaign. Venues with more than one sports franchise have even more challenges related to booking events around playoff dates.

Prime tenants are very important to the economic viability of most venues because they offer the following benefits:

- Guarantee a number of events each year
- Significantly enhance the value of certain commercial rights, such as:
    - Naming and beverage rights
    - Advertising signage
    - **Premium seating** (suites, club seats, loge boxes, party suites, etc.)
- Generate media coverage and exposure for the venue
- Are generally the best and most reliable drivers of **ancillary event revenues**, such as concessions and parking

For example, most venues hold dates for annual multi-day family shows, major concerts, trade or consumer shows, or one-of-a-kind special events. This information must be provided to the prime tenant to assist in establishing their final schedule. Likewise, performing arts venue managers will reserve prime dates for commercial touring productions while still hosting a nonprofit performing arts organization's season events.

McCaw Hall at Seattle Center - Seattle, WA

Holding Dates

A promoter may hold dates in a venue at three distinct levels: **tentative**, **confirmed** (i.e., contract pending), or **contracted**. While different venues or venue types may have different names for these levels and some may have intermediate levels, ultimately, there remain only three distinct categories. The booking agent attempting to **route an event** (i.e., process of sequencing dates for traveling from venue to venue in the most expeditious and economical manner) will ask the booking manager to place a tentative hold for an open date(s) on the venue's calendar. This tentative hold simply tells the booking manager the promoter is interested in leasing the venue.

Once the booking manager agrees to hold a specific date, the promoter can assume the following:

- The event can occur on that date(s);
- There are no conflicting scheduled events;
- The venue has the production capabilities to host the event; and,
- The date(s) will remain on hold and not be reassigned without consent of the promoter.

The booking manager, by placing this hold on a date(s), believes the promoter:

- Is serious about producing the attraction;
- Has the authority to book the date;
- Has the financial capacity to produce the event; and,
- Will release the date(s) promptly, if it is deemed no longer viable.

Experienced managers will normally release holds according to an agreed-upon timetable, unless contractually confirmed by the promoter. Booking agencies or artist representatives often offer acts to various promoters seeking the best financial opportunity. Therefore, it is not uncommon for several promoters to hold dates for the same event. As a result, it is extremely important that holds are act specific. If a date is being held by Promoter A for Act Z, and Promoter A loses Act Z to Promoter B, then Promoter A also loses control of the date. In other words, *whoever gets the event, gets the date*. In order to be fair to all promoters, the booking manager must remain neutral.

Efficiently routing shows to venues in various geographical areas is a difficult task. There are many moving parts that must come together. As a result, while it is prudent for a venue manager to have an automatic cut-off built into the date-hold process, the venue manager should be willing to extend that date if requested by the promoter. Granting extensions is also beneficial in maintaining a good relationship with the promoter.

Once routing is completed and the exact date(s) have been selected for the event, the booking manager should be notified so any unused dates on hold are released and returned to inventory. When a hold is confirmed, a contract is issued with a deadline for its return along with a rental deposit and other venue requirements, such as event insurance. When the signed contract and deposit are returned, the event's status becomes "contracted," at which point the process for putting tickets on sale may begin (refer to Appendix C for detailed information regarding contract components). Any remaining holds for the now-confirmed event are released at the point of contracting, and the dates are reclassified as open and available to potential users as the process begins anew. Figure 4-4 outlines a sample process for holding space/dates.

HOLD IS:	PROCESS SEQUENCE
TENTATIVE	Inquiry: ✓ Is the date available? ✓ Is the attraction / event desired? ✓ Potential user qualifies? ✓ Basic contract terms agreed? If yes, issue a "Tentative Hold" for X days (subject to challenges).
CONFIRMED (contract issued)	✓ Promoter qualified ✓ Contract terms agreed ✓ Contract issued ✓ Return required in X days ✓ Deposit required with contract
CONTRACTED	✓ Contract is signed and returned ✓ Deposit returned with contract (subject to bank clearance) ✓ Facility signs contract ✓ Prepare to put tickets on sale

Figure 4-4 : Sample Process for Holding Space/Dates

Challenging Hold Dates

Promoters desiring to hold a date(s) already held by another promoter might ask the booking manager for a *second hold* or issue a challenge for the date already on hold (Figure 4-5 outlines a sample process for challenging a hold date). A second hold enables the requesting promoter to immediately gain top priority if the event promoter currently possessing the hold date(s) relinquishes it or does not meet the venue's timelines. When a challenge occurs, the venue's booking manager contacts the promoter who has the first hold on the date and announces that another promoter is seeking the same date(s). The first promoter then must either enter into a contract for the date(s) within a specified period of time or remit a non-refundable deposit in order to keep the tentative hold status. If the original promoter does neither, the date(s) is relinquished and awarded to the challenger.

PROMOTER	REQUEST	ACTION
Promoter A "Mike"	Mike requests a tentative hold on specific date(s).	Venue booking representative grants tentative hold if: ✓ Date is available ✓ Event / attraction is desired ✓ User qualifies ✓ Basic contract terms agreed Hold has a deadline within which it must go to contract and is subject to challenge.
Promoter B "Teresa"	Teresa challenges Mike's hold (assume Teresa and her event meets criteria for contract). Venue booking agent may require Teresa to provide a non-refundable deposit and understand that she will have to go to contract immediately if the date(s) become available.	Venue booking representative notifies Mike of the challenge and issues a short deadline for Mike to submit a signed contract with deposit. If Mike cannot or will not commit to contract, the booking representative may cancel the initial tentative hold and make the date available to Teresa.

Figure 4-5: **Sample Process for Challenging a Tentative Hold**

The venue may require the challenger to submit a deposit, up to the minimum rental fee, prior to contacting the first-hold promoter to ensure the challenge is legitimate and not just a means to control dates. The challenger should be required to immediately execute the contract if the date becomes available.

It is not unusual for a promoter to attempt to tie up venues with tentative holds. If successful, the promoter is then able to leverage the date(s) to gain an advantage in competing with other promoters for the event. Venue managers normally follow a policy that sets the date aside for whoever gets the event. A key consideration is that venue managers must structure the process so that they control the venue's schedule and do not allow others to gain that control.

A challenge may only be issued against a "tentative" hold. If a contract has been sent to a potential user for a date(s), that promoter has until the stated deadline to sign and return the contract along with any required deposit. If the deadline passes, the date(s) becomes available for the venue manager to allocate as desired.

Circumstances will determine how much time and flexibility to give promoters during this process. The releasing of dates is a very sensitive issue. The experienced manager must remember that promoters book events critical to the venue's success and releasing the date of an established promoter could have negative consequences.

Date Protection

Different promoters often request dates for events that may appeal to the same audience or exhibitor base. This typically is not in the venue's best business interest, and it also often serves to confuse the public. For example, booking two circuses in the same month or two country concerts in the same week in an arena is generally considered an unwise practice. Likewise, in a convention facility, similar trade or consumer shows should not be booked too close together. To avoid such conflicts and preserve financial viability, some venue-governing bodies have instituted scheduling criteria requiring a reasonable degree of separation between similar events. Policies of this nature are termed "*protection policies*" and are designed to facilitate financial success for all parties. Consumer shows and traditional touring family shows commonly request protection from similar events.

Date protection shall apply to events that have 20% or more similar exhibitors, are charging an admission to gain entry to the event, and/or are open to the general public rather than being limited to a well-defined class of persons who normally belong to a trade or professional association.

Similar events renting the entire ballroom or more than 30,000 gross square feet of exhibit hall space and which are actively competing for specialized and specific local markets shall maintain the following clearance periods prior to the first event day and following the last event day:

- ✓ 45 Days: Public / consumer shows (e.g. boat shows, RV shows, home shows, etc.)
- ✓ 30 Days: Hobby / arts & crafts shows (e.g. antique shows, auctions, bridal shows, etc.)

Events not falling into any of these categories will be spaced at the discretion of the venue. Although booking and protection policies exist, the venue manager makes the final determination regarding the venue calendar and decisions most compatible with the venue's mission.

Figure 4-6 : Sample Date Protection Policy for a Convention Center

---

Clearly outlined and fairly enforced protection policies tend to be good tools for enhancing the success of an event. However, providing protection as a matter of policy may lead to other challenges. For example, a booking manager, working with a policy that provides a two-week window of protection, books a small-attendance, local wrestling event for the venue. Shortly thereafter, the manager discovers an opportunity to host a large national professional wrestling event. In order to book the larger event, the two-week window of protection provided to the smaller event would have to be compromised. Does the manager then abide by the protection policy and lose the larger event or ignore the policy and schedule both events? A situation of this nature requires the manager to demonstrate creative flexibility. Possible solutions may include the venue manager offering to reschedule the smaller event at a reduced rental rate, offering to buy out the smaller event, or making some other accommodation.

Booking managers realize that protection policies may protect events within the venue but do not necessarily protect events in the market. In most instances, it does not help the venue or **promoter** to prohibit another similar event from happening in their venue if the event will end up at another venue in the area. In fact, the manager may want to book both events to not only maximize revenue but also give both events the best chance for success by controlling advertising and **on-sale dates** for each event. It is advisable for any protection policy to be reviewed and approved by the venue's legal counsel to protect against liability concerns.

Freedom of Speech Issues

A manager may be asked to book an event that, although deemed "safe and legal," is so controversial in nature that hosting it would undoubtedly create problems. Venue managers and their booking personnel must remember, however, that a controversial event may have the same legal protection as any other event. While a manager, supported by venue policies, may reject any event that might distress either the community or the venue's governing body, the prudent manager will not refuse to lease the venue unless the intended activity is unsafe for the general public or fails to meet legal requirements. A venue with a history of leasing its public space is obligated by that history to continue this practice, without regard to performance content, so long as the building's protection policies remain intact, space is available, the event is properly scheduled and booked, and the activity is both legal and safe.

The operative word here is content. Based on freedom-of-speech considerations, neither the booking manager, the venue's governing body, the law-enforcement authorities, nor local civic leaders may discriminate against an event or attraction based strictly on its content. For instance, a venue leasing space to traditional religious congregations cannot legally forbid religious cults from use of the same space even though a majority in the community might disapprove. In this instance, the booking manager would be on more solid legal ground by simply denying use of the public assembly venue for all religious activities rather than trying to accept some while rejecting others.

Contracting

Once the promoter agrees with the conditions of use for a public assembly venue and the hold is confirmed, the booking manager will issue a contract. The specific details of the agreement should be itemized succinctly and include, but are not limited to, the following:

- Name and description of the event
- Event date(s) and times
- Contracted space
- Financial terms and considerations

Additional language should be included stipulating such items as the following:

- Deadline for contract return
- Lead time for delivery of insurance and performance riders
- Overtime charges
- Merchandising rights and fees

- Equipment service and labor rate sheet references
- Communication of fundamental performance expectations

The act of issuing a contract constitutes an offer. Before the agreement becomes legally binding, the recipient must accept the offer and provide consideration in the form of a deposit or collateral. In some instances, prior to executing an event, contract venues may be required to submit a **license application** to the local municipality for the purposes of using municipal services.

As previously stated, when the signed contract and deposit are returned, the event's status becomes "contracted" and the event management process begins (refer to Appendix C for additional information regarding contract components). While it may appear the venue has nothing to lose in a straight rental scenario, it is also very important for the promoter to enjoy success. The long-term success of many venues depends on repeat business, and the only way for that to happen is for the venue owners to adopt operating philosophies that allow both the venue and the event promoter a reasonable chance to succeed. If promoters are successful, they likely will generate repeat business. In the end, success breeds success.

Creating the proper business relationship with the venue's clients is the responsibility of venue management. Whether clients are promoters, presenters, vendors, subcontractors, or meeting planners, the objective of developing strong and positive relationships remains consistent. It is important for the booking manager to create a strong working relationship, even though the official agreement between client and venue may not call for the sharing of revenue, expenses, or risk. This particular type of relationship requires the sharing of information and ultimately a concern for the welfare and success of each party. It also requires an effort for each party to understand the problems and concerns of the other, a willingness to share resources, and creativity in identifying mutually beneficial solutions to issues that may arise.

SUMMARY

The booking process is designed to maximize yet protect the venue's two most important commodities: *time and space*. Efficient management of these elements is vital to maximizing the number of event bookings and the number of potential revenue streams. Successful programming of a venue's calendar should take into consideration the venue's mission, along with the needs of the community. Priority for bookings must always take into consideration prime tenants and major annual events. These events form the foundation for a diverse and dynamic schedule. Additional events can then be added to complete a schedule that offers something for the community the venue was built to serve.

As part of the booking process, the promoter places a tentative hold on a particular date(s). Once the promoter and booking manager are confident the event will take place, the event is transferred to a confirmed status. At that point, the contract is issued and the date is taken out of inventory and no longer available for booking by other promoters. When the contract is signed and other requirements, such as receipt of the rental deposit and insurance certificates, are met, the event is transferred to a contracted status and tickets may be placed on sale.

When governing bodies institute scheduling criteria requiring a reasonable separation between similar types of events, they are establishing date protection policies. Such policies should be written and communicated to any event promoter affected and should be reviewed and approved by the venue's legal counsel prior to implementation.

Although a public assembly venue manager may not agree with or like the content of a prospective event, freedom of speech issues may prohibit the manager from barring the event based on content alone. The essential question is, What is the venue manager's role in determining the values, needs, and desires of the community? Nonetheless, it is understandable that a manager may seek to protect the venue from negative publicity generated as a result of a controversial event. It is also important for the venue manager to consider the logistical needs and safety concerns and to determine whether the venue is capable of accommodating the event requirements.

Once both venue management and the promoter agree to the terms and conditions for use of the venue, details should be committed to in writing through a legal and binding contract. All specific details of the agreement should be included in the contract, which becomes a legally enforceable document. The event contract outlines the business relationship between venue management and the promoter and should be as specific and detailed as necessary to protect the interests of both parties.

CHAPTER 5

MARKETING AND SALES

INTRODUCTION

The difference between success and mediocrity is often the ability of a venue to market and promote both itself and its events. Marketing departments have to be the voice of the public assembly venue. They must make the industry, as well as their local community, aware of all the events and sales opportunities available. Venues are designed to present events and, in so doing, enhance the quality of life in the community, generate direct and indirect economic impact, and provide opportunities for a variety of sports, entertainment, conferences, and cultural events in a safe and comfortable gathering place.

Fulfilling this public mandate is no easy task. It takes daily effort, commitment, and attention to detail on the part of venue management, and particularly the marketing and sales department, to succeed in an increasingly competitive environment. Successful event marketing and sales involve the following:

- Constant salesmanship
- Industry recognition
- A marketplace that supports events through ticket sales
- Cooperation of the media and local businesses in advertising, promoting, and sponsoring events
- Supportive **governing body**
- Effective venue management

Marketing and sales encompasses many areas. In the context of venue management and for purposes of this book, our focus in this chapter is on the marketing and sales of the following:

Marketing

- Attracting events by marketing the venue and its capabilities
- Driving ticket sales through advertising, promotions, and publicity
- Evaluating the customer experience at the venue
- Stimulating public, media, and community relations

Sales

- Commercial rights to generate long-term, contractually obligated revenue, such as:
  - Naming rights
  - **Premium seating**
  - Advertising signage
  - **Pouring rights**
  - Branding of food and beverage products
  - Memorial gifts
- Event sponsorship to generate additional revenue on an event-by-event basis

The expansion of available public assembly venues, along with escalated competition, fewer events, shorter concert tours, and the need to generate revenue demands an aggressive marketing and sales strategy. Prudent venue managers know that waiting for business to appear on their doorstep will result in a very limited schedule. Researching touring attractions, cultivating industry relationships, and seeking out profitable events are the hallmarks of a highly successful venue. Consequently, a comprehensive strategic marketing plan becomes an absolute necessity for the venue to achieve success. The purpose of this chapter is to provide the basics of how an effective marketing and sales department should function.

MARKETING AND SALES DEPARTMENT

A vital part of many public assembly venues is the marketing and sales department. Overall responsibilities of the marketing and sales department may include the following:

- Manage and extend the venue's brand to all key stakeholders essential to the venue's success
- Produce an annual venue marketing plan, including advertising, promotions, and publicity strategy and tactics
- Develop and monitor marketing department budgets
- Arrange for industry-wide publicity about the venue and its events, achieving positive public/industry awareness
- Provide an in-house ad agency to assist in event advertising, marketing, and promotion
- Place event-related advertising
- Place industry advertising for the venue
- Sell advertising signage, sponsorships, premium seating, naming and pouring rights, and other commercial rights
- Maintain positive ongoing publicity, media, and community relations
- Conduct marketing and customer satisfaction research
- Oversee digital marketing activities, including website, e-mail content/design, and social media activities
- Facilitate the design and distribution of brochures and other **collateral materials**
- Manage and administer any outside marketing-related service contract(s)
- Monitor competitive events in local and regional venues
- Track current social media trends and use them appropriately
- Perform regular database management, data mining, and analytics
- Market and manage **group ticket sales**
- Coordinate marketing efforts with local CVB and other appropriate organizations
- If requested, assist with event booking

Every venue, regardless of size and type, should have a strategic marketing plan. The marketing plan presents a strategy for positioning the venue within the marketplace in order to maximize its business potential and accomplish established performance objectives. Consumers enjoy a continually expanding number of available options for spending discretionary income. These additional opportunities increase the level of competition among venues for available events and customers. Each venue, as part of its marketing strategy, must address several questions that get to the heart of its competitive standing, which include:

- What makes the venue different from its competitors?
- Why should event **promoters** and organizers book the venue rather than a competitor's venue?
- What effective strategies can be employed to maximize ticket sales and attendance?
- What are the venue's strengths and weaknesses?
- What competitive threats exist?
- What competitive opportunities are available?

The purpose of the marketing plan is to guide the establishment of a **market position** to achieve stated objectives in concert with the venue's purpose and mission statements. The venue manager needs a plan that is practical and applicable in a variety of business environments. Most importantly, the plan must be tailored to fit the unique, local market. Ultimately, the job of the marketing and sales department should be to maximize venue revenues through effective marketing strategies.

MARKETING AND SALES DIRECTOR

Every venue, regardless of size, should have at least one staff member whose primary focus is to sell and market the venue and its events. The primary responsibilities and skills of the marketing and sales director may include:

- A thorough knowledge of marketing strategies and tactics
- A thorough knowledge of the local market
- A good understanding of the marketing capabilities of the venue's ticketing systems
- An effective analysis of the venue's customers and the customer database
- Establishment of mutually beneficial relationships with event promoters and producers
- Strong and active relationships with local, regional, and national media
- Production of creative promotional campaigns for traditional and digital platforms
- Encouragement of positive stories that highlight the venue and its upcoming events
- Creation, monitoring, and regular updating of the venue crisis communications plan
- Action as the liaison between the venue and key stakeholders, such as the local convention and visitors bureau (CVB), chamber of commerce, and sports commission
- Implementation of a comprehensive marketing plan

Effective marketing and sales directors must be versatile professionals with a wide variety of skills. They play a critical role in the overall mission of the venue and can contribute greatly to the success of the venue's events.

VENUE MARKETING

Most public assembly venues are dependent on promoters for events. One of the most critical elements for sustained success is the ability for venue management to develop key industry relationships. The most successful venues have several common characteristics, which include the following:

- A well-respected, high industry-profile sales/booking team that serves as a magnet for events

- Solid and continuously reinforced relationships with entities that control event bookings, such as artist reps, talent agencies, promoters, show producers, association executives, sports leagues, and other similar groups and individuals

- Effective working relationships with local stakeholders that help make events successful, such as the CVBs, chambers of commerce, hotel-motel associations, retail associations, or other similar organizations

- Developing relationships with local media and business partners that allow for the delivery of effective advertising, marketing, and promotional campaigns to sell tickets

- Providing outstanding service to tenants and customers, resulting in high levels of satisfaction and repeat business

- Because of intense competition for events, venues must consistently work to attract event promoters and identify potential new sources of business. The marketing department must develop creative ways to get the attention of new promoters, as well as keep the attention and loyalty of existing promoters. There are two primary ways for the venue manager and marketing department to get the attention of promoters: *direct selling* and *industry advertising*.

- Direct or personal selling is a marketing strategy in which the seller establishes direct sales contact with its product's final users (Boone & Kurtz, 2002). In venue management, direct selling is used to reinforce to promoters the positive attributes of the venue. Some direct selling techniques include attending industry conventions and award shows, visiting promoters and agents in their corporate offices, and inviting promoters and meeting planners to the venue city for special events or familiarization tours. The ultimate goal of direct selling is to get one-on-one time with a promoter or meeting planner to encourage interest in utilizing the venue.

- Advertising is intended to create and maintain awareness (Shank, 2009) and includes any paid, non-personal communications about an organization or product intended to inform or persuade members of a particular audience (Boone & Kurtz, 2002). Advertising is also important in attracting the attention of promoters and meeting planners, particularly those not familiar with the venue. Venues always seek to create awareness and communicate the positive attributes of the venue and the market in an effort to attract events. For example, the marketing department may place advertisements in industry publications, create dynamic websites, and use social media to reach a diverse group of potential clients.

EVENT MARKETING

In-House Advertising Agencies

One of the primary goals of any marketing department should be to support the promoter's efforts to maximize event ticket sales by creating and implementing a successful marketing plan. The venue's marketing department often acts as an in-house marketing agency working on behalf of the promoter. Although the promoter has specific knowledge of their event, it is the responsibility of the marketing department to use their understanding of the local market to determine the most cost-effective and efficient means to maximize sales. For example, a viable ticket price in Chicago may be unrealistic in Charlotte. In order for promoters to make informed decisions on the viability of an event, they need accurate information on market demographics, acceptable ticket prices, preferred event days and start times, previous history in the market, and projected event attendance. Marketing departments that develop their own in-house advertising agencies can offer promoters the following at reduced costs or through value-added services:

- Advertisement placement in local and regional media
- Reduced advertising rates through venue relationships created by volume purchasing with local media
- Involvement with the media and local business partners in event sponsorship
- Willingness to minimize cash expenditures by securing advertising in return for **complimentary tickets**
- Creation of positive public relations stories that apply to a specific event
- Ability to pre-sell tickets through the venue's customer database
- Potential to procure corporate sponsorships to further reduce the cost of advertising and promotion
- Capacity to present the promoter with a clear and well-documented media settlement/reconciliation

While some venues may generate revenue through ad placement and other services, the primary reason for offering an in-house advertising agency is to provide a value-added service to those using the venue. An effective in-house ad agency may serve as a competitive advantage when attracting events to the venue. Those in-house agencies that do charge for their services generally receive a 10 to 15 percent agency commission. In-house advertising agencies should display to promoters an enthusiastic and honest effort to promote each event successfully.

Event Advertising and Promotions

As previously stated, marketing can help with the achievement of specific venue objectives. While objectives may differ for each venue, a commonly shared objective is to increase revenues generated through rent, ticket sales (i.e., if the rental fee is based on a percentage of the ticket sales), and income derived through **ancillary services**. Effective marketing through advertising and promotions is the key to achieving these objectives.

Effective **advertising campaign** strategies are crucial to achieving ticket sales goals. Typically, the event promoter provides the local marketing staff with an advertising budget, which the local marketing staff must best allocate. Once the advertising plan is approved by the event, the local marketing staff implements the plan with the designated media outlets.

The marketing manager must weigh the following questions when creating an advertising plan:

- What is the target audience?
- When should the campaign begin and end?
- When should ads run in selected media?
- Should direct marketing be included in the plan?
- How will digital media be utilized?
- What role should social media play?

Target Audiences

Target audiences for media buying are typically identified by some combination of the following: age, gender, ethnicity, geographic boundaries, incomes, education, and interest areas. The goal is to achieve the highest reach and frequency possible within the budget constraints. The marketing manager must determine what combination of media ("media mix") will allow the marketing campaign to reach the largest portion of the target audience (" reach") the most times ("frequency"). Media sales representatives from the various media outlets can provide specific data regarding their reach. The venue marketing manager can use this information to evaluate which media outlets and which programming will give the greatest exposure to the desired target. However, the media sales representatives are trying to sell their advertising inventory, and the prudent marketing manager will weigh the value of all options.

Campaign Duration

The marketing manager must determine when the campaign should begin and end. There are two primary considerations when determining the campaign duration: budget and event sales history. For example, popular events that are likely to sell out may only need a few days of advertising prior to the **on-sale date**. Other events may sell slowly but steadily for several months. It is important to know the likely sales pattern for the event before making advertising timing decisions. The marketing manager should also research the event sales pattern and advertising schedule in other markets.

Run in Selected Media

Along with determining campaign timing for traditional media, individual advertisements must be scheduled in specific programming slots or **dayparts** on radio and television. The size and location of print ads must also be decided. It is important in evaluating these decisions to consider the creative aspects (i.e., the actual ads themselves) and the impact of each. If one has a strong TV ad and a weak radio ad, one may opt to do more TV and less radio. The best way to begin this process is to ask the media sales representative to produce a suggested schedule that delivers the highest possible reach and frequency for the budget. This can then be adjusted slightly to include any specific programs that are of special appeal to the target audience.

Direct Marketing

Direct marketing refers to advertising e-mailed or mailed directly to potential ticket buyers. The best predictor of future behavior is past behavior, so often the best source of ticket buyers for an event is the venue's customer database. Sending e-mail alerts or direct mail to ticket buyers who have attended similar events in the past is typically the highest return of any marketing activity. Offering advance sales to these prospects also provides an early indicator on how sales are likely to unfold, generates early momentum through social buzz, and provides analytic data.

Digital Media

With the continued growth of digital media, traditional media channels, including newspapers, radio, and TV, are proving less effective as advertising options, particularly among younger audiences. Today, a venue marketer can place tracking pixels on its website, which allows the marketer to track site visitors across the Internet after they leave the venue site. This is why consumers may see repeated ads popping up for golf clubs after they visit a site selling clubs or search that term. This type of advertising is called re-targeting.

Search engine marketing is also essential. This means buying likely search words on search engines so that your date and link appear when customers search for shows or entertainment options. Other digital metrics allow the tracking of ticket sales back to ads and even send follow-up e-mails to customers who abandon their sales carts prior to final purchase. Some of the latest technology in mobile advertising allows advertisers to "geo-target" a message within a specific geographic zone. For example, you could advertise a special one-day discount offer to everyone who travels within a five-mile radius of the venue box office.

Social Media

On the social media front, digital marketers have options for advertising on social media platforms, but many marketers believe social channels are most effective when employed to create awareness and buzz rather than hard-sell advertising. Creating effective social media presence for a venue and its events is a role that is becoming critically important for venue marketing managers. Because of the technological complexity and the rapid rate of change in all things digital, venues should consider regular consultations with digital marketing specialists.

As discussed previously, one of the primary objectives of the marketing department is to increase tickets sales, which, in turn, has a positive impact on ancillary revenue. The main sources of ancillary revenue include parking, food and beverage sales, and merchandise sales. The marketing effort may also involve a number of other strategies, including price scaling for the event, **dynamic ticket pricing**, **group ticket sales**, promotional packages, discount offers, and incentives. The marketing department may also coordinate additional activities to benefit local charities while helping promote the event and drive ticket sales. These strategies not only help to grow ancillary revenue but also build an increased customer base through exposure to new events.

Media Channels

Once the target market is identified, the marketing director must decide what combination of media will most effectively and efficiently reach that market. Factors such as the advertising budget, length of time before the event, competing events in the market, and available advertising inventory will impact this decision. The most common forms of media include social media, radio, television, and newspapers.

Social Media

The availability of social media has dramatically changed the way venues advertise their events. This ever-changing medium allows artists and event promoters to connect with fans in a dynamic way. One mention on social media of an appearance by a performer at a particular venue can sell out a concert. With its low cost and ability to reach literally thousands, or tens of thousands of potential customers, social media is an advertising vehicle that must be used for almost every **advertising campaign**. As with other forms of advertising, it is important for the marketing director to identify the target audience in order to determine the most effective form of social media.

The use of social media channels is essential, but, in order to be effective, the marketing staff must devote a substantial amount of time to provide fresh and engaging content (i.e., posts). As a result, many venues are hiring a designated social media manager to oversee all efforts in this area. Social media is constantly evolving, and, therefore, venue marketers may also consider regular consultations with digital and social media marketing specialists in order to stay abreast of current trends.

Radio

Even with the advent of satellite radio and MP3 players, radio advertising continues to be an effective advertising vehicle in some markets for some events, especially concerts that feature artists the station is playing. A major advantage is that radio stations are normally formatted to appeal to specific market segments, making it is easy to identify which station aligns well with a venue event. Media scheduling refers to setting the timing and sequence for a series of advertisements (Boone & Kurtz, 2002). The frequency and length of these advertising messages, along with the optimum choice of schedules for running the ads, is an important consideration in development of a promotional plan. **Run of Schedule (ROS)** is the airing time of a radio commercial left to the discretion of the station (a sample run of schedule can be found in Appendix A 5-1). Securing ads to be broadcast at a specific moment (time slot) or during a particular program usually requires payment of a premium. Many radio stations also offer strong promotional support through disc jockey (DJ) endorsements and on-air promotions. For some events, this promotional support is extremely valuable and should be considered in evaluating the ad buy.

Television

With the popularity of digital video recorders (DVRs), fewer people watch live television today. However, television can still be a very effective form of advertising for events with broad appeal and strong visual creative. This medium uses sight, sound, and motion to convey the advertising message. For events that deliver strong visuals, like family shows and sporting events, television is the strongest medium. A disadvantage of television advertising is its cost, particularly if you buy primetime programming. To evaluate value, a buyer can compare the cost and reach of a TV buy versus a radio buy to see which delivers the most exposure as measured through reach and frequency. Typically, radio will be less costly, but this is not always the case. You also may consider cable TV programming options, which tend to serve narrower audiences. For example, a venue presenting a food show with celebrity chef demonstrations may be best served by running commercials on the *Food Network* rather than selecting more costly network spots. Like radio, **Run of Schedule (ROS)** is also used to refer to the airing time of a television commercial left to the discretion of the station. Television commercials broadcast at a specific time or during a particular program usually require payment of a premium. Another important consideration is whether the event has produced a TV spot that simply needs to be customized to the local market, as opposed to the venue having to produce a newly created ad, which may be cost-prohibitive.

Newspapers

Although readership of newspapers continues to decline, they still provide some advantages, including flexibility, community prestige, coverage, and control of the exposure to the advertising message (Koolbeck, 2013). Newspaper ads are most effective for audiences over forty, and it is important to check current circulation figures and weigh those numbers against the quoted advertising rates. **Run of Press (ROP)** refers to placement of an advertisement in a newspaper or magazine left to the discretion of the publisher. Its placement in a particular location or a specific page usually requires payment of a premium. Most newspapers also offer online advertising as part of their advertising packages. When evaluating this option, it is important to determine if reading the on-line content is limited to any degree by a pay-wall and, if so, how many subscribers have access to the part of the site where your ad will appear. Most newspapers also participate in national digital ad networks like *Google* and *Yahoo,* and it is often more cost-effective to buy local media sites through these national channels, which typically are sold on a pay-per-click basis versus impressions.

Other Media Options

Other media forms may include electronic billboards, which may be stationary or mobile. Both provide the flexibility to change the message more frequently and to potentially reach larger numbers of people at a more reasonable cost than traditional billboards. Additional media options may also include grassroots efforts, sidewalk chalk drawings, and traditional signage and posters.

One of the exciting facets of event marketing is the development of creative promotions that ultimately inspire people to buy more tickets. The marketing department, with the help of the promoter's representative, always has the ability to leverage assets associated with an event. Promotions, which may include ticket giveaways, promotional giveaways, two-fers (i.e., entitle customers to purchase two tickets to a specified theatrical production for the price of one), booth space discounts, and autographed artist memorabilia, are just a few of the popular promotions used to create excitement around an event. Creative promotions can be accomplished with little expense to the venue or promoter. The marketing department can use social media to engage potential customers in interactive promotions, such as an event-related scavenger hunt to win tickets. With limited resources and intense competition for customers, the marketing department must be creative and innovative to be successful.

Analytics and Customer Databases

Analytics is an important component of most modern businesses, including public assembly venues. Business analytics refers to the analysis of data in search of meaningful patterns that may assist in decision making. In venues, analytics are used to track the return on investment (ROI) for marketing campaigns. Venue management, in conjunction with their ticketing partners, are able to track click-throughs and follow up with customers who abandoned ticket purchases prior to completion. Analytics can also be used to track or confirm trends in website traffic and methods of access. Generally, venues must focus on long-term trends, as website traffic may vary dramatically based upon event announcements, on-sales, and event dates. For example, with a large event social media views or website visits may increase 2,000 percent during one week but be down 1,500 percent the following week. While professional sports teams and other sports and entertainment organizations have been using analytics for quite some time, it is relatively new for public assembly venues, and venue management must work to identify how to make the data actionable.

Customer databases have become a standard tool in the promotional arsenal. Promoters expect the venue marketing department to provide access to their customer database to promote their event at no cost. Customers in the venue database are alerted via e-mail regarding upcoming events and may be provided access to pre-sales and special promotional offers.

Many ticketing systems automatically download existing ticket buyers into the database according to a pre-determined schedule. The marketing director must determine whether customers are provided a blatant opt-in or an opt-out of the database. Databases may also be built through opt-in opportunities at off-site events, the venue website, and media contests.

In order to increase effectiveness of the communication, the marketing director should create dynamic e-mails that engage the customer. Lastly, the marketing director must determine the philosophical approach to communications with customers through the database, including the content, frequency, and whether or not they target segments of the database based on past purchasing history or customer preferences.

Public Relations

As the voice of the public assembly venue, the marketing department must work to strategically place positive stories related to the venue and its events in local media and industry publications. "Public relations is a strategic communication process that builds mutually beneficial relationships between organizations and their publics" (PRSA, 2014). The marketing staff tends to be more effective in securing coverage when they have a positive relationship with the media.

Almost every event has some positive human-interest story. The artist performing in the event may have ties to the community, the marketing department may facilitate a visit by circus clowns to the local children's hospital, or a visiting professional athlete reads to students at his former elementary school. These are stories that would appeal to local media outlets and, if covered, would also generate publicity for the event.

One vehicle the marketing department uses to communicate information about the event or the venue is the press release. Press releases are advertising disguised as news. An effectively written press release can prompt the local media to generate a story related to the upcoming event. An interesting story on the local evening news may reach more potential customers than a paid, thirty-second commercial airing at 10:00 a.m. on a Monday.

With advances in cameras and computer editing, the venue marketing manager also should consider generating original video and audio content for posting to social media channels. Furnishing broadcast quality footage to stations unable to cover an event is also a possibility.

SALE OF COMMERCIAL RIGHTS

Commercial rights are opportunities for venues to derive non-event revenue from the sale of certain assets. These rights represent a value to corporations and businesses that can benefit from the affiliation with the venue, tenants, and events. The sales of these assets represent long-term, contractually obligated sources of revenue and may include the following:

- Naming rights
- Beverage pouring rights (exclusive and non-exclusive)
- Branding of food and beverage products
- Sponsorships
- Advertising signage (static and electronic)
- Additional advertising opportunities
- Memorial gifts

Ideally, before a venue undertakes the sale of commercial rights, an inventory of all rights, sponsorships, advertising signage (electronic and static), media mentions, branding relationships, and trade/barter is prepared. This inventory is intended to help establish:

- Size/dimensions
- Location
- Possible categories of exclusivity
- Contract terms
- Value/pricing
- Fulfillment to the buyer (i.e., tickets, premium seating, parking, and VIP amenities/ access)

Once inventory has been identified, rates representing the value of each asset and the corresponding fulfillment obligations can be established. Due to the importance of this process, venue management may seek assistance from a third-party source that specializes in the valuation of the inventory.

The venue is obligated to fulfill requirements as outlined in the commercial rights agreement. For example, the XYZ Corporation purchases the naming rights to a stadium for a ten-year period at a cost of $2 million per year. While this may be treated as operating income, a portion of the revenue may be used for contract fulfillment requirements. Typically, a naming rights sponsor is provided a fulfillment benefits package that might include a complimentary suite, club seats, signage, and parking privileges. If the value of these elements accounted for $200,000 of inventory, the net incremental revenue to the venue for naming rights is $1.8 million.

The selling of commercial rights may rest with the venue's sales department, the marketing department, or a third-party contractor that specializes in the sale of commercial rights. Regardless of where the responsibility lies, it is vitally important to ensure the commercial-rights client is happy, satisfied, and inclined to renew its contracts at the appropriate time.

Naming Rights

The sale of **naming rights** may be a critical component in funding new construction or revitalization of a venue, or it may be treated as operating income. Further, in some cases, naming rights are also a significant part of the economic mix to attract or retain a major or minor league sports franchise in a growing number of venues. Venues of all types have the opportunity to capitalize on this revenue source either through the naming of the venue or individual spaces within the venue.

Naming rights agreements vary in length and magnitude based upon a number of factors, including venue size, type, location, and tenants. For example, a small arena in a **secondary market** with a minor league tenant may garner $100,000 annually for ten years, while a stadium in a major market with an NFL team may garner up to $20 million annually for twenty years.

One of the things that must be considered when naming rights are sold is the time and **fulfillment cost** associated with branding the venue. A common misconception is that naming rights implies venue ownership. However, branding may include signage throughout the venue, staff uniforms, **collateral materials**, letterhead, and other tools associated with sales and marketing. When naming rights change, management must consider the lead-time and cost necessary to re-brand the venue.

Barclays Center - Brooklyn, NY

Staples Center - Los Angeles, CA

Beverage Pouring Rights

Beverage **pouring rights** refer to the exclusive rights of a beverage maker or distributor to have its products sold at a particular venue, event, or institution (Oxford Dictionaries, 2013). Similar to naming rights, beverage pouring rights agreements may include inventory such as signage, **premium seating**, and promotions. Beverage sponsors often place a premium on these elements to gain "exclusive" pouring rights, thereby excluding their competitors. A beverage pouring agreement is usually the result of a **Request for Proposal (RFP)** process and decided by competitive bidding. The larger soft drink companies are well versed in this process and often have a revenue formula based on volume sales they use to generate a proposal.

Alcoholic beverages pose a different set of circumstances since federal and state laws regulate the relationship between alcoholic beverage companies and retailers with regard to sponsorships and pouring rights. On the federal level, these laws are called "tied house" laws and basically state that a retail license holder cannot accept inducements (cash or equipment and sometimes even service) to sell a specific brand of alcohol to the exclusion of other brands (Alcohol and Tobacco Tax and Trade Bureau, 2014). Therefore, whoever holds the retail liquor license (typically the **concessionaire**) cannot be the same individual or company that solicits alcoholic beverage companies for sponsorship (typically venue management) (Bigelow, 2013). There must be a legal separation between the two parties. The beer companies, in particular, will look for some kind of advertising exclusivity, if available. It is important, as with all exclusives, to define them as narrowly as possible so that revenue can be maximized in the category.

Branding of Food and Beverage

In an effort to maximize food and beverage sales, many venues find it advantageous to brand certain offerings with popular local or national products. The **branded products** are generally selected based upon the financial incentives provided to the venue. Whether the food and beverage operations are in-house or contracted out, the concessionaire may also sublet to third-party providers for a percentage of their revenues (Steinbach, 2008). While most industry experts agree that hot dogs, peanuts, and other ballpark staples account for two-thirds or more of a venue's total concession revenues, many consumers still prefer to see branded products (Steinbach, 2008).

Sponsorships

Venues offer a variety of sponsorship opportunities, and the creative marketing department should identify those areas offering revenue potential. This may include sponsorship of a concourse, ticket office, ticketing system, food court, interactive kiosks, or some other interior space or feature even though a title sponsor has its name on the venue as a whole.

Sponsors may also wish to associate their name with a particular event. These opportunities may include title or presenting sponsor designations and may be shared with media sponsors. In most cases, the venue does not benefit from the revenue generated by event sponsorships, but their efforts serve to support the **promoter** relationship.

Advertising Signage

Perhaps the most traditional form of commercial rights sales is advertising signage, both static and electronic, and both interior and exterior. Advertising signage may include:

- Scoreboards
- LED (light emitting diode) boards
- Electronic message boards
- Backlit display cases
- Outdoor marquees
- **Vomitories**
- Concourse TV monitors

These opportunities may be priced at affordable levels, enabling smaller businesses to become advertising partners. Typical business categories targeted for venue advertising include the following:

- Airlines
- Automotive
- Banks
- Communications (wireless)
- Financial
- Alcoholic beverage companies/distributors
- Insurance
- Media
- Real estate
- Technology

Yankee Stadium - Bronx, NY

Kauffman Stadium - Kansas City, MO

In some cases, the prime tenant teams and the venue share advertising inventory. For example, an NHL prime tenant would most likely have the rights to advertising on hockey dashers and the **Zamboni** (an ice resurfacing machine). The team would also most likely have rights to on-ice advertising, although the venue would retain the right to include the logo of the naming rights sponsor, or simply the name of the venue. In some cases, the venue and team cooperate by combining their inventory and selling it through one sales team. This system reduces costs for both entities and offers buyers a much broader package of options that can be tailored to their specific needs.

Additional Advertising Opportunities

There are additional opportunities to expand revenue streams through advertising sales in the following areas:

- Tickets (paper or electronic)
- Event programs
- Venue newsletters
- Playbills and theater season brochures
- Seating charts
- Event schedules
- Venue website
- Merchandise

- Seat cupholders
- Promotional giveaways

The possibilities for raising additional monies through marketing/advertising channels are virtually endless, restricted only by the depth of the marketing department staff's imagination. With this in mind, the marketing department must be careful to resist selling too much advertising, which might create clutter, diminish the venue's attractiveness, and reduce value. In addition, an overload of advertisements makes it very difficult for the venue's guests to recall the advertising messages. The level to which guests are able to recall advertisers is very important to the companies seeking to gain a return on their advertising investment. The guest's level of advertiser recall is also important to the venue manager seeking to attract new and/or retaining current advertisers. Astute venue managers will implement periodic research studies to ascertain their guest's recall levels. The resulting data can be very influential when negotiating with current and potential advertisers.

Memorial Gifts

Donor programs are designed to attract individuals or businesses wishing to assist the venue financially or through the provision of goods and services. The difference between donors and sponsors is that contributions made by donors are generally altruistic. They are intended to honor a family member or patron of the arts and generally do not afford the donor any additional benefits. The benefit to the donor is more likely to be satisfaction and recognition through memorials, such as commemorative plaques on benches or seats, a meeting room or hospitality area named for the donor, or commissioned artwork. In addition, donor programs may offer the donor a tax deduction for their gift. Memorial gifts are not generally considered sources of annual operating revenue.

Institutions of higher education have developed excellent donor programs to solicit contributions from their graduates, as well as the business community, philanthropic organizations and the general public. Venues can institute similar donor programs when seeking contributions from foundations, benefactors, and businesses wishing to support the community. The performing arts represent one segment of the entertainment industry that has benefited greatly from donor programs. Even though donor programs may not seem as profitable as sponsorship agreements, they can create substantial amounts of good will in addition to providing needed revenue or goods and services.

MARKETING AND SALES OF PREMIUM ACCESS

Regardless of the industry, sales can be enhanced through creative marketing and value-added packaging. The public assembly venue is no exception. In some types of public assembly venues, exclusive seating options are in limited supply and often more desirable. This marketing concept is based on the premise that individual guests and businesses are willing to pay a premium price for seating in areas that offer added amenities. These added amenities might include proximity to the attraction, exclusive access, optimal sightlines, and/

or physical comfort. Sale of premium access may represent a substantial percentage of the venue's revenue and includes suites and club seats.

Suites now represent the ultimate in upscale seating. They have evolved from skyboxes added at the top of the venue to luxury suites placed in prime locations. In recent years, these spaces have been re-named "hospitality" suites to satisfy concerns of corporate accountants regarding tax-deductible expenses and shareholders concerns regarding "luxury expenditures." Hospitality suites have now expanded into other areas in the venue and may include a variety of seating and viewing combinations, such as bunker, dugout, and locker room suites. These concepts are addressed in more detail in chapter 6.

The marketing of the premium access products requires the marketing and sales department to conduct research resulting in the identification of target businesses and individuals. In addition, these businesses need to be convinced that premium-access products will help grow their business and enhance their bottom line.

While the structure of the lease agreement varies at each venue, selling suites offers a variety of avenues by which revenue can be generated in addition to the basic suite lease. These opportunities may include:

- Food and beverage
- Suite ticket sales for additional events (if not included in the basic lease)
- Priority access to additional non-suite event tickets
- Access to other venue amenities
- Concierge service
- Valet parking

Distribution of the revenues generated from suite sales and related amenities is normally predetermined by contractual agreements between the venue and its tenants. The percentage of distribution varies but most often is heavily weighted to the tenant. The venue still benefits from this process, and, therefore, the efforts by the sales and marketing department are an important function of venue management.

The marketing of suites is enhanced when venues allow suite holders the opportunity to sublease their suites on a per-event basis. This option is appealing to suite holders not wishing or able to attend every event, because it provides the opportunity to re-capture a portion of their leasing costs. It is also beneficial to the venue because it brings guests to the events who purchase tickets and ancillary products or services. Empty seats do not purchase food, beverages, merchandise, or produce parking revenues. Subleasing can also provide an opportunity to introduce the suite concept to potential suite holders.

For some customers, premium or "club" seats offer an opportunity to enjoy some of the same amenities available to suite holders, but at a lower price. Like suites, some of these amenities may include preferential parking, food and beverage delivery service to the customer's seat, access to the venue's restaurants and clubrooms, private restrooms, and admission to the venue through a private entrance. In addition, one of the primary advantages useful in the marketing of club seats is the ability of the club seat holder to purchase premium seats to other events. The market for club seats is much broader than for suites because of the available inventory and relative affordability.

Suites and club seats have become such vital revenue producers that they can significantly influence the design of new venues, especially amphitheaters, arenas, and stadiums. As stated previously, successful marketing of suites and club seats is extremely important and demands a concentrated effort to maximize the potential. Therefore, venue management must provide the necessary resources to ensure the marketing and sales department is able to focus sufficient time and energy to this vital revenue source. Though the prime tenant may manage premium access, the venue must still support their efforts.

Premium Seating

SUMMARY

Creating awareness of the venue and its events is an important ingredient in the venue's success. The marketing and sales department must be skilled at selecting advertising to reach the target audience, as well as generating public relations stories and creative promotions that excite the community.

Identification of the target audience is critical to venue and event marketing. Once the target audience is identified, the marketing and sales department must select the best form of advertising to reach that audience. Although event promoters know their events, it is up to the venue's marketing and sales department to provide the promoter with the best way to sell their event in the local market. The marketing and sales department often serves as the advertising agency for promoters and is able to take advantage of discounted rates afforded the venue.

The marketing department must create strategic marketing campaigns for each event. There are various forms of advertising available, including social media, radio, television, newspapers, and billboards. The marketing department must identify the best type of advertising for the event based on the potential audience. It is important for the marketing and sales department to monitor tickets sales and determine if the advertising strategies are effective or need to be adjusted to increase event awareness.

The marketing and sales department may also be responsible for the sale of commercial rights, including naming rights, beverage pouring rights, sponsorships, advertising signage, and memorial gifts. These commercial rights may represent lucrative sources of revenue for the venue. Of course, the marketing and sales department is responsible for contract fulfillment to ensure the satisfaction of the entities that purchase these opportunities.

The essence of venue management is booking viable events and then working to maximize tickets sales. Venues that accomplish this generate more event activity and more repeat business from event promoters and show organizers. Often, promoters may schedule their events in one venue over another because of the quality and effectiveness of services they receive from the marketing and sales department.

CHAPTER 6

TICKETING AND ACCESS MANAGEMENT

INTRODUCTION

The issuance of tickets is almost as old as the management of public assembly venues itself. Historically, in the latter part of the first century, admission into many of the events held in the Roman Colosseum was free to the public. However, their social classes in Roman society determined where attendees were allowed to sit and stand. Attendees were issued colored pottery shards that corresponded to color-coded entrance portals and seating sections in the venue. These served as the first control of assigned seating and were the foundation that led to today's ticketing process (Coarelli, et al., 2000/2001).

Ticketing or granting a "right of admission" into a venue today has evolved from its earliest forms into today's ticketing technology. Whether shards, preprinted hard tickets, or e-tickets, tickets serve three primary functions, which include:

- Limited Contract and Revocable Permit
- Means of Communication
- Means of Financial Accounting and Inventory Control

The ticketing process is part of the overall venue access control system and has transcended simply selling and taking tickets at the entrance of a venue into a fully integrated access management and information control process. The ticketing process includes two different elements: *ticketing operations* and *sales*.

Ticketing operations refers to the tasks that take place prior to putting the event on sale, which include determining ticket prices and the seating configuration, creating a seating chart and **ticket manifest**, and developing an equitable system to sell the tickets.

Ticket sales refer to the process of transferring a ticket to the customer and marking it as sold within the ticket manifest. Venues have the responsibility of making this transaction as convenient as possible through primary authorized channels, which include the ticket office, phones, retail outlets, and online through the venue's ticketing system.

The information in this chapter will highlight the various facets of the ticketing process and will discuss the importance of developing an accurately managed, time-sensitive, ticketing operation and sales process. The venue type will determine the significance of the ticketing process to the specific venue. Some venues, such as arenas, stadiums, and theaters, are dependent on a successful ticketing process. On the other hand, convention and exhibition centers use a ticketing process but to a much lesser degree.

TICKET OFFICE

Few experiences match securing a ticket for your favorite artist, the big game, or the annual car show. For many customers, purchasing a ticket represents their first interaction with the venue and can affect their perception of the overall event experience. To support the ticketing process, it is important to have a properly designed, high-functioning ticket office, including knowledgeable personnel and state-of-the-art systems.

While some venues, especially theaters, manage their ticket operations in house, requiring additional personnel and space, many venues require reduced space due to the increased percentage of tickets being sold online. When designing ticket offices in new venues, architects need to account for whether the ticket operations are managed in house or contracted, which in turn will dictate the necessary square footage, facilities, and amenities. Additional consideration must be given for customer access and event-day crowd flow.

The role of ticket office personnel has significantly changed since customers now purchase the majority of tickets online. Nonetheless, for the customers who purchase tickets through the ticket office or pick up reserved tickets, the process must be conducted efficiently and with a high level of customer service.

TICKET OFFICE MANAGER

A ticket office manager has a tremendous amount of responsibility, which directly impacts the ability of the department to effectively meet objectives. The ticket office manager is responsible for the following:

- Oversight of the ticketing system
- Managing of the ticket office staff
- Establishing ticket office policies and procedures
- Liaison to the promoter
- Accountability for ticket revenues
- Generating daily ticket sales reports
- Developing ticket manifests and seating charts
- Preparing event settlement sheets
- Troubleshooting ticket issues

The person in this position must have extensive technology, accounting, and management experience, plus exceptional communication skills. Ticket office managers communicate with a variety of stakeholders, including promoters, tenants, ticketing companies, venue personnel, customers, and sponsors. In addition, an effective ticket office manager exhibits effective time management, the ability to work under pressure, the ability to multi-task, attention to detail, and creative problem solving.

FUNCTIONS OF A TICKET

Limited Contract and Revocable Permit

A ticket for admission to a venue and an event is both a limited contract and a revocable permit. For the ticket holder, it provides evidence of authorization to enter the venue, with restrictions, and a guarantee that the promoter will deliver what has been purchased as advertised and promoted. In addition, the ticket may identify a specific seating location purchased by the ticket holder.

The event name, date and time of the event, name of the venue, and ticket price are generally printed on the face of the ticket. This information becomes part of the ticket's guarantee obligating the promoter to produce what the ticket promises. Substitution of one attraction for another and/or changing the time and place of the performance may give the ticket holder the right to request a full or partial refund.

If the venue and promoter cannot deliver the event as advertised and promoted, the ticket holder may have the right to compensation that can include, but is not limited to, a partial or full refund of the ticket price or a complimentary ticket to a future event. For example, when the headliner performs an abbreviated show or the lead performer in a play does not appear for a particular performance, the audience may have the option of requesting a refund depending on the circumstances.

In some instances, the ticket holder may have the option to be relocated to an area within the venue that enables the ticket holder comparable or better proximity to the event. For example, customers who buy a ticket to watch a baseball game have the right to complain if they were not informed in advance of an **obstructed view**. In this instance, the venue or team representative would either relocate the customer to a seat with an unobstructed view or, if none were available, refund the price of the ticket.

Often, when extremely popular attractions are being promoted, seating that is obstructed or offers a limited view of the event is made available to the public once the purchaser has been informed in writing on the ticket that the seats have sightline restrictions. Tickets for these seats should be clearly marked "Limited View" or "Obstructed View." In rare cases, seats that only provide the purchaser with a video screen to view the event rather than a direct live view have been sold and are referred to as "No Direct" or "No Live" seats.

In most venues, each ticket shows the price paid for the ticket as well as, in some instances, the tax and service charges. Indicating the price paid on the ticket protects the ticket office in the event a refund is necessary. Complimentary and **trade tickets** should have $0.00/zero value included on the ticket, which would indicate they are not eligible for a refund since they were not purchased. There may also be discounted tickets, which should in some manner indicate their value. Computerized ticketing facilitates the ability of venues to display accurate ticket pricing information correctly.

Each ticket is also a revocable license, the conditions of which may prevent a guest from entering the venue or lead to removal from the venue based upon a number of reasons. For example, a guest who is clearly intoxicated may not be permitted to enter the venue. In addition, another guest's behavior after entry may negatively impact the event experience for other guests and result in removal from the venue. Depending on the circumstances, revoking the ticket (i.e., license) may initiate a refund of the ticket price. If the customer does not comply with terms of the event disclaimer, waiver, or release of liability on the ticket, then the venue has the right to remove the customer from the venue for cause and without reimbursement of the ticket price.

Means of Communication

In addition to event-related information and safety warnings, the ticket is an effective and efficient means for communicating venue-specific information directly to the customer, particularly policies relating to prohibited items, camera policies, and specific entry points. In addition, the ticket sales process has also become an effective means of pre-event communication, as well as a post-event evaluation tool enabling the venue and promoter to more effectively and efficiently reach the ticket-buying population. Generally, guests ordering tickets online have provided their e-mail address, which creates a usable database for that particular event. This database enables the venue to notify guests in advance of pre-event activities or expected traffic delays, as well as invite guests to participate in an online survey rating their experience. Tickets can also be used as marketing and promotional opportunities, acknowledge an event or venue sponsor, and create value-added benefits.

Ticket Front & Back - Fenway Park - Boston, MA

Means of Financial Accounting and Inventory Control

The ticketing process has evolved into a means of financial accounting and inventory control. Once venues began controlling tickets sales activities and admissions, promoters and entertainers began to demand an accurate accounting of gate receipts. Consequently, ticketing became an extremely important facet of the venue accounting process. It was a simple process to compare money collected at the ticket office with ticket stubs collected at the door. The introduction of turnstiles in some venues provided an even more efficient and effective means for managers to reconcile the amount of money collected at the ticket office against the number of customers passing through the gate. The comparison of the ticket sales report, ticket stubs count, and turnstile counts served as a positive auditing system.

Today, the final ticket sales reconciliation process is illustrated through the ticket office event audit. The audit uses the sold ticket inventory to calculate the total gross sales figure, which is compared to money on hand from ticket sales and **drop counts** or bar code reports. Figure 6-1 is an example of a basic ticket office event audit.

Category	Ticket Totals	Amount
Available ticket inventory	20,000	
Ticket price (face value)		$ 50
Gross potential ticket sales		$ 1,000,000
Sold tickets	10,000	
Complimentary tickets	100	
Total tickets out	10,100	
Gross revenue from ticket sales		$ 500,000
Money on hand from ticket sales		$ 500,000
Drop count (actual attendance)	9,750	
Unused inventory	9,900	

Figure 6-1 : Basic Ticket Office Event Audit

The primary function of the ticket office is to accurately account for all tickets and gross receipts, including complimentary and promotional tickets. The venue must accurately reconcile the tickets and receipts back to the original **ticket manifest** for the promoter. Proper financial accounting and inventory control is the cornerstone of an effective and efficient ticket office.

TICKET FORMAT

Technology continues to change and improve the ticketing industry. One of the most significant technological changes is the ability of the consumer to purchase tickets online, download and print their ticket(s), or receive an e-ticket. The technology and security feature that allows an e-ticket to be printed at home is the use of a bar code. When consumers download an e-ticket, they also download a corresponding unique bar code, a format that—to date—has not been susceptible to counterfeit or fraud. While each ticket can be copied, as can other types of hard tickets, the bar code is the determining factor as to the authenticity of the ticket. Consequently, an e-ticket can be used for entrance into a venue/event only if it is the first time the barc ode is scanned. Once the bar code has been read at the entrance, all other copies of the same bar code are null and void, even if the first e-ticket used to gain entry is not the original e-ticket.

Although e-ticket technology has been a significant convenience to both the venue and customer, the ticket companies, in cooperation with venues, are making great strides in reducing the opportunity for counterfeiters to sell bogus tickets. An e-ticket can be electronically communicated instantaneously and at no cost, contains unique customer identifiers on the ticket itself, and holds ticket holders accountable for all use of that ticket while in their possession.

Sports teams, theater companies, and cultural organizations are converting season tickets into a digital format. In this instance, the season ticket holder does not have to carry physical tickets to each event and is provided the convenience of using a branded card or mobile identifier. In addition, this debit-type card may be pre-loaded with funds to purchase merchandise, food and beverage, parking, and other in-venue amenities. Organizations utilizing a digital format eliminate the expense of printing and distributing season tickets.

MANAGING THE TICKETING PROCESS

The ticketing process is a combination of both operational procedures that need to be completed prior to putting an event on sale, and a system to track tickets when they are on sale to determine if additional advertising and marketing are necessary to maximize sales. It is important to remember that a venue's events are time sensitive to the extent that once the event happens, it is over and one cannot turn back the clock. Therefore, tickets are considered to be a perishable commodity that must be marketed and sold before the start time of the event. Once the event is over, the ticket has no value.

Appendix A 6-1 includes a sample checklist a ticket office manager might use for planning. The following sequence is the process by which most venues prepare, sell, and reconcile ticket sales:

Prior to On-Sale

1. Research event potential
2. Determine the event configuration
3. Determine ticket prices
4. Scale the house
5. Determine service charges and fees
6. Create ticket manifest
7. Determine seating holds
8. Determine on-sale date
9. Prepare for ticket distribution

On-Sale

10. Put event on sale and monitor sales

Event Day

11. Event-day will-call and walk-up
12. Ticket office audit
13. Event/promoter tax collection
14. Ticket revenue distribution

This process is designed to ensure success for the event, the promoter, and the venue. Venue management will inform and advise the promoter, but, ultimately, the promoter makes the final determination in most aspects of the ticketing process.

1. Research Event Potential

An important part of the ticket process is to research the event's potential. This includes researching similar events in the market to review ticket prices, number of tickets sold, and event date. It is also important to determine how many tickets the potential event is currently selling in other markets. Finally, the ticket office needs to research competitive events that may draw consumer's discretionary income away from the show being contemplated. The size of the market and number of ticket buyers in an event's potential market is a finite number. Therefore, if there are similar events in the market currently selling tickets, it may be advisable to seek an alternative date. It is important that both the venue manager and the promoter are aware, based on the research, of the event's potential to sell tickets.

2. Determine Event Configuration

Once the venue manager and promoter have agreed on the event's potential, they must address the ability of the event to achieve the desired gross ticket sales. Both want to be able to proclaim the event is sold out. This can be accomplished by selecting an appropriate seating configuration. For example, arenas typically have several locations in which to place a stage. Depending on whether the venue is set up in end-stage, center-stage, or half-house (refer to Figure 6-3), all have a bearing on the capacity of an event. Therefore, if an event sells all 6,000 seats of a half-house configuration in a 12,000-seat arena, the event is technically sold out. The sold-out designation provides the event, promoter, and venue with a sense of accomplishment and credibility.

Therefore, the venue manager and promoter must determine which event configuration and seating chart will be used to maximize ticket sales and provide the best possible sightlines to customers. When determining the most appropriate configuration, the manager must consider both the venue capabilities and the requirements outlined in the event **production rider**. The production rider stipulates event-specific requirements in terms of stage location and size, sound and lighting equipment, sound and lighting mix location, and other information required for the event set-up. Refer to Appendix A 6-3 for sample venue configurations.

In addition, the promoter, as the spokesperson for the event, will work with venue management to determine the most appropriate seating format, which may include reserved seating, general admission seating, or festival seating.

- **Reserved seating** requires a separate ticket for every seat, fixed or portable, sold on a section, row, and seat basis for an event.
- **General admission seating** is the seating format in which all seats are available on a first-come, first-served basis. The general admission format can also be used when the house is scaled by identifying individual seating sections that are sold at different prices but seating within each seating section is still available on a first-come, first-served basis. This format may produce additional safety concerns as guests attempt to secure the best available seats. Therefore, some venues may not allow general admission seating.
- **Festival seating** is a form of general admission. Often, the area directly in front of the stage or platform is simply an open space with no actual seating, providing the audience space to gather to observe a performance. Festival seating in an amphitheater is more often at the back of the seating area, where the audience observes a performance while seated on the lawn.

Based on the nature of the event, seating configuration, production-rider requirements, and the venue, the event may use one or a combination of seating types. Some venues are designed to have both reserved and general admission types of seating. For example, an amphitheater may have reserved seating under cover in front of the stage and festival seating in the grass area behind the fixed seats.

All public assembly venues receive a governmental **capacity rating,** which is based upon a number of factors, including use of the space, available exits, and fire suppression systems.

This capacity may be changed based upon the set-up for a particular event, such as staging, portable chairs, and tables. When hosting an event with an unusual set-up, it is recommended that a local fire marshal review and make any necessary changes to the seating chart prior to developing a ticket manifest for an event.

Once the capacity for the event is established and the seating configuration and seating format have been finalized, the venue manager and ticket office manager have the information required to develop the seating chart and ticket manifest.

3. Determine Ticket Prices

The next task in the ticketing process is for the **promoter** and venue management to determine what price can be charged for the event in the market. Determining the correct ticket pricing is an important element in ensuring the financial success of the event. If the price is too high, it may restrict ticket sales. If it is too low, it may compromise potential maximum revenue. The promoter relies on information gathered about ticket prices of similar events recently in the market, as well as the ticket price for that specific event the previous time it was in the market. Once this research has been completed, the promoter makes a final determination regarding ticket pricing.

It is becoming more common for venues and events to utilizing **dynamic ticket pricing**, where pricing is based on demand, similar to airline and hotel pricing. For example, when a visiting star pitcher will be on the mound, tickets for that game may be 30 percent higher. This concept is addressed in greater detail later in this chapter. Other pricing strategies may also include ticket auctions, added-value ticketing, such as buying merchandise or other artist-related items along with entry to an event, or an entertainment "experience" such as a *meet-and-greet* with artists or athletes.

4. Scale the House

Scaling the House refers to pricing tickets at different values based on sightlines and proximity to the event. Most venues, regardless of type, have the ability to scale the house. Promoters are able to capitalize on those customers willing to pay for a premium location, while still offering affordable tickets for other seats. By doing so, the promoter can maximize their ticket revenue. Family shows often not only use multiple ticket prices based on sightlines and the proximity to the event but also for specific demographics of the population, such as children, senior citizens, military personnel, and large groups.

It is advised that scaling a house should be done along hard breaks in the venue seating setup, such as along cross aisles and/or different levels of the venue. Different ticket prices within seating areas not divided by hard breaks may create disgruntled customers and the potential for refund requests.

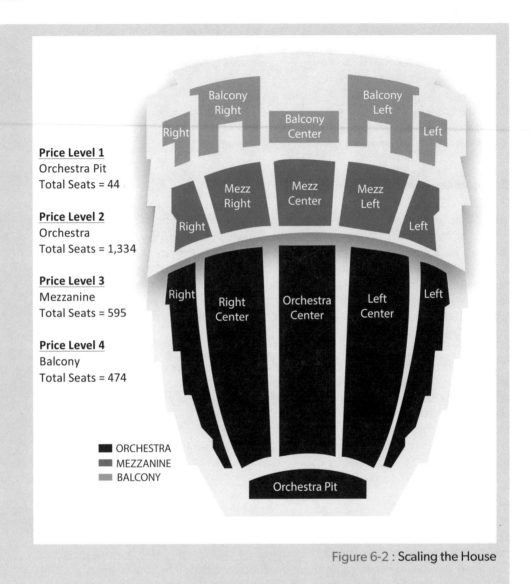

Price Level 1
Orchestra Pit
Total Seats = 44

Price Level 2
Orchestra
Total Seats = 1,334

Price Level 3
Mezzanine
Total Seats = 595

Price Level 4
Balcony
Total Seats = 474

Figure 6-2 : Scaling the House

Ultimately, the venue manager, in consultation with the ticket office manager and operations manager, can advise the promoter regarding the scale for the event. The final decision on ticket prices and scale rests with the promoter.

5. Determine Service Charges and Fees

If applicable, ticket service charges should be specified in the contract between the venue and the ticketing company. It is important to understand that ticket service charges vary based on a number of factors, which may include the ticket price. It is also important to verify that the ticketing company is applying the appropriate service charges, based on the contract for each and every event. Typically, the venue manager prefers to pass on the cost of ticketing to consumers. Therefore, service charges often include credit card fees and per-ticket costs normally charged to the venue by the ticketing company.

The primary recipient of the event ticket revenue is the event promoter or producer. However, the venue can collect revenue through a variety of fees, such as venue fees, maintenance fees, parking fees, traffic management fees, or venue restoration fees. As a general rule, the venue fees assessed to each ticket are minimal yet can generate a sizable revenue source when considering the total number of tickets sold at a venue during the year.

6. Create Ticket Manifest

Creating a ticket manifest is a process by which the ticket office manager places seats on the seating chart in exactly the location and to scale (or, price) that they will appear when the event is set up. This manifest will be the document that the ticketing company will use to create the event on the ticketing system used to sell tickets to customers. It will also be the document used by the operations manager to set up all available seating for the event. If the ticket manifest is not accurate and does not match the actual seating set-up, guests may have tickets for seats that do not exist. Therefore, it is important that the promoter approves the manifest in advance of the on-sale and the set-up is verified prior to opening doors.

7. Determine Seating Holds

Once the event configuration, seating chart, and manifest have been established, the event is almost ready to go on sale. Prior to the on-sale, the ticket office manager must identify the seating holds. Seats put on hold are not available for public sale. Seating holds are generally designated by their purpose and may include promoter holds, building holds, production holds, artist holds, relocation holds, or accessible seating holds.

In the United States, the Americans with Disabilities Act (ADA) requires venues to provide reasonable accommodations for customers with disabilities, renovations, such as appropriate signage, seat armrests that rise or seats with no armrests at all, assistive listening systems, and special seating platforms. Therefore, before tickets are made available to the general public, the operations manager, event manager, and the ticket office manager must identify seating for customers with disabilities. Most venues provide permanent seating locations for guests with disabilities. These areas must be located throughout the venue and at each available ticket price. Many other countries also have laws and regulations similar to the ADA. It is important to remember that ADA guidelines may impact each type of public assembly venue differently. Therefore, it is the responsibility of the venue manager and staff to understand how the ADA impacts their venue and its events. The ADA guidelines may change depending on the type of event being held at the venue.

Once the ticket office manager has compiled a complete list of seating holds, the promoter will review the list for final approval. Only the ticket office manager or designees should be able to change the status of any seating holds. The ticket office manager may release the holds for public sale; they may sell them to specified individuals; or if directed by the promoter, they may release them as **complimentary tickets**. When the ticket office manager releases the holds they should have some type of printed or electronic documentation that provides verification for why the tickets were released, to whom the tickets were released, and at what price they were sold or issued as complimentary.

8. Determine On-Sale Date

Usually, the **on-sale date** of the event is determined by a consensus of the promoter, venue manager, marketing manager, ticket office manager, and ticketing company. It is important that the first day of ticket sales is as strong as possible, developing a sense of urgency and creating momentum, resulting in a high demand for tickets. Considerations when determining on-sale dates include the following:

- Day of the week when the customer base is most likely to buy tickets
- Similar events that may be on sale or going on sale in the market
- Existing on-sale protection policies in place for other events
- Date when event information is released through social media

The ticket office manager may manage a number of pre-sales to specified groups, which may include artist fan clubs, credit card membership groups, loyalty programs, or others. This may result in multiple pre-sales prior to the general public on-sale. For some events, a multitude of pre-sales may result in the sale of the vast majority of tickets, leaving only a small percentage for the public on-sale. The ticket office manager should work to ensure ticket allocations are handled as stipulated for each group. For example, promoter holds may be located within the first ten rows or venue holds must be located outside row ten.

9. Preparation for Ticket Distribution

When all essential information has been confirmed between venue management and the promoter, the ticket office manager needs to verify the readiness of the system with the ticketing company to ensure the correct building and event information is in place at all points of sale. This is a critical step because the majority of tickets are not purchased at the venue ticket office. They are more commonly sold online, at remote locations, or through phone centers where the ticket office manager has little control over the customer service provided. The ticket office manager must ensure the ticketing company is conveying accurate information to their staff and that they are providing the highest quality customer service possible to meet the needs of the customers buying tickets for the venue's events.

10. Put Event On Sale and Monitor Sales

Prior to the public on-sale, the **promoter**, on behalf of the event and in conjunction with venue management, may restrict the number of tickets purchased per transaction. These restrictions are implemented so more people have an opportunity to purchase tickets for the event. The ticket office manager and the ticketing company carefully monitor ticket sales. This information is useful in a number of ways:

- It alerts to any potential network issues;
- It is useful in determining the level of demand for the event; and,
- It is useful in modifying the marketing campaign as necessary.

The venue and ticketing company share the responsibility of guarding the integrity of the ticket sales process to the maximum extent possible.

11. Event-Day Will-Call and Walk-Up

Will-call and walk-up are two terms that deal with ticket operations on the day of the event. **Will-call** are the tickets that have been pre-purchased and/or assigned prior to the event and are picked up at the ticket office on the day the event. **Walk-up** is the term used for the tickets purchased on the day of the event. By its nature, general admission events do not guarantee a particular seat and, therefore, do not encourage customers to purchase tickets in advance. As a result, general admission events often result in greater levels of walk-up sales.

It is very important for the venue manager and ticket office manager to correctly anticipate the potential for walk-up sales and will-call of an event. Checking recent event history and verifying pre-sold tickets can help determine the level of staffing required. Customer service issues can develop if the venue has not properly staffed and prepared for an orderly processing of both of these types of ticketing functions.

12. Ticket Office Audit

The ticket office audit may be the most crucial responsibility of the venue manager and the ticket office manager. The audit includes the following:

- Audit of tickets sold
- Tickets scanned/**drop count**
- Complimentary ticket report

The audit enables the venue to account for every ticket and all ticket revenue. Keeping track of ticket sales has become more complex because tickets are now sold in four primary locations (ticket office, phones, retail outlets, and online through the venue's ticketing system), as well as many secondary locations. Most of the money for an event comes into the ticket office or its designated bank account electronically, and, consequently, the ticket office manager must be able to account for tickets and the money associated with them.

13. Event/Promoter Tax Collection

It is the responsibility of the ticket office to collect all governmental taxes and any additional venue fees or charges. All charges are shown on the event settlement statement, and it is the responsibility of the ticket office manager to see that those taxes and fees are sent to the proper governmental agency when the event has concluded and all monies disperse. To eliminate any late charges or penalties, venue management must make, on a pre-approved regular basis, the payment of these applicable taxes.

14. Ticket Revenue Distribution

When the ticket office manager has completed the final ticketing report, that information, along with all supporting documents, is sent to the finance director or a designated individual to be reviewed and approved. Finally, the ticket office audit is included in the overall event settlement, and, based on the event contract, the venue manager determines any deductions from the final ticket proceeds due the venue, including fees, extra charges, and marketing expenses relating to the event. The ticket office manager should not distribute any funds to the promoter until the venue manager has approved and signed the **settlement sheets**. Finally, payment is made to the promoter, either by venue check or bank wire to a specified bank account. A sample ticket office statement can be found in Appendix A 6-2.

SELECTING AND DEVELOPING A TICKETING SYSTEM

Ticketing systems today are capable of providing ticket office managers and, in turn, venue managers and promoters, with sophisticated database information regarding customers' buying history and behavior. It is essential, given the wide variety of opportunities people have to spend their discretionary dollars, to understand and cater to the likes and dislikes of its unique audiences.

Venue managers have the responsibility to select a ticketing system that enables the venue to reach as many customers as possible. This can be accomplished by creating an in-house system or by selecting a ticketing company to provide these services. If selecting a ticketing company, it is advisable for a venue manager to go through the **Request for Qualifications (RFQ)** and/or **Request for Proposal (RFP)** process to ensure the system under consideration will serve the best interest of the venue, promoters, tenants, and potential customers it serves.

Along with distribution, one of the important issues to be considered when selecting a ticketing system is the ability to collect and maintain a database of customer information. The venue can collect this information through the online ticketing transactions as well as through active recruitment of customers into a preferred customers group who receive notice of upcoming events and access to certain pre-sales. Maintaining direct contact with venue customers is an important marketing tool for selling tickets to events.

TICKET MARKETS

Whether using an in-house or a contracted ticketing system, there are four authorized primary points of sale: ticket office, telephone, retail outlets, and online sales. Any tickets purchased through primary points of sale can be used for admission to the event. Tickets may also be purchased through the **secondary market**, but caution must be exercised since the secondary market is often unauthorized by the venue or event.

The secondary ticket market gets its name from the fact that the tickets have been purchased, in some form, from the primary market and are now being resold, hence the name secondary market. As discussed previously, the primary ticket market refers to *authorized* points of sale. The secondary market is, in some instances, the *unauthorized* points of sale for tickets that have been purchased once and are now being resold by **ticket brokers** and **ticket scalpers**, generally for a higher price. Currently in the United States, there is no national law prohibiting the resale of tickets. In fact, many state laws are becoming less restrictive, thereby making it easier for ticket brokers to exist and flourish.

In many instances, the secondary ticket market may actually be authorized. While it is the venue manager's primary focus to maximize ticket sales through the primary market, it may be beneficial to work with the secondary market. For example, due to the ever-increasing ticket prices for professional sports and the venue and team's goal to maximize ticket sales, some ticket brokerage companies have developed partnerships with venues and teams.

Some ticketing companies have also developed software and system platforms that allow venues, teams, and season-ticket holders to legitimately resell unwanted or unusable ticket inventory on the open market. The development of these partnerships and platforms allows customers to purchase tickets through the secondary market with confidence. In addition, creating these partnerships enables the venue and tenants to mitigate the potential negative aspects of the secondary market.

PREMIUM SEATING

Early construction of venues provided for separate locations designated for distinguished guests. The new generation of public assembly venues demonstrates how these areas for dignitaries and other VIPs has evolved over time.

In the last forty years, venues began to add seating options for those customers who wanted an exclusive area to entertain clients for business purposes and experience the event. Often, those locations were known as "skyboxes" because they were usually constructed above the existing seating areas to avoid major and expensive renovations to the venue. When this idea began to generate a significant amount of additional revenues, architects began to design venues to optimize the sightlines of these exclusive seating areas. The evolution of these spaces enabled the marketing staff to sell them at a premium price, thereby maximizing venue and tenant revenues.

This next generation of exclusive seating was referred to as "luxury suites." The name was appropriate, as many of these seating areas began to take on the appearance of living rooms and boardrooms that you would find in more expensive homes and offices.

For some, the term *luxury* was considered elitist and often a difficult expense for corporations to justify to their employees and shareholders. As a result, these premium spaces were then renamed hospitality suites. In addition, venues began to sell exclusive seating in the form of club seats, which also provided exclusive access to private clubs or other amenities within the venue.

Many types of **premium seating** have been added to enhance venue and team revenue. These areas vary based on size, location, amenities, cost, and contract terms. Many public assembly venues use other premium seating concepts, such as the following:

- Party Suites are usually rented on an event-by-event basis. The price of the suite usually includes tickets and sometimes food and beverage.

- Bunker Suites are usually located under the seating area with no direct sightline to the event and are used before, during, and after the event. While bunker suites include television for in-suite viewing, they often also include seats in the premium spectator area.

- Founders Suites are sold during construction and include premium amenities. These founding partners hold a prominent position in the venue and generate a significant amount of financial support for construction.

- Grand Suites are large suites that can accommodate more than 100 people.

- Celebrity Suites are similar to party suites and are usually rented on an event-by-event basis. These suites often include celebrity hosts, such as retired players from the resident teams.

Premium seating has evolved into a major source of revenue for both the venue and tenant. While the development of these locations is costly, venues and tenants have realized that the level of financial return justifies the investment. In some instances, retention of tenants is dependent upon the venue's ability to maximize revenue streams in these premium areas.

PRIORITY SEATING

The selling of priority seating, often referred to as a **Personal, Permanent**, or **Preferred Seat Licenses (PSL)**, represents yet another vehicle for generating additional revenue. In purchasing a PSL, fans pay a one-time fee in order to gain ownership of a specified seat, and they retain ownership with the annual purchase of a season ticket for a specified period of time, up to lifetime. As a revocable license, if the PSL owner does not purchase tickets as required or violates other policies, the seat license may be revoked.

Although not limited to sporting events, the PSL can produce significant amounts of new money in markets with passionate sport fans. However, it must be kept in mind that the sale of a PSL only produces one-time money which may help offset construction costs rather than annual operating revenue unless the PSL is for a limited period of time and then must be repurchased.

In the collegiate setting, the PSL concept is the same, though it may be applied somewhat differently. Rather than selling a PSL, fans are often encouraged to become members of the institution's booster club. Most booster clubs offer a variety of membership levels, each requiring a specified minimum financial contribution. Each contribution level provides stated benefits with the number and quality of the benefits increasing as the contribution level increases.

SEASON TICKETS AND SUBSCRIPTIONS

Packaging or bundling through season tickets or subscriptions may help to promote events in public assembly venues. Season tickets or subscriptions provide customers with a number of advantages, while encouraging them to make a season-long commitment to the team or event series. One of the advantages for the customer is the ability to keep the same seats for the duration of the season. Also, often, the price for the season ticket or subscription is less than the combined individual rates of each event. However, if there is high demand, the season ticket or subscription price may not be less, but the purchase of season tickets or subscriptions may provide access to tickets prior to a public sale. In other words, a season pass to a series may simply guarantee you an exclusive opportunity that individual purchasers may not have, not a less expensive price.

Another method of adding value to season subscriptions is to package a specified genre of talent together and schedule the performances over several event dates. Using this tactic, a creative entrepreneur can produce a subscription series by contracting for a well-known and recognized act/talent and then include some lesser-known talent in the season package. Combining a more prominent act with lesser-known acts as a package can produce a very marketable series.

In the United States, some professional leagues and major college teams are using this same basic approach. They are using access to the games with the more attractive opponents to create value. For season tickets, there may be an added cost included in the price for the prime opponents, or there may be no added cost but the fan is induced to buy the season ticket and ensure access to the game(s).

Sports Authority Field at Mile High - Denver, CO

GROUP TICKET SALES

Ticketing campaigns for certain events may include **group ticket sales**, most often referred to as group sales. Group sales refer to blocks of tickets ordered by a group, usually meeting a minimum order quantity and sold at a discount. Family shows, cultural events, and consumer shows often offer group rates as a means to encourage ticket sales. In some instances, this provides a means to sell blocks of tickets in less desirable locations. While this service may be contracted out, it is still the responsibility of the ticket office to coordinate with the group sales representative to fulfill the ticket orders.

Providing blocks of group tickets at significant discounts or as complimentary tickets is also an excellent way for many events to engage segments of the community that would not otherwise be able to attend the event. In addition, this has a positive impact on ancillary revenues while enabling promoters to expose potential customers to their event, which may lead to future ticket sales.

DATABASE MANAGEMENT

Database management is the collection and use of the information that can be gathered from ticket transactions. This information, which includes credit card information, addresses, phone numbers, and e-mail addresses, is used to code types of tickets purchased and frequency of tickets purchased. This information can be used in many different ways. This historical data can be used to track the frequency with which people attend events, the types of events they attend, and the ticket prices they have paid. This enables the venue to target marketing efforts to those customers most likely interested in a particular type of event. This is also an example of how analytics are used within public assembly venues.

Database management also requires the staff handling such sensitive data to be responsible for the safety and security of the data. Identity theft is a real issue affecting millions, and it is incumbent upon any in-house or contracted ticketing company to make sure personal buyer information is protected from theft or loss. Further, the government requires all companies, including venue operators, to comply with laws that were enacted to protect consumer information from being used in unlawful or disruptive ways. Information management laws also require venue managers to offer each customer the opportunity to "opt-out" from receiving additional information, similar to how customers can state their preferences for Do-Not-Call lists.

Database management and the gathering of credible, reliable information pertaining to the customers who visit public venues is essential for that venue's success. Moreover, that same data, if used carelessly, will discourage customers from visiting the venue. Effective information gathering is an important tool for business growth but a liability if used improperly and without rules and regard for patron privacy.

DYNAMIC PRICING

The practice of dynamic pricing, yield management, or revenue management involves the manipulation of prices in order to price event tickets and seating differently based on customer demand. Unlike retail goods priced the same for all customers, some seat locations and tickets for those seats lend themselves to multiple pricing plans constructed using dynamic pricing techniques.

Dynamic pricing is a process that enables venue managers to maximize the potential financial yield on seats they manage. They do this by systematically adjusting the ticket price based on demand analysis in order to maximize yield. Figure 6-3 outlines five characteristics of products or services that make good markets for using dynamic pricing techniques.

Characteristic	Industry Application / Description
Fixed Capacity.	The number of seats in a particular configuration is fixed.
Customer demand can be identified and separated into distinct market segments based on willingness to pay.	Those willing to pay for better seats or locations, and can be separated from those customers unwilling to pay premium prices for the best seats.
Product or service is perishable.	When the event begins, the opportunity to sell the ticket is over.
Product sold in advance of consumption.	Event has advance ticket sales.
Consumer demand fluctuates.	Weekend, mid-week, or seasonal demand for event tickets.

(Kimes, 1989)

Figure 6-3 : **Characteristics of Products/Services Well Suited for Dynamic Pricing Techniques**

The hotel and airline industries appear to be successfully marketing their inventory by either increasing prices or discounting prices, based on unsold inventory, as the product expiration date draws near. When the expiration date is very close, both airlines and hotels put their product out to bid to other outlets with a belief that getting a lesser price is better than nothing at all. In addition, dynamic pricing may have a positive impact on ancillary revenues, strengthen consumer-buying patterns, and enhance brand loyalty. Like the hotel and airline industries, the inventory of tickets offered by public assembly venues is dramatically affected by time. An unsold seat to a performance or event might have a $100 value minutes before the starting time but becomes worthless once the performance or event has concluded. For those venues hosting long-running shows, venue managers prefer to pre-sell the earliest shows in a long run because once those events have ended, unsold seats mean lost revenue on a hit show. Therefore, it is an advantage for the venue manager to advertise the early weeks of a performance and withhold or prevent the latter weeks of a long-run attraction from the initial on-sale date. This strategic manipulation of ticket availability is critical from the venue manager's perspective and very different from a professional sport ticket sale announcement.

One example of how using dynamic pricing increased revenue relates to a struggling auditorium housing a summer entertainment series. The venue manager noticed that ticket demand was highest on weekends and lowest Monday through Thursday. Tickets were priced the same ($30) for all performances. However, demand for weekend tickets was twice that of the venue's seating capacity, while only one-fourth of available tickets for the mid-week performances were sold.

Through the use of dynamic pricing techniques, the venue manager or promoter increased revenues by changing two pricing levels. First, the price for weekend performances was increased to $45 to capture those willing to pay the higher price in order to attend the weekend performances. Second, the price for weekday performances was reduced to $20, thus attracting larger audiences, including those unable to get weekend tickets but willing to attend a weekday performance rather than not attending at all. In this case, new revenue was generated from the higher prices on weekends without affecting demand, and new revenue was generated from weekday performances due to the reduced price that produced an increase in ticket sales. The new pricing rules evolved from management's ability to divide the total market into segments based on demand and the consumer's willingness to pay.

Many sports teams that use stadiums and arenas are in the early stages of transforming their standard full-price ticket into a higher revenue, yielding tickets in two ways. One is to charge a premium price for weekend games, as in baseball and basketball. The second is to charge a premium price for specific games against high-profile teams or traditional rivals.

The concept of dynamic pricing is not new but has evolved into its current form. It has long been common for some events to charge one price for advance ticket purchases and a higher price for day-of-event sales, rather than reducing the prices as expiration time nears. The strategy behind this pricing format is to encourage advance ticket sales.

At times, however, the application of the dynamic pricing approach could result in stimulating day-of-event sales as opposed to advance sales. If this were to occur, it may result in making a decision not to book additional events because of poor advance ticket sales when, in fact, a demand actually exists for those additional events. The end result would be too little supply for the actual demand and the creation of an ideal market for scalpers. In addition, some event producers are now concerned that they may have trained or conditioned their audiences to wait for discounts, resulting in less gross potential revenue.

TICKETING TRENDS AND ISSUES

Ticketing is one of the most complex and constantly evolving systems in a venue. Managers must work diligently to keep abreast of the continual changes in ticketing services and technology. Current trends include, but are not limited to, the following:

- **New Terminology**—The term ticketing and ticket office is evolving into "access management," which includes management of all access to the venue through ticketing, media credentialing, and other access options.
- **Bar Codes/QR Codes**—While some venues already use bar codes and **QR codes (Quick Response codes)** on both hard tickets and e-tickets, potential future applications of this technology may include use of these bar codes/QR codes to purchase other venue services.
- **Paperless or Digital Ticketing**—A paperless ticket simply means that a ticket is delivered exclusively via electronic means and then authenticated and redeemed at the venue. The venue may save some expense via the elimination of the need to print, handle, and mail hard tickets. While this seems convenient for customers, it

is not without challenges. This option provides new opportunities for venues and ticket office managers to learn about their customers' buying habits and to thwart counterfeit attempts.

Figure 6-4 : e-ticket Sample

Figure 6-5 : e-ticket Sample, Mobile Version

- **Universal Personal Identification Card**—This card could hold all personal identification information, serve as a driver's license or passport, be used as a debit/credit card, and serve as a ticket for access to events. This would enable the consumer to swipe the card and gain entrance to the venue, as well as use the card for the purchase of parking, merchandise, food and beverages.

- **Secondary Market**—Venue managers must grapple with the ethics and complexities of this growing segment of ticketing and access management. The **secondary market** and **ticket brokers** are now an established part of the ticketing process, and venue managers and promoters must find ways to capture a greater share of the revenue derived from the secondary market.

- **Scalping Tickets**—Scalping is, simply put, the process of reselling a ticket for more than face value, which may or may not be legal depending on where you live. The beneficiary of the profit usually has no affiliation or responsibility to the building or persons who are at financial risk for the event. Scalping has become more prevalent as ticket prices have increased.

- **Counterfeit Tickets**—Fraudulently duplicated tickets sold to unsuspecting customers as valid tickets for an event are referred to as counterfeit tickets. With new technology, tickets can be duplicated to look just like the original tickets, and the potential exists to deceive unsuspecting ticket buyers, as well as venue ticket takers. Venues must continue to use technology to counteract counterfeit tickets, such as bar codes and QR codes.

- **Ticketing Kiosks** – As consumers become more comfortable using technology, many venues provide self-service ticketing kiosks for the purchase or pickup of tickets. Successful implementation of this technology allows ticket office managers to reduce staffing levels.

Venue managers and ticket office managers must be vigilant and stay current on emerging trends in ticketing and access management. Advancing technology is the manager's best resource in addressing these and future issues.

SUMMARY

As complex and sophisticated as ticketing systems have become, they will continue to have their roots in the fundamentals of access management; the ability to control capacity; the ability to count the revenue based on tickets sold; and the ability to value seating locations based on sightlines and the public's perceived value of the entertainment.

Venue managers and ticket office managers are constantly refining their skill sets relative to the changes occurring in the modern ticketing marketplace. Technological advances have brought significant change to the venue management industry. Ticket office managers and, by extension, venue managers, must be technologically-savvy and leverage technology to maximize ticket sales and ancillary revenue.

Tickets protect the legal rights of the venue and promoter through the use of limited contract and hold-harmless language, while corresponding service fees and advertising serve as an additional revenue stream. In addition, ticketing and associated programs, such as online ticketing and targeted e-mail campaigns, have become a significant means of communication between the venue and the consumer.

CHAPTER 7
EVENT AND ANCILLARY REVENUE SOURCES

INTRODUCTION
PROMOTER-GENERATED ANCILLARY REVENUE
- In-House Marketing and Advertising Agency Fees
- Television Production Fees
- Utility Fees
- Labor Fees
- Additional Space Rental
- Equipment Fees

GUEST-GENERATED ANCILLARY REVENUE
TICKETING
- Venue Fees
- Ticket Service Charges
- VIP Order Fees
- Interest Income from Ticket Sales Escrow Accounts

FOOD AND BEVERAGE
- In-House vs. Contracted Food and Beverage Service
- Food and Beverage Contractor Compensation
- Physical Layout and Design of Food and Beverage Service Areas
- Food and Beverage Marketing
- Foodservice as a Marketing Tool
- Alcohol Sales

MERCHANDISE
- Structure of Merchandising Agreements
- Merchandise Operations
- Permanent Tenant Merchandise Stores

PARKING
- Parking Services
- Parking-Related Ancillary Revenue Sources
- Parking Lot Events

SUMMARY

INTRODUCTION

Public assembly venues, regardless of type, share a common challenge. Each operates to host events, and each venue must focus on those events as their opportunity to make a positive impression on the attendee and, as a result, produce the perception by the attendee that the event experience met their expectation.

Each event is an opportunity for the venue to solidify its image in the community by providing a safe, clean, and inviting location for the conference, concert, sporting event, theatrical presentation, trade show, or other public gathering. These events also serve as opportunities for both the venue and event **promoter** to produce revenue, allowing them to support their businesses. It is extremely important that these revenue-generating opportunities be maximized in every way possible to sustain healthy business operations.

The venue manager often serves three groups. First is the entity that rents the venue, often referred to as the promoter, producer, presenter, or team. The second group includes the individuals who actually attend the events, referred to as the guests, customers, or attendees. Third, the venue's owner, which may be a public entity, sports team, or private company. In this chapter the term "promoter" will refer to the producer, presenter, or show organizer, "guests" will refer to the customers or attendees, and "owners" will refer to the entity that has ownership responsibilities.

While renting event and meeting space is one of a venue's major functions, it may not be its primary source of income. In addition to rental income, the venue can generate a variety of additional revenue streams outside of space rental or ticket sales generated by the promoter and guests. This chapter will focus on both promoter-generated and guest-generated **ancillary revenue**.

The wide variety of venues in terms of size, capacity, design, and purpose results in differences in their interest or ability to offer programs and services that generate ancillary revenue. Consequently, it is important for venue management to set expectations and educate event promoters and prospective guests prior to the event. For example, a small theater may present events without issuing tickets, serving food and beverage, or selling merchandise. In most cases, however, the venue manager must think entrepreneurially. Every possible ancillary service needs to be considered for its potential to generate additional venue revenue through purchases, fees, and surcharges.

For most venues, the growth potential for certain revenue categories is limited. Event capacity is regulated by code, and, therefore, the maximum capacity is a fixed number. The promoter or team usually retains revenue from ticket sales, while venue rental and ticket service charges typically go to the venue. Venue rent potential is limited, especially in competitive markets. Therefore, for many venues, the opportunities for increasing total revenue are largely concentrated around ancillary revenue sources.

The scope and number of possible **ancillary services** and, consequently, venue revenue generators are very large. To maximize ancillary revenue opportunities, venue management must maintain the highest standards of quality with respect to service, products, and presentation.

PROMOTER-GENERATED ANCILLARY REVENUE

Promoter-generated ancillary revenue may be generated through in-house marketing and advertising agency fees, television production fees, utility fees, labor fees, additional space rental, and equipment fees. Obviously larger venues tend to collect more of these secondary revenues than smaller venues, but that does not reduce the need for these revenue opportunities to be maximized when possible.

In-House Marketing and Advertising Agency Fees

In some venues, in-house marketing and advertising fees may create a venue revenue source, while allowing the **promoter** to realize advertising rates enjoyed by the venue on the basis of advertising volume. Promoters can maximize their event advertising cost-effectiveness by enlisting the venue marketing staff to purchase and place their ads. This can significantly increase the amount of advertising the venue places in the local media and, therefore, decreases the expense to the promoter. That savings is then passed on to the promoter, who in turn may pay a portion of the savings to the venue through a straight fee or a percentage of the advertising budget.

Another advantage to the promoter for using the in-house agency would be the expertise of the venue staff on the market's demographics. This enables the agency to provide the promoter the most advantageous approach to directing the event advertising to the targeted audience.

Television Production Fees

Television, radio, closed circuit services, and fees may also present themselves as possible revenue streams for the venue. When a promoter has indicated that an event will be televised, ancillary revenue may be generated through a number of fees as outlined in Figure 7-1.

FEES	DESCRIPTION
Origination Fees	These fees may be charged to the promoter of the event and/or the telecast producer as well. This is usually a negotiated fee that can range from several hundred to several thousand dollars.
Connection Fees	These fees may be charged by the venue to the telecast producer to pay technicians to make connections for TV and radio trucks used for remote location broadcasts. This service enables producers to connect directly to the venue's internal cabling system limiting the amount of temporary cable required for the telecast.
Production Fees	These fees are usually charged by venues with in-house production capability to produce closed circuit feeds to TVs the venue and/or for in-house security.

Figure 7-1 : Television Production Fees

Utility Fees

Utility expenses are hard costs and need to be paid to the utility provider. In many venues, utility costs are calculated into the rent. However, in some instances, especially convention and meeting venues, the promoter is responsible for reimbursing the venue for actual or negotiated utility costs. The venue also has utility expenses on non-event days, which are an expense of the venue's operating budget. In order to charge promoters for event utility expenses, the venue must be able to accurately separate non-event day utility expenses from the increased utility expenses as a result of an event. Modern venues are often equipped with systems and software that allow management to track utility usage. The following utilities may be negotiated into the event contract:

- Natural gas
- Electricity
- Water
- Heating, ventilation, and air conditioning (HVAC)
- Pressurized air
- Refrigeration
- Satellite/cable television connections
- Telephone and data connections

While utility fees can be charged in any venue at any type event, the most frequent example of passing these costs along to the event is evident in the contracts for convention center or meeting and exhibit space.

Labor Fees

Labor fees are a source of revenue when the event promoter is charged for personnel the venue hires for the safe and secure operation of the venue during an event. Personnel numbers and labor rates are usually provided in a venue **rate sheet** that lists the rates for all front and **back-of-house** personnel, both union and non-union. The rate sheet also addresses labor requirements, including overtime, holiday pay, and minimum call. These rates include the base rate, benefits, processing percentage, and a venue mark-up cost. The labor categories may include the following:

- Police
- Security personnel
- Fire personnel
- First-aid personnel
- Ushers
- Ticket office personnel
- Load-in/load-out personnel
- **Stagehands**
- Decorating personnel
- Service desk staff
- Freight handling personnel
- Trades personnel

Working Stagehands

Additional Space Rental

The promoter may rent additional space beyond the primary event space. Especially in convention and conference centers, this is usually a one-time charge to the promoter and may include additional amenities, such as phone and data connections or coffee service. Areas that fall into this category may include a production office or additional meeting space not included in the event needs.

In addition, some events may request a cyber café, which not only requires additional space but also requires Internet access for attendees. The Internet access is often provided for an additional fee.

Equipment Fees

Additional charges may include equipment fees. Venues may rent equipment on an hourly, daily, or event rate to the promoter. Some types of venue equipment that may be rented include:

- Staging
- Tables
- Chairs
- Linen
- **Pipe and drape**
- Crowd control barriers
- Spotlights
- Forklifts
- Scissor lift
- Risers
- Carpet
- Portable dance floor
- Cable trays
- Podiums
- Metal detectors
- AV equipment
- Scoreboards and ribbon boards
- Sound systems
- Sports surfaces

GUEST-GENERATED ANCILLARY REVENUE

The venue may have, through a variety of channels, the opportunity to produce guest-generated ancillary revenues in addition to promoter-generated ancillary revenues. The areas where these revenues might be realized include ticketing, food and beverage, merchandise, and parking. The growth of social media and personal apps may provide greater access to these services, thereby enhancing the potential revenue streams.

TICKETING

Ticketing services can be an additional venue revenue resource. This revenue may be generated through venue fees, ticket service charge rebates, VIP ticket order fees, and interest income earned from ticket revenue being held in escrow accounts. In some cases, the law requires that any fees charged be fully disclosed on the face of the ticket.

Venue Fees

A venue fee is a small charge added on to the base ticket price and is generally used for venue maintenance, repairs, renovations, and **capital improvements**. This fee may be called a restoration, renovation, or capital improvement fee.

Ticket Service Charges

Service charges are often added to the base ticket price, whether utilizing an in-house or a contracted ticketing company. This charge is used to help offset the expense of the ticketing system and ticketing personnel. If using an in-house system, the venue retains the full fees. If using a contracted ticketing company, the venue may receive a negotiated percentage of the fee in the form of a rebate from the ticketing company.

VIP Order Fees

Venue management usually has important business relationships that require special attention. When these relationships require fulfillment of ticket requests, they are usually accomplished without the purchaser going through the normal ticket-buying process. These requests are often handled through a special allotment of premium ticket holds. Often, there is a service or handling fee for this privilege, which may become a source of ancillary revenue for the venue.

Interest Income from Ticket Sales Escrow Accounts

In most instances, advance ticket sales revenue is collected by the venue and held until the event occurs. These dollars can be substantial but are not the property of the promoter until the event is concluded. The entrepreneurial venue manager and finance director may work with local banks to place these funds into short-term, no-risk financial accounts that may net the venue some ancillary revenue in the form of interest earned.

FOOD AND BEVERAGE

For many venues, food and beverage (F&B) service to guests represents one of the most important revenue-producing **ancillary services**. Many guests attend events planning to spend money on food and beverage. Such expectations represent an opportunity to generate substantial ancillary revenue, and the venue must be prepared to accommodate those expectations. In addition, with increased competition, food and beverage services can be used as a marketing tool to attract businesses and consumers.

Food and beverage service operations have grown exponentially in recent years in terms of sales and profits. The food and beverage service operation may range from the traditional concession stand and basic catering to fine dining and banquet facilities.

Older venues may still offer only traditional concession stand operations, while new and renovated venues with refurbished food and beverage service facilities are designed to offer an expanded menu with a variety of culinary options. As discussed in chapter 5, in an effort to maximize food and beverage sales, many venues find it advantageous to brand certain offerings with popular local or national products. As a result, menus today may offer items from local restaurants, nationally recognized brands, or specialty items. These special menu items may provide opportunities to charge premium prices.

Venue Concession Stand

Though individual tastes may vary, food and beverage operations seek to provide an array of popular items, as well as those popular within the geographic region. Having these items available tends to enhance the guest's overall event experience, as well as increase the **per caps**, a measuring standard used to define the average amount of sales derived per person for the event. Per caps are calculated by dividing the total **gross revenues** by the event **drop count**.

Food and beverage ancillary revenues are generated through the concessions, catering, suites, clubs, and restaurants. Concessions operations include traditional concession stands, as well as portable concession carts, in-seat wait staff, and hawking services. Traditional concession stands are strategically located throughout the venue to accommodate guests. Portable concession carts provide flexibility in locations and product offerings to best serve guests in attendance for any particular event, such as beer at a sporting event or cotton candy, sno-cones, popcorn, and soft drinks for family events.

Depending on the type of event, many guests make purchase decisions based upon the convenience of having food and beverages brought to their seats. Therefore, many venues offer in-seat service, whereby guests in premium areas may have the opportunity to order from a menu and in-seat wait staff delivers the items. In addition, **hawkers** roam the general public seating areas selling select food and beverage products. At sporting events, hawkers work continually during the event, while at concerts or theatrical events where house lights are off during the performance, they may only service guests during intermissions. By providing in-seat services, management is enhancing convenience and is providing the guest with value-added service.

Hawker Selling Beer

Catering operations include foodservice in both **front-of-house** and **back-of-house** areas. This may include a banquet for 5,000 at a convention center, a luncheon for ten at a business meeting, or service for twenty in a hospitality suite during a concert. Back-of-house catering may include meals for the media, artists, crew, or employees.

Many venues offer the guests an opportunity to dine in a restaurant, which may be operated by the venue or contracted to a popular regional restaurateur. These restaurants may be available to all guests attending the event or may be restricted to guests who purchase premium access. In addition to restaurants, many venues feature bars and club-level dining. While venue restaurants cater to event guests during normal **event operations**, they may be open to the public on non-event days.

In addition, there are a number of important considerations that must be addressed by venue management to maximize the ancillary revenue opportunities in this area:

- In house vs. contracted food and beverage service
- Food and beverage contractor compensation
- Physical layout and design of food and beverage service
- Food and beverage merchandising
- Foodservice as a marketing tool
- Wait service and hawking sales
- Beer and alcohol sales
- Trends in foodservice

In-House vs. Contracted Food and Beverage Service

With the proven potential for increased profits from a properly managed food and beverage operation, prudent venue managers must give this venue function a significant amount of attention. This then gives rise to the question of how best to manage the venue's foodservice operation. A venue manager has the option of managing the service in-house or contracting it to a private company to operate all or part of the food and beverage business.

In-House Operation	Private Contractor
■ Ability to retain control ■ Ability to retain flexibility ■ Ability to retain all financial control	■ Capital investment management ■ Use of proven systems ■ Provides liability protection from operations, especially alcohol service

Figure 7-2 : **Advantages of In-House and Contracted Operations**

The venue infrastructure must be assessed to determine whether in-house or contracted services would be most profitable for the venue, as well as meeting the needs and guest service expectations of the market. The assessment should include the following considerations:

- Labor pool analysis
- Culinary skills of potential foodservice staff
- Foodservice staff training requirements
- Foodservice labor laws
- Financial resources
- Required capital equipment

Beyond the assessment of the venue and labor issues, a particularly important consideration is whether or not the venue manager has the desire, time, and ability to oversee such an operation. When a venue contracts its food and beverage operations, the venue's manager is allowed more time to focus attention on the other aspects of the venue's operation. Depending on the structure of the contract, the contracted company might assume the responsibility for the following:

- Labor expenses
- Hiring and training of labor
- Health department permits and compliance
- Alcohol licensing
- Alcohol and general insurance liability
- Compliance
- Food product costs, storage, and inventory

In addition, depending on the agreement reached, the contracted company might also provide and amortize necessary furniture, fixtures, and equipment (FF&E), as well as the costs required to design and construct the food and beverage areas.

There are distinct advantages to both in-house and contracted food and beverage management. If foodservice is operated in house, venue management maintains total control of labor, products, services, and profits. If it is allowed to function in a for-profit mode, many venues generate substantial profits from that operation. At the same time, in-house operations must assume liabilities and significant risks associated with food and beverage operations. In-house operations work best when these services are allowed to operate without bureaucratic restrictions and the focus is on a for-profit service that produces quality products at reasonable prices.

When contracting services, management will normally use the **Request for Qualification (RFQ)** and the **Request for Proposal (RFP)** processes in a systematic effort to select the best contractor for their particular situation. This decision will have a substantial impact on the overall operation and will be a major contributor to the venue's ancillary revenue streams.

The RFQ is used to pre-qualify interested food and beverage companies by assessing their experience, financial strength, and knowledge of the business. Consideration should be given to their history in other similar venues, the level of service they are able to deliver, and the quality of product they use in their service. The RFP is then sent to those firms who exhibit the qualities deemed important to the venue's management with a request for a financial proposal that will compete with other interested companies for the venue's food and beverage service. Due to the complexities of the process and importance of the outcome, some venues may contract a foodservice consultant to assist in the selection and design process.

It is important, however, that the selection process for the contracted service focuses on which company is most responsive to the stated requirements and can provide the highest quality of products and service at the best price, rather than focusing strictly on financial return. Initial increases in revenue may not be sustained if the quality of product and service does not meet guest expectations.

Regardless of the direction finally taken, the venue's decision on food and beverage is as important as any decision venue management makes. If managed properly, food and beverage service can become a signature feature of the venue and create a positive impact on the guest experience. The convention or meeting guest may not necessarily remember the speaker's message but will always remember whether or not the food and service was good at the final banquet.

Food and Beverage Contractor Compensation

While the percentage of gross sales is the most common form of food and beverage contract, the food and beverage contractor compensation can take other forms, including a management fee-based contract or a profit-percentage-based contract.

CONTRACT TYPE	DESCRIPTION
Percentage of Gross Sales	The contractor pays the venue a percentage of gross sales.
Fee Based	The contractor receives a management fee, often combined with a profit-percentage-based incentive.
Profit Based	The contractor receives an agreed upon percentage of the profits.

Figure 7-3 : Food and Beverage Contractor Compensation

In each contract, incentive bonuses may be negotiated based on pre-determined benchmarks and goals. In all options, there are potential penalties for both the venue and contractor. The venue may be penalized for failing to deliver an agreed-upon number of events or attendance levels, while the contractor may be penalized for failing to meet pre-determined sales goals.

Whether in-house or contracted, the venue manager is responsible for efficient food and beverage operations with outstanding levels of guest service. Regardless of the contract type, the venue manager must reserve the right to approve product quality, menu selections, product pricing, and the availability of alcohol. It is also critical that venue management retain the right to approve the hiring and/or removal of key food and beverage personnel.

Even when the contractor appears to be performing effectively, it is the responsibility of the venue manager to continually monitor the level and quality of service being provided. In the same manner, managers operating in-house food and beverage service should be constantly examining their operations. Given the importance of food and beverage revenues and the role the service plays in the customer satisfaction and, therefore, repeat business, venue management must strive for exemplary foodservice to all guests (Bigelow, 2008).

Physical Layout and Design of Food and Beverage Service Areas

When new venues are being planned and designed, careful consideration must be given to food and beverage service operations including the following:

- Kitchen
- Prep kitchens
- Permanent concession stands
- Strategic location of full-cooking sales locations versus non-cooking or warming kitchens
- Portable concessions kiosks/mobile carts
- Restaurants, bars, and lounges
- **Premium seating** (suites and club seats) foodservice support stations
- Storage
- Offices
- Data lines for all permanent and portable sales locations for both digital signage and **point-of-sale** register with credit card readers

A particular concern is to correctly select the size, design, and location of food and beverage service areas in the venue so as to maximize revenues. Venue management, along with the architect, foodservice consultant, and building contractor, should examine the venue's capabilities and design foodservice areas that can accommodate the anticipated event schedule and projected attendance levels. This process will help determine type, number, location, layout, and size of the food and beverage areas required. Financial and capital resources must also be considered when shaping this decision. The elimination of potential flaws during the design process will serve to minimize operational problems and allow for maximizing revenue once the venue is in operation. Products will be more easily marketed when patron flow, including **ingress** and **egress**, and the positioning of concession stands are planned as a package.

An important consideration is the availability of venue support facilities, which must be properly sized and positioned in locations that allow them to support their required production. This is especially important to convention centers or other meeting venues because those venues rely heavily on the ability to cater large meals and other social functions. Adequate refrigeration and dry-storage space are necessary for a kitchen to function properly. The location of shipping and receiving areas and the proper placement, capacity, and dimensions of freight and service elevators in multi-level venues can further maximize the productivity of food and beverage service employees. Venues often use staging or prep areas to accommodate **hawkers**, as well as provide secure product storage. Failing to provide an area to accommodate the needs of these hawkers will negatively impact efficiency of service, as well as have a negative impact on sales. Other common design flaws within concessions operations include the following:

- Inadequate number of concession stands relative to seating capacity (industry standard is 1 permanent **point-of-sale (POS)** per 150 seats in venues selling beer and 1 per 250 in venues not selling beer).
- Lack of concession stands in high-traffic flow locations to spur impulse sales.
- Inconvenient kitchen location and insufficient space without direct access to sales or banquet locations.
- Service elevators poorly located relative to storage facilities and improperly sized to handle weight loads and equipment that need to be transported.
- Inadequate size and inconvenient location of loading docks and storerooms.
- Inadequate ventilation for cooking capabilities in concessions (current standard is 50% of all concession stands should be vented for grilling and frying capabilities).
- Insufficient energy availability, which should be sized based on projected menu with allowance for growth.
- Insufficient concourse areas to accommodate traffic flow.

(Bigelow, 2014) (Russo, 1980)

Managers of existing venues without financial resources to create an optimal infrastructure for their food and beverage service operation should still evaluate potential improvements that may assist in maximizing their operation's success. This analysis should include:

- A return on investment (ROI) analysis
- Attractiveness of existing food and beverage service areas
- Cost of making them more attractive
- Projected additional revenues resulting from renovations
- Projected impact on the level of service, product quality, and guest experience

In essence, venue managers should be knowledgeable about current needs and trends and open to making changes based on expected future demands.

Food and Beverage Marketing

Food and beverage sales are enhanced through the implementation of strategic and timely marketing techniques. This can be done in a variety of ways, including exhibition cooking, effective signage, and overall presentation to the customer. In addition, at certain events, especially sporting events, strategically placed closed-circuit television screens may encourage guests to visit concession stands without missing any of the action.

To effectively motivate customers to purchase food and beverages, attention should be given to creating appeal by stimulating customers' senses, both sight and smell. Providing potential purchasers with a view of food in preparation, such as popping popcorn, smoking barbeque, and sizzling cheesesteaks, may stimulate their sense of smell and sight in a way that might persuade them to purchase the item. The same is true for displaying the various sizes of beverages, French fries, popcorn, and other specialty options. Enhanced lighting highlights the presentation of food and beverage items and is an effective marketing tool.

Posted menus, whether digital or static, must clearly list available items and prices. To assist in the successful marketing of menu items, there must be compelling signage throughout the venue, especially in close proximity to the concessions stands. In the same vein, many venues contract with regional and national brand name companies to sell their products on an exclusive basis. When this occurs, the names of these products should be included in all product-related signage. Brand recognition may induce the guest to purchase an item. When an outside company provides branded signage, it reduces expenses for the venue and, consequently, increases ancillary revenues produced from food and beverage operations. Regardless of who provides the menu boards and signage, they should be positioned to enable customers to quickly and easily see what specialty items the concession stand has to offer.

Purchases from concession stands and portable carts, as well as dining at on-premise restaurants, are often spontaneous decisions. Food and beverage managers seeking to create and maintain a successful operation must present and package their offerings in an enticing and appetizing manner. They must create an appropriate menu and price each item reasonably based on attendee expectations and industry standards for their geographic region.

The marketing of food and beverage services can substantially increase ancillary revenues produced by this operation. Figure 7-4 provides estimated ranges for foodservice per capita spending for a variety of event types. Methods and specific strategies vary based on upon the venue and event type but are always a crucial element of the overall food and beverage operation.

EVENT	LOW	HIGH
High School Sports	$0.25	$2.00
Family Shows	$2.50	$5.50
College Basketball	$2.50	$10.00
College Football	$3.50	$12.00
Minor League Baseball	$7.00	$15.00
MLS	$7.00	$15.00
NBA	$13.50	$19.00
MLB	$13.00	$25.00
Concerts	$1.25	$25.00
NHL	$13.50	$25.00
NFL	$15.00	$35.00
Championship / Super Bowl	$20.00	$95.00

(Bigelow, 2014)

Figure 7-4 : **Foodservice Per Capita Spending**

Foodservice as a Marketing Tool

Although food and beverage is considered an ancillary service, it also has the potential to significantly enhance the venue's overall image. As an increasing number of venues seek to generate additional revenues by renting space for private events, the availability and quality of the venue's food and beverage service operation becomes paramount. In convention centers, catering is often the primary source of revenue, exceeding even rental income.

For instance, stadiums, arenas, and performing arts venues with on-premise restaurants, suites, and clubs may rent these areas for private parties, weddings, and banquets on non-event days. It is important to market the availability of venue space and ancillary services jointly to potential customers in order to take full advantage of additional revenue-generating opportunities. Of course, this type of activity is common for convention centers and community centers, as well as other conference and meeting-oriented venues.

The core function of foodservice operations in convention centers is to address the foodservice needs of groups meeting in the venue. Convention centers must strive to keep their prices in line with competitors, such as local hotels and other banquet venues, in order to successfully compete for meeting and convention business and accompanying food and beverage service. When convention centers host international, national, regional, and local meetings and conventions, the food and beverage service should be marketed in a manner that demonstrates the venue's ability to adapt to varying event needs. These events have a positive economic impact on the community through hotel stays and additional business for area restaurants and retail stores. Hosting local meetings and conferences can generate a substantial amount of new revenues and allows the convention center to support community activities that enhance the image of the venue. In every instance, the same rules apply with respect to the high quality of the food and beverage service, its efficient and convenient delivery, and its appearance at presentation.

Alcohol Sales

Alcohol sales are a significant ancillary revenue source and a staple product that enhances the customer's experience while attending events. The ability to purchase beer, wine, and spirits during events has become such an established customer expectation that its availability may be a determining factor for customers when making a decision whether or not to attend an event. An increasing number of colleges and universities now provide alcoholic beverages in some or all of their sports and entertainment venues, even those located on campus (Bigelow, 2014).

The economic benefits of selling alcohol is balanced by the vendor's complete responsibility for safe and effective alcohol management. Dram shop laws specify that commercial establishments can be held liable if an employee sells alcohol to a visibly intoxicated person who later is involved in an accident or injures third parties (Sharp, Moorman, & Claussen, 2007). As a result of those liability concerns, training of servers and attendants is an essential part of managing the alcohol service environment. Several good programs are available, such as Training for Intervention Procedures (TIPs) and Techniques for Effective Alcohol Management (TEAM), which can augment employee training. Figure 7-5 outlines alcohol service guidelines from TEAM.

ID GUIDELINES

Serving alcohol to underage people is illegal in every state. Use the three ID guidelines to help avoid problems:

1. Ask to see the ID – don't take the guest's word for it that he/she is over the legal drinking age.

2. Ask for more proof if you have any doubts. The second form of ID should be any credit/debit/loyalty card in the guest's wallet with the same name as on the ID.

3. Know where the alcohol is going. If a guest asks for two different types of alcohol drinks (a beer and a wine), ask who will be drinking the other drink.

CUT-OFF GUIDELINES

Sometimes it becomes necessary to refuse a sale and inform a guest that he/she will not be given any more alcohol. Follow these guidelines to help diffuse the situation:

1. Say "I'm sorry. I cannot serve you alcohol now. I would be happy to get you water or a soft drink." Move the transaction along. Reference the long line of other customers to avoid a drawn-out conversation with the guest.

2. Give clear reasons and don't judge the guest. Never say "You're drunk."

3. Call for backup from co-workers, a manager, security staff, or law enforcement if the guest makes trouble.

SAFE DRINKING GUIDELINES

Keep your guests safe and having a good time while they're drinking by following these guidelines:

1. Buy time. At an outlet, limit the number of drinks a guest can buy. In the stands, limit the number of times you walk by people who may be misusing alcohol.

2. Offer alternatives to alcohol. Suggest food and non-alcohol beverages to guests who show signs of impairment.

3. Use the personal touch. Make eye contact and some friendly conversation with every customer as often as you can.

Figure 7-5 : TEAM Alcohol Service Guidelines

A risk analysis using a variety of criteria can assist venue management in evaluating the potential risks and implementation of alcohol management techniques, such as limiting size of containers, number of cups that can be sold per person at one time, and early cut-off of sales. Management's determination regarding the availability of alcohol is often based on event type and audience demographics, as well as feedback from the event promoter.

Beer and alcohol companies enjoy the benefits of associating with high-profile events and are often great advertisers and event sponsors. It should be noted that, unlike soft drink distributors, venues are not permitted under federal law to negotiate an exclusive vending agreement with alcohol beverage manufacturers and distributors. Likewise, an alcoholic beverage retail license holder may not be able to accept promotional funds from an alcoholic beverage manufacturer. This is another reason having a contracted **concessionaire** may make financial sense. With that in mind, venue management must be cognizant of the proper way to structure relationships with beer and alcohol vendors within legal guidelines.

MERCHANDISE

Customers attending venue events often seek some tangible reminders and evidence of their experience. Branded items with a team or touring event logo are especially popular. Therefore, selling authentic, exclusive, event-related merchandise and novelty items is another ancillary service and potential revenue source that has proven popular with customers and lucrative to events, artists, and teams. The terms merchandise and novelty items refer to tangible, non-perishable souvenir products. Early souvenir and merchandise items included pennants, programs, and buttons and were sold at carnivals, circuses, and sporting events. Later, popular music tours wanting to increase the sale of artists' music, introduced new types of merchandise.

While overall merchandise sales continue to be strong, the venue's percentage of sales has been shrinking in recent years as a result of more competitive contract negotiations. Nonetheless, it is still a viable source of ancillary income. These opportunities primarily come from concerts, family shows, Broadway productions, and other touring events. Touring shows typically sell their merchandise rights to a third party, or merchandiser, who travels with the show and negotiates with the venue for the sale of their event-specific products. While professional and collegiate sports teams may generate significant revenue from the sale of merchandise, those revenues are rarely shared with the venue.

The three best times to sell merchandise are during **ingress**, intermission, and **egress**, often referred to as the **blowout**. Capturing the moment of excitement from a grand finale or the exuberant high of a competitive victory can extend the sales opportunity exponentially. Special attention and emphasis should be given to take advantage of this unique opportunity. To do so, management must ensure that proper staffing levels are maintained to accommodate customers in a timely manner and offer pertinent information to enhance the sales opportunity.

Venue managers have several options for managing merchandise operations. As with the food and beverage service, venue managers may elect to operate their merchandising in-house, contract the operation to a private merchandising company, or include it in the rights and responsibilities of their food and beverage contractor. In most instances, the event travels with its own merchandise operation, including all product and key staff.

Regardless of who is responsible for merchandise operations, there are risks associated with merchandise sales that are assumed by the responsible party. These potential risks include customer and employee theft of merchandise and cash, credit card fraud, overstocking, and overpriced merchandise that goes unsold and is printed with a specific date. Venue managers must consider these risks during the booking and contracting process.

Structure of Merchandising Agreements

The venue provides the opportunity to sell merchandise to a captive audience and, therefore, generally receives a portion of merchandise sales. During the event, contract negotiations, the venue representative and the merchandiser or promoter must address the merchandise revenue distribution. Typically, one of three types of merchandising agreements is used: a flat-rate fee, a per-person fee, or a percentage-of-sales fee (Bigelow, 2008).

The **flat-rate fee** is a one-time, fixed-rate dollar amount paid to the venue. This method does not produce maximum revenue results for a venue, and the venue manager has little control over what or how much is sold at the event. This method is often used in smaller buildings and markets or for performing arts events that produce low merchandise sales. This system is also used at convention centers when a show promoter wishes to sell ancillary products such as tapes, books, or other similar merchandise.

The **per-person fee** is based on a pre-determined amount to be charged by the venue for each person attending the event. This number is usually determined by using verified attendance figures. This method can be an effective approach if the historical per capita sales for the event are researched. However, if this information cannot be obtained, then this fee base may be ineffective as a maximum revenue producer.

The **percentage-of-sales fee** is probably the most common and accepted fee arrangement for the right to sell merchandise at events. Under this arrangement, the venue receives a percentage of the sale of merchandise and novelty items. While this fee arrangement is more common, it requires additional supervision, control systems, and marketing knowledge from the venue staff and retailer. The retailer's role under this fee arrangement is to provide personnel to inventory, display, sell, and account for the merchandise and novelty sales (Bigelow, 2008). Venue management must also verify the beginning and ending inventory in order to ensure collection of the venue's percentage of sales.

Both the flat-rate and per-person fee provide income to the venue with little or no involvement from venue management. The venue also has no reporting requirements for payment of wages or product. The percentage-of-sales method is more labor intensive for venue management, especially in exercising inventory controls of the products being sold. The prime issue in collecting a percentage of sales is determining the total sales amount.

In general terms, the event receives 75 to 90 percent of gross merchandise sales after applicable taxes. The venue typically receives 10 to 25 percent of gross sales. Whoever is responsible for the sale of the merchandise is responsible for paying the sellers. To protect the interests of the venue, the manager must take the required steps to ensure that all parties involved in the merchandising operation are held accountable for fulfilling their tax obligations.

The final amount the venue receives from merchandise sales may be impacted if merchandise operations have been contracted out to a third party. In that instance, the third party provides the services involved and pays the venue a percentage of gross sales. It is likely this would be less than if the venue directly handled the merchandise operation, but the venue has transferred risk and responsibility to a third party.

For venue managers to negotiate the most lucrative agreement, they must have knowledge of projected merchandise per capita spending. While merchandise **per caps** varies greatly due to an event's popularity, color and style fads, geography, event types, and customer demographics, Figure 7-6 illustrates common industry ranges based on event type.

EVENT	LOW	HIGH
Performing Arts	$0.15	$2.00
College Sports	$0.25	$3.00
Major League Sports	$0.75	$4.00
Family Shows	$1.00	$4.00
R&B Concerts	$2.00	$12.00 *
Country Concerts	$2.00	$15.00 *
Rock Concerts	$3.50	$20.00 *
Professional Wrestling / MMA	$3.00	$20.00
World Series / Super Bowl	$15.00	$50.00

* It is not unusual for exceptional events to generate as much as $10.00 per person more than the above ranges.

(Bigelow, 2014)

Figure 7-6 : Merchandise Per Capita Spending

Merchandise Operations

As with other venue functions, the venue manager should be knowledgeable about the current merchandising environment in order to maximize profit, regardless of the fee structure negotiated. For example, just like in the foodservice areas, all sales areas selling merchandise, whether permanent or portable, need to accept credit cards. Given the high prices of products and the trend for customers to carry little, if any, cash with them, credit cards are a basic necessity to maximize sales.

Regardless of who is physically selling the merchandise, venue management must clearly communicate their expectations regarding display and service. An attractive and clearly visible display of available merchandise, combined with an efficient sales system and staff, will produce the most successful financial results. Merchandise points-of-sale should be adequately staffed, and there should be a variety of payment options available. Sales personnel should be uniformly dressed, knowledgeable about the products, helpful, and trained to be courteous and professional at all times.

In the venue management industry, bootlegging refers to the unauthorized sale of unlicensed or stolen merchandise, as well as any items that infringe on the copyrighted logos or marks. Precautions must be taken to prevent the sale of this type of merchandise. When appropriate, local law enforcement should be hired and retained to enforce laws and regulations governing unlicensed vendors selling merchandise on venue property. These personnel expenses are typically the responsibility of the event.

Permanent Tenant Merchandise Stores

Venue managers are normally required as part of tenant negotiations to provide permanent locations for merchandise sales. While the venue rarely receives any of the profit from the sale of team merchandise, they are often compensated for use of the space and utilities. This may be negotiated as a flat monthly fee, a square-foot charge, or may be included in the tenant's venue rental agreement. In any event, this arrangement can be beneficial to both parties, as it creates the opportunity for continual presence, offering the ability to enjoy revenue streams throughout the year. These stores often mirror normal retail hours and are open on non-event days, which may encourage the public to visit your venue throughout the year.

Colts Pro Shop - Indianapolis, IN

PARKING

One of the first impressions a customer has when arriving at a venue for an event will be derived from the efficiency and effectiveness of the parking, traffic, and transportation plan. For venue management, parking revenues may produce an important ancillary revenue source, as well as other related services. It is imperative that the venue manager devotes ample time to these services in order to encourage repeat business and increase ancillary revenues.

Parking Services

Parking and parking lots produce another ancillary revenue source. While some venues may not have dedicated parking options, those that do should work to develop parking plans that maximize these revenues. The venue manager should carefully assess the parking inventory, available staff, and the venue's event schedule in order to determine what types of parking services might be appropriate and profitable. There are expenses associated with the traffic and parking operation, which may include parking personnel, uniformed traffic police, utilities, snow removal, trash removal, necessary equipment, signage, and closed-circuit television systems, as well as the cost of printing and distributing parking passes.

Although most parking operations charge guests a flat fee to park while attending an event, some people are willing to pay for added conveniences. Depending on the number and location of available parking spaces, the venue manager may construct a variable fee schedule, charging higher prices for parking located in closer proximity to the venue. A venue parking operation may generate additional revenue through the following programs:

- Selling parking passes to season ticket holders and frequent users of the venue
- Making daytime parking available to the general public on non-event days
- Monthly or annual parking space leases for individuals who work near the venue
- Providing valet parking service during scheduled events
- Parking lot events

Since cash transactions are common in parking lots, an accounting system with appropriate audit controls must be adopted and implemented to protect revenues and discourage potential theft. Employees allowing guests to park for free or pocketing a portion of the collected fees represent two forms of theft that may occur if proper supervisory and accountability measures are not continuously monitored and enforced. Venue managers, in conjunction with the finance department, must develop safeguards to prevent theft. Many venues have a parking or transportation fee in the price of each event ticket. Other venues have customers buy their reserved or general parking space at the time they buy their tickets. Both options significantly reduce the need for parking staff as well as the potential for employee theft.

Parking, just like food and beverage and merchandise, requires credit card acceptance at all entry locations as well as online for pre-paid parking. Many venues are now utilizing software online that directs customers to the best available venue parking option, provides detailed directions, and may even allow them to reserve a parking space. This may help alleviate traffic congestion prior to events, particularly when customers new to your venue are driving around looking for a parking lot (Bigelow, 2014). Likewise, pre-paid parking increases the efficiency of parking lot ingress because cashiers do not have to make change or process credit cards.

Venue Parking & Event Tailgating

Parking-Related Ancillary Revenue Sources

Typically venues can charge a higher rate for recreational vehicles (RVs), buses, and limos because they use more than one parking space or may be using the space for an extended period of time. Some venues also provide utility hookups for RVs for an additional fee. RV parking is a staple at football games and auto racing events but is also popular at trade shows where exhibitors are in town for extended periods of time. Venues also generally have designated areas and traffic flow plans for RVs, buses, and limos to allow for efficient parking operations.

Valet parking service represents another potential source of ancillary revenue for the venue and a value-added service for the customer. Because of the liabilities, venues offering this service may contract it out to a third party. Even if the revenue derived from this service is merely equal to the expense of employing the service, it may be worth the effort to enhance the customer's event experience.

Parking Lot Events

There are two basic types of parking lots: surface lots and multi-level parking decks. Surface lots are significantly less expensive, per car, to develop, construct, and maintain than a parking deck. However, surface lots require more land to meet the needs of the venue when compared to a parking structure. Venues built in metropolitan areas must often opt for parking decks since land is expensive to obtain. Those venues with large surface parking areas may use the parking lots for a variety of revenue-producing events. Parking lot events may include flea markets, outdoor trade shows, traveling circuses, and auto events, such as car shows, ride-and-drives, road rallies, and races. Events such as these can be used to create supplemental revenue when parking areas are not being used for normal venue events.

SUMMARY

One of the greatest pressures on the venue manager is to generate revenues in an effort to meet annual goals and financial expectations. Ancillary revenues are an important part of achieving those goals and expectations. Traditional sources of revenue must be supplemented to ensure success, and there are a number of ancillary revenue sources that the venue manager can pursue. These ancillary revenue sources may include:

- Promoter-Generated Ancillary Revenue
    - In-house ad agency fees
    - Television production fees
    - Utility fees
    - Labor fees
    - Additional space rental
    - Equipment rental
- Guest-Generated Ancillary Revenue
    - Ticketing
    - Food and beverage
    - Merchandise
    - Parking

It is important for the venue manager to investigate every option available to identify those ancillary opportunities and develop them as completely as possible. This area will test the venue manager's ability to negotiate and think entrepreneurially. It will be one of the most significant areas where the venue manager can have a positive impact on both the venue's bottom line and the overall guest experience.

CHAPTER 8

VENUE OPERATIONS AND SERVICES

INTRODUCTION

The Operations Department is responsible for making the public assembly venue functionally ready, safe, and secure for everyone who works in, uses, or visits the venue. Depending on the event calendar, venues are constantly being transformed from one event to the next. Even when the venue is not booked, venue personnel should work productively to make necessary repairs and maintain the venue to assure it operates efficiently and effectively.

This chapter will focus on the **back-of-house** operations or functions that facilitate the delivery of services to the users and guests. Back-of-house refers to the portion of the venue where public access is not permitted and incorporates the activities that take place behind the scenes to deliver the event and all its requirements. Operations personnel and their attention to the many details required to host an event will greatly impact the venue's overall success.

OPERATIONS DEPARTMENT

Fundamentally, achievement of the venue's objectives depends on a skilled operations department. Regardless of type, size, ownership, and number of events, common operational services and activities must occur in order for the venue to function as desired. The operations department is generally responsible for the venue's physical environment, including the following:

- State of maintenance, repair, air quality, and air temperature
- Management and control of building systems
- Logistical delivery of event-production requirements
- Life safety/security

To successfully meet these challenges, the operations department must operate within a well-defined organizational and management structure that enables the venue and its personnel to prepare and adapt to each event. Excellent communications within its staff is a critical element of a successful operations department. The functional areas that typically define an operations department vary depending on the venue type and geographical location but typically include:

- Personnel and labor sources
- Regulatory compliance
- Shipping and receiving
- Inventory management

- Capital replacement
- Sustainable practices
- Engineering (HVAC/refrigeration/life safety systems/utilities)
- Technical services (IT/AV/phone/Internet)
- Maintenance and repair
- **Trades** (electricians, plumbers, mechanics, and carpenters)
- Housekeeping and custodial requirements
- Grounds maintenance
- Pest control
- Sanitation, recycling, and trash removal
- **Event production**
- **Back-of-house** security/24-hour security
- Coordination and management of event contract riders
- **Conversions/changeovers**
- **Rigging** requirements
- **Stagehands** and event labor
- Union labor relationships
- Customer/client services
- Event equipment

The typical back-of-the-house organizational chart (see sample in Figure 8-1) may include some of the following positions, again depending on size, type, and geographical location:

- Director or VP of operations
- Operations manager
- Assistant operations manager
- Engineers
- Electrical/mechanical technicians
- Technical director/production manager
- Stage manager
- Conversion/changeover supervisor
- Trades steward
- General trades (union) employees
- Maintenance staff
- Custodial supervisors

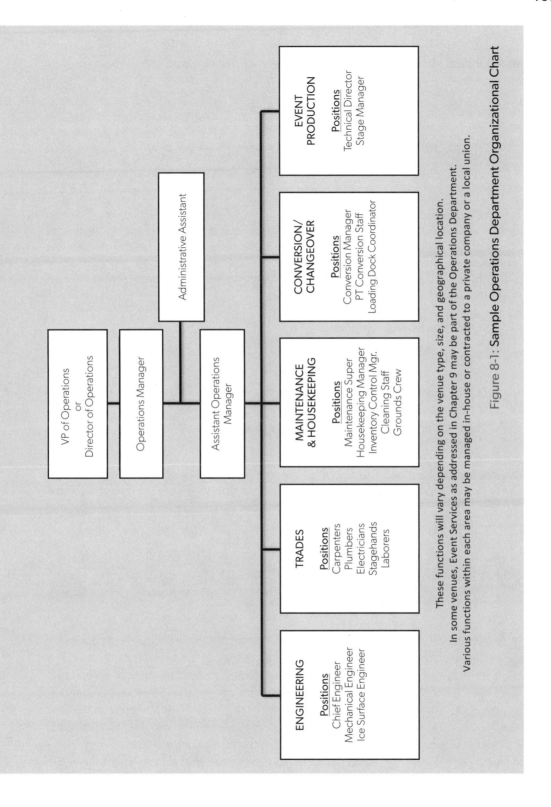

These functions will vary depending on the venue type, size, and geographical location.
In some venues, Event Services as addressed in Chapter 9 may be part of the Operations Department.
Various functions within each area may be managed in-house or contracted to a private company or a local union.

Figure 8-1: Sample Operations Department Organizational Chart

The information in this chapter is intended to describe the internal workings of an operations department and the levels of cooperation and communication that are essential between the **front-of-house** and **back-of-house** functions to successfully and safely manage and operate a public assembly venue before, during, or after an event, or on a day with no event.

DIRECTOR OF OPERATIONS

The typical director of operations has a tremendous amount of responsibility, which directly impacts the ability of the organization to meet objectives and fulfill their mission. The director of operations manages a variety of venue functions and needs to have a basic understanding of all areas within the operations department. Strong leadership skills are required, along with the ability to work with diverse clients and employees. As in other key management positions, this position also requires the following:

- Effective time management
- Ability to work under pressure with strict deadlines
- Ability to multi-task
- Attention to detail
- Strong written and verbal communication skills
- Creative problem solving
- Skilled budget management
- Strong negotiating skills

The director of operations, like all operations employees, works long and irregular hours. The available support depends on the venue size and type, as well as the type and volume of events.

VENUE OPERATIONS MANAGEMENT

As a general rule, a public assembly venue operations department has two distinct components, both of which are critical to the success of the venue and its mission. The first is devoted to the operational aspects of the venue, including mechanical systems and maintenance, and the second is focused on the delivery of events. The venue's operational services must continually keep the venue safe, clean, and in good repair while also coordinating building **conversions** or **changeovers** to fulfill all event-related requirements. To achieve the venue's objectives, the operations department must be flexible and responsive to the varying event-related needs of guests and clients while working to maintain the venue and its equipment, which enables the venue to continue hosting events.

The organization of the operations department is generally based on the tasks to be performed. The director of operations is responsible for the supervision of various managers within the operations department, as well as any applicable union labor. The number of managers varies depending on factors, such as size, venue type, and volume of events.

Figure 8-1 provides a sample organization chart for an operations department. Depending on the type, size, and organizational structure, the operations department may include another area, Event Services. In some cases, Event Services functions as a stand-alone department. Regardless of the organizational structure, the event services department generally addresses the needs of the front-of-house, defined as the areas of the venue and event operations experienced by the guests. Front-of-house event services are addressed in more detail in chapter 9.

Management should implement techniques that encourage full-time and part-time employees to focus on the venue's mission and appreciate their contribution to the venue's overall success. The venue and both operations and event services managers may accomplish this objective by insisting that all full-time managers and supervisors implement the venue's recruiting, hiring, training, and rewards systems for all employees. Other management tools include having up-to-date job descriptions, providing manuals and handbooks that clearly explain personnel policies and procedures, scheduling required employee training sessions, requiring documentation of employee skill levels, and using effective employee evaluation and reward techniques.

Personnel and Labor Sources

Public assembly venues employ individuals with varying skills, and some tasks may be unique to the venue type. A stadium may have a grounds crew, a theater may have a technical director, an arena with an ice floor may have an ice engineer, and a convention center may have a banquet manager. Each department supervisor is charged with the responsibility for directing and supervising their staff. That staff may be made up of full-time or part-time employees, but most likely a combination of both depending on the venue's event schedule. Although engineering, maintenance and trades, housekeeping and custodial, and sometimes event services generally reside in the venue operations department, the tasks assigned to each area can be significantly different. A manager who is knowledgeable and experienced concerning the specifics of the work to be performed should supervise each area of an operations department.

The support required for maintenance, engineering, housekeeping, and other services might come from any of the following sources or a combination of these sources:

- In-House support where the employees are directly employed and managed by the venue
- Support provided by other entities (e.g., municipalities, universities, etc.)
- Support provided through a contractual arrangement between the venue and a third-party contractor

For example, a municipally owned venue might have an on-site operations department to deal with general maintenance and housekeeping services but rely completely upon the municipality's public works department for major repairs and support of the mechanical systems. It is not unusual for a university-managed performing arts center, particularly one with a modest event schedule, to draw all of its maintenance and housekeeping support from the university's maintenance, grounds, and housekeeping departments. In all probability, the performing arts venue would receive its water, electrical power, and HVAC support from the respective university departments as well. In situations of this nature, the venue may employ a superintendent to oversee the venue's operations and to serve as a liaison between the venue and the service providers.

Regulatory Compliance

Federal, state, and local regulatory codes must be diligently monitored by all types of public assembly venues. Compliance with these codes is most often the responsibility of a venue's operations department. Local regulatory jurisdictions usually will oversee venue compliance in a number of ways but invariably will refer to various national codes. In the United States, some of the most common are the Occupational Safety and Health Administration (OSHA) regulations, which seek to protect the safety and health of workers; the Americans with Disabilities Act (ADA), which protects both employees and guests from discrimination due to both mental and physical disability; and fire, life safety, and building codes such as those developed and recommended by the National Fire Protection Association (NFPA). Local building codes may also greatly impact the operation of a venue, and management should be aware of those regulations. Similar code requirements can be found worldwide.

In addition, the operations department is responsible for monitoring and scheduling periodic inspections ranging from elevator maintenance certification to fire extinguisher validations with respective local agencies. Failure to comply with some of these responsibilities not only places guests, clients, and employees in danger, but also can put the venue in a position of liability for the safety of those same individuals. During winter months, many venues are faced with the issue of snow/ice removal and making **ingress** and **egress** for guests safe. Many venues, especially in warmer climates, opt to contract out snow and ice removal services due to the infrequency of that need or lack of necessary equipment.

The operations department should require periodic inspection by their engineers in the areas of fire suppression, fire sprinklers, and smoke detection systems. Auxiliary generators used to produce electric power for emergency lighting and public address systems during periods of electrical outages should also be routinely tested and maintained. It is imperative that, during periods of electrical outages, emergency power be available to provide for the safety of the venue's guests, clients, and employees. Emergency power systems are a legal requirement for most venues.

Shipping and Receiving

Public assembly venues that host **trade shows**, **exhibitions**, or similar events require vendors to ship materials to the venue in advance of the event and, upon its conclusion, ship those same materials back to their place of business or to another site. Therefore, venues may have an in-house shipping and receiving unit specifically to oversee the shipping and receiving functions. However, it is not unusual for trade show or exhibit events to use a private contractor, referred to as the Official Services Contractor, to perform these functions. In this instance, venue operations personnel will coordinate needs with the Official Services Contractor to ensure efficiency and accuracy. Shipping and receiving responsibilities include the following:

- Scheduling adequate staff to receive deliveries in a timely and organized manner
- Providing secure storage for deliveries upon arrival
- Managing a tracking system to coordinate deliveries with the appropriate activity
- Organizing deliveries to maximize efficient movement
- Coordinating removal of materials at the conclusion of the event
- Preparing materials for shipping, if necessary
- Managing required documentation associated with the receiving and shipping processes

Clients rely on the venue to receive and properly manage their shipments of materials. Therefore, it is imperative that the operations department efficiently coordinates the shipping and receiving process.

Inventory Management

In many public assembly venues, the operations department is responsible for managing an inventory control system that adheres to the budgetary requirements of the finance department. This may include recordkeeping, periodic scheduled and unannounced inspections, lock and key controls, and surveillance and security systems. The event schedule and the number of guests accommodated at those events make it necessary for tracking substantial venue assets. Inventory management is a responsibility for which all venue personnel must be accountable. It can be a daunting and endless task, and, as a result, some venues hire specialized personnel to manage the inventory.

In some venues, the inventory control system includes a labeling and numbering system whereby each item is etched, labeled, and numbered with a tag. These labels, in addition to identifying the item, may also display a bar code that when scanned provides additional information about the product. Knowing pertinent information about the product may enable operations personnel to track usage and plan for replacement based upon the life expectancy of the product.

In addition, the operations department must monitor and inventory supplies, such as paper products, cleaning supplies and chemicals, and light bulbs. These supplies are ordered based on anticipated use, which can be difficult to predict. However, the operations manager can review past history and examine expected attendance for upcoming events when making purchasing decisions.

Operations department staff responsible for inventory control may randomly spot-check selected items from the venue's inventory list. Should a discrepancy be discovered or some item appear to be unaccounted for, a more thorough and complete physical inventory may be required. Maintaining the venue's assets and keeping them in good working order is at the heart of ensuring successful events. Effective and efficient inventory controls help in that effort. An important part of any inventory management system also involves establishing procedures for removing any outdated, non-functional, or sold items from the inventory control list.

Another important element of inventory control is a venue access management system. Management must designate who requires access to which areas of the venue and provide access accordingly. When utilizing a traditional key system, creating an inventory of all keys to locked areas, and recording the recipient of each key, is central to maintaining the venue's security and access control. This is a critical step in protecting the venue's inventory. A part of the key inventory may also include conducting periodic inspections of all locks and noting any required maintenance. Many venues have incorporated a card-access system, whereby personnel are able to access areas with their employee identification card. Keycard systems and biometric indicators identify employees who have access to any secure area and are also helpful in the process of controlling inventory and assuring security.

As mentioned earlier, it is also a good business practice to have controls in place to track receipt, use, and replacement of materials and supplies. Controlling costs is essential in any business, and tracking the use of expendable supplies can help assure the best use of materials such as paper goods, cleaning supplies, and other products used in the venue's operation. An inventory system for these items provides many benefits including the following:

- Recording materials and supplies when they arrive documents that a transaction is complete and payments may be made.
- Tracking the use of materials and supplies to enable staff to reorder in a timely manner
- Enabling the venue to monitor usage and trends over time
- The existence of an inventory control system may serve as a deterrent to misappropriation or misuse of venue resources.

Tracking supplies used during an event, such as paper goods, enables the operations manager to calculate inventory used on a per-person basis. This information is an important management tool in determining the amount of product necessary for an event or series of events. It is also an excellent tool when creating an annual budget. When actual event usage is determined, those amounts may be used for budget projections, thereby enabling management to more accurately predict actual costs for upcoming events.

Capital Expenditures

Public assembly venues are built for the guests and clients they serve. More events means more guests and more wear and tear on the venue and its equipment. While preventative maintenance programs can prolong the life of equipment, all physical assets have limited lifespans and eventually wear out. Therefore, new equipment must be purchased on a regular basis.

Capital expenditures refers to the amounts spent for real estate, furniture, fixtures, equipment, and certain major repairs or improvements. These funds are not usually included in the operating expenses but are shown as a separate section of the financial statements. Examples include purchasing a floor scrubber, replacing all the seats in a theater, purchasing a new scoreboard, or major venue renovations.

Planning ahead for **capital improvements** and replacements is an important responsibility of the director of operations, in cooperation with the venue manager and director of finance. Knowledge of the equipment's lifespan is a key component in planning for its replacement. A capital replacement plan provides a schedule for such expenditures and may be viewed over a three-to five-year period, enabling management to anticipate line-item expenses for each year's budget. It is important to note that publicly owned venues must comply with local regulations regarding capital asset disposal when applicable.

Sustainable Practices

Like executives in many organizations, venue managers have become increasingly aware of the need to operate their venue with awareness of the environmental impact generated by the building and the events it hosts. While sustainable practices may have a positive impact on a venue's public image, it is more important to recognize the obligation to operate in an environmentally responsible manner. In addition, some artists/performers are cognizant of a venue's sustainable practices and may make decisions regarding where to perform based on the venue's environmental awareness. Venue operations departments can implement sustainable programs by focusing their efforts on the following key areas of sustainability:

- Waste management and diversion
- Energy conservation
- Water quality and conservation
- Air quality
- Environmental purchasing
- Community engagement
- Staff buy-in

While specific strategies may vary depending on the characteristics of the venue, the use of sustainable practices will continue to be the expected standard operating procedure for all venues. In addition, those involved in the design, construction or renovation of public assembly venues are working to create more environmentally friendly buildings.

A critical first step in implementing a sustainability program is to establish baseline data in the areas of waste diversion, energy consumption, and water consumption. Once the venue has an understanding of its environmental impact, it can then begin to develop a plan to address these specific areas. By continuing to track this data, a venue can then evaluate the effect of certain programs, equipment upgrades, and/or revised operational practices. Many resources exist to help gather this information, such as the EPA's EnergySmart tool.

Specific strategies and goals may vary depending on a venue's needs and the resources in the community. For example, some municipalities may not offer commercial compost collection. Therefore, this waste management technique may not be available to the venue, and other strategies for waste diversion would need to be explored.

There are several environmental standards that address venue operations, which serve as helpful guides and resources in identifying industry agreed-upon best practices. The most widely recognized of these standards are:

1. **Leadership in Energy and Environmental Design (LEED)**

   LEED certifications include programs for LEED New Construction (LEED NC) and LEED for Existing Buildings: Operations and Maintenance (LEED EB: O&M). LEED is a green building tool that addresses the entire building lifecycle, recognizing best-in-class building strategies. The LEED program provides third-party verification of green buildings. Building projects satisfy prerequisites and earn points to achieve different levels of certification. Rating systems are groups of requirements for projects that want to achieve LEED certification. Each group is geared towards the unique needs of a project or building type. Additional information can be found at www.usgbc.org/leed.

2. **ASTM/APEX Venue Standard**

   ASTM International provides a global forum for the development and publication of international voluntary consensus standards for materials, products, systems, and services. The Accepted Practices Exchange (APEX) is an initiative of the Convention Industry Council that promotes development and implementation of industry-wide accepted practices to create and enhance efficiency throughout the meetings, conventions and exhibitions industry. Additional information can be found at www.astm.org.

3. **International Organization for Standardization (ISO) 14001 and 20121**

   ISO 14001 is a management system that addresses environmental management. It provides practical tools for companies and organizations looking to identify and control their environmental impact and constantly improve their environmental performance. ISO 20121 is a management system standard designed to help organizations in the events industry improve the sustainability of their event-related activities, products, and services. Additional information can be found at www.iso.org.

While these best practices have environmental benefits, they also often save time and money. For example, by replacing outdated lighting systems with new LED technology, a venue saves money from the decrease in energy consumption, but because these bulbs have longer lifespans, the venue also saves the staff time and cost of replacing older bulbs more frequently.

On a smaller scale, many venues have established recycling programs. The high volume of people in one place at one time results in a high volume of waste and potential recyclable materials. The IAVM 2012 Sustainability Study indicated that 99 percent of the venues responding have some form of recycling program. In addition, well over half of the respondents indicated that they use green cleaning chemicals, floor-care products, and paper products (IAVM Sustainability Study, 2012).

As discussed previously, sustainable practices are part of the expected standard operating procedures for all venues. Each venue manager must determine which practices will be most effective and provide the greatest impact. Venue managers must seek opportunities to implement sustainable practices within the context of their venue and financial resources.

Example of a Waste Recycling Program

ENGINEERING

Engineering, which in some larger venues may be a stand-alone department, is one of the most critical areas of venue operations. If this department and its systems do not function efficiently and effectively, it may negatively impact the guest's experience and could even result in life safety and financial consequences. The vital areas that require engineering servicing and monitoring may include:

- Maintaining air quality and temperature through the heating, ventilation, and air conditioning (HVAC) system
- Monitoring water quality and flow pressure
- Monitoring electrical consumption and maintaining electrical power distribution equipment
- Maintaining emergency power systems
- Monitoring life safety systems such as fire suppression and sprinkler systems
- Maintaining ice rink refrigeration systems

Mechanical systems have become very sophisticated. In order to provide constant and vigilant oversight of these systems, many venues use web-based monitoring systems for centralized master control of the venue's mechanical, life safety, security, and comfort environments. Some of these systems are referred to as:

- BAS – Building Automated Systems
- EMS – Energy Management Systems
- CAFM – Computer-Aided Facility Management
- FMIS – Facilities Management Information Systems

These systems enable engineering and operations personnel to pre-program scheduled settings, as well as monitor and control the systems from mobile devices. For example, depending on weather conditions, the HVAC system may be programmed to provide comfortable air temperature only when the venue is in use. Effective use of this system eliminates unnecessary utility expenses. Also, when freezing temperatures or roof snow loads become a concern, engineers are able to make temperature adjustments from remote locations to address the issue. These systems are efficient to operate and minimize utility use and labor.

Because of ever-evolving technology, in-service training and licensing is required for many of these specialized mechanical areas. Therefore, many venues choose to use service contractors for these systems, which may include:

- Elevators and escalators
- Fire suppression equipment
- Security alarm and surveillance systems
- HVAC systems
- Refrigeration systems
- Life safety systems

These services are generally outsourced to the manufacturer or private companies through service and maintenance contracts.

In venues with ice making capabilities for hockey, traveling ice shows, and/or public skating, it is not unusual for a venue engineer to have the responsibility of maintaining the refrigeration system. In addition to the engineer, other operations staff may be responsible for the following:

- Installing and removing the ice based upon the venue's event schedule
- Maintaining the ice surface, which may be modified based on the event type
- Logo placement and painting
- Maintaining the ice resurfacing equipment (such as a **Zamboni**)
- Managing the maintenance program for the ice making equipment
- Installing dasher boards, glass, and safety nets

Ice Resurfacing Equipment

Exactly where the line is drawn between the operations department and engineering services depends on the venue size, mission, event types and volume, and whether the venue has access to other external departments for required areas of support. Regardless of the structure, the work done by engineering personnel may not be immediately recognized or appreciated by guests but remains one of the most critical components of a successful venue operation.

PREVENTATIVE MAINTENANCE

Extending the life of the venue and its operating equipment and systems is an important and ongoing process. Venues with financial constraints may often delay necessary maintenance in an effort to control expenses. Unfortunately, when venue owners or management are confronted with the need to reduce expenses, one of the first cuts tends to be the venue's maintenance and repair budget. Deferring maintenance may be a short-term solution but will likely result in long-term consequences. The cost to repair or replace neglected equipment far exceeds the cost of providing routine maintenance. In other words, deferred maintenance decisions predictably result in very expensive long-term costs and will inevitably negatively impact the experience for customers, clients, and employees.

It is the director of operations' responsibility to generate adequate preventive maintenance schedules and to ensure the completion and documentation of all assigned maintenance tasks. A complicating factor in adhering to a maintenance schedule is the venue's schedule of events, which must take precedence. However, a venue manager may need to block time on the event calendar for major maintenance projects such as **rigging** inspections and re-finishing a portable basketball or dance floor. While some preventative maintenance can be accomplished between events, others require consideration to assure they can be completed safely and without endangering guests or staff.

A well-designed preventive maintenance program takes into consideration the life cycle of the venue and especially its equipment. To initiate such a program, the operations department may categorize the various properties of the **physical plant**. A maintenance schedule for each category's elements can be assigned a timeline for attention and formalized in a departmental action plan. The key is to have a system in place for upkeep to reduce the effects of normal wear and tear and to minimize the aging process as much as possible.

Adequate funding for scheduled and preventive maintenance is also critical to the venue's life span. Often, venue managers will dedicate a certain percentage of the venue's operating budget to preventative maintenance expenses.

Responsibility for the venue's preventative maintenance may be assigned to either in-house personnel or service contractors. Exactly which approach best benefits the venue depends upon a number of variables, such as the availability of services and skilled labor, costs of service, and type of maintenance and repairs required. Regardless of who is assigned responsibility for the venue's preventative maintenance program, the best approach is one that considers all options and produces the desired results at an acceptable cost and on time.

TRADES

A **trade** is defined as an occupation requiring manual or mechanical skills and often requiring licensing. In the operations department, there are several types of positions that fall under this description. The trades used in most venues include electricians, carpenters, plumbers, painters, and mechanics. Depending on venue location, trades in a venue may be covered by a local union. Labor unions can supply a trained, skilled workforce as determined by the terms of a **collective bargaining agreement**. Unions are addressed in greater detail later in this chapter.

Tradesmen often hold a license in one or more of the common maintenance areas such as plumbing, electrical, mechanical, or carpentry, and they are expected to have a general working knowledge of each. These employees may also possess skills in general shop work, general mechanics, electrical and gas, welding, metal fabrication, HVAC, painting, and computer applications. Most maintenance workers are hourly employees paid based on their skill level and seniority and are usually eligible for overtime compensation and shift differentials.

Trades are important to a venue because they supply necessary skills, knowledge, and experience to address specific critical elements of the overall operation of the venue and functions associated with the events.

HOUSEKEEPING SERVICES

Housekeeping services relate to those tasks directed toward keeping the venue safe, clean, and appealing to clients, customers, employees, and owners. The housekeeping services unit faces many challenges. One is to establish a standard for cleanliness and sanitization. Another is to successfully identify, recruit, train, and supervise employees and to motivate them to work difficult shifts such as overnight, weekends, and holidays. There are many tasks that fall under the housekeeping services domains which, if not properly performed, may result in lost business or negatively impact the venue's public image. While a clean venue may not be the reason people attend an event, it may be the reason they choose not to return.

Within every venue, housekeeping services are required, and each area may have its own standard by which acceptable cleanliness is measured. The cleanliness standard for the office area, for example, may be quite different from the standard for a private dining room. Housekeeping attention provided to open-air seating in a sports stadium is different from that afforded to **premium seating** areas in many types of venues. The key dynamic affecting the level of housekeeping service provided is based upon guest's and client's expectations. Consequently, it becomes the responsibility of the housekeeping supervisor to recognize the differences and develop operating procedures for the housekeeping services staff that specify what must be done in order to meet these expectations.

Housekeeping personnel can often be divided into two groups: non-event and event. Venues may employ full-time housekeeping personnel to maintain the administrative offices and those areas open to the public or used by staff during non-event days. Cleaning the venue following an event usually requires more personnel than just the full-time housekeeping staff. Tasks of this magnitude are often assigned to in-house or contracted cleaning crews employed on a part-time, as-needed basis. Some venues use full-time staff to serve as crew leaders. Cleaning a venue after a large event may require a crew of one hundred or more workers. Such work often begins late in the evening and must be completed in time to allow the venue to host another event the following morning. If the venue chooses to use a contracted cleaning service, it is important that the venue reserves management rights and quality control in monitoring the work performed.

Of all the work that occurs in a venue, keeping the venue clean, sanitary, and presentable is undoubtedly the least glamorous activity. However, housekeeping and custodial services are critical components to the successful management and operation of a venue. Although housekeeping services may be underappreciated and undervalued, a clean and comfortable venue may greatly impact a customer's event experience and, subsequently, their decision whether or not to return.

BACK-OF-HOUSE EVENT MANAGEMENT

Responsibility for managing the event from the back-of-house perspective usually falls under the supervision of the operations manager or technical director, depending on the type of venue. Areas of the venue usually associated with the back-of-house operations include the stage, dressing rooms, mechanical rooms, loading docks, equipment storage rooms, and operations staff-support areas.

One of the fundamental functions of a public assembly venue is to provide a space in which events are produced. Bringing all of the various elements together that comprise an event is referred to as **event production**.

Production Rider

The event client or **promoter** often provides a **production rider** that includes a detailed description of the support and assistance required to produce their event (a sample rider is provided in Appendix A 8-1). The venue operations department is responsible for carrying out many of the specific requirements of the rider. Depending on the size of the production, the rider may address the following needs:

- Staging requirements
- Set-up requirements (registration, meeting room set-ups, production offices, etc.)
- Production and technical requirements (sound, lights, **rigging**, special effects, etc.)
- Dressing room requirements
- Food and beverage requirements

- Transportation and hotel requirements
- Labor requirements

Touring attractions and exhibitions usually provide their own production crew, often referred to as the **road crew**. Depending on the size, type, and technical requirements of the event, the show may bring its own sound and lights and personnel to operate them. Generally, touring shows do not provide their own laborers, such as loaders, forklift drivers, riggers, wardrobe assistants, and general labor. It is usually the venue's responsibility to provide such personnel as specified in the rider. The expense of providing these workers is usually the responsibility of the promoter and is addressed during event settlement. The venue may be asked to provide personnel in any or all of the following categories:

- Riggers to hang and detach equipment above the stage
- **Stagehands** to load/unload trucks and operate event-related equipment
- **Runners** to perform pickup and delivery tasks
- Certified personnel to operate forklifts and other equipment
- Electricians to handle power/energy connection and distribution for the event
- Carpenters to build sets/props
- Wardrobe staff to help arrange, clean, organize, and sometimes repair costumes
- First-aid/emergency medical technicians (EMTs) to deal with medical emergencies that may occur while the event is being set up, during the event itself, or while the event is being broken down
- Physicians to attend to the specific needs of an artist

Venue security personnel, either in-house or contracted, normally provide protection in the back-of-house areas. As a general rule, the production rider will outline the requirements relating security coverage in these areas. While the production rider addresses these requirements, venue personnel must remember that the production rider likely has been prepared for an entire tour and is not venue-specific. Venue managers are ultimately responsible for the safety and security of the clients, customers, and employees, and, therefore, the final decision-making authority resides with the venue manager. Most often, the venue will provide security as requested in the production rider at a minimum and will schedule additional security as needed based on the layout and access points for their particular venue.

Conversions/Changeovers

A conversion or changeover is defined as the act of transformation that occurs between events that provides the necessary environment for the next use. The result of the conversion is the creation of the foundation for the event that is ready for the client upon their arrival. Fundamentally, the venue production staff is responsible for assisting the client with producing the physical and technical environment required to achieve the successful and desired event objectives. In some cases, this may simply be the elimination of all obstacles by providing a clean and open space. Other situations, as in the conversion from a basketball game to an ice hockey configuration, may require significant conversion activities necessitating considerable physical changes to the venue set-up.

Conversion in Progress

Rigging

Nearly all venues have **rigging points**, which in many venues is referred to as a **rigging grid**. Rigging for events involves the use of cables and motorized hoists to lift and position lighting, audio, video, scenery, signage, special effects, and related items. This practice poses unique and serious risks for venue management because these objects often are suspended over the heads of performers, guests, and/or employees. Venue management is liable for all rigging that takes place in their venue, even if installed by clients and their contractors. Therefore, a rigging safety plan is critical and usually includes the following:

- **Building load capacities** certified on a **rigging plot plan** by a structural engineer
- Fall protection plan and equipment, such as safety harnesses and life lines
- Training programs and certificates of ability for rigging staff
- Constant monitoring and evaluation of safety procedures and OSHA-required rigging equipment and use
- Regular inspection of rigging points and grids by certified personnel

It is the responsibility of the engineers to monitor activities held in the venue in order to ensure weight limits are not exceeded. The weight limits for all of the load points and structural steel should be sent in writing to prospective clients and promoters during the booking process. In some instances, a venue may lose the opportunity to host an event because the venue load capacity is not sufficient to support the event rigging requirements. The venue operations manager, the venue structural engineer, and stagehands should always be involved when questions arise concerning venue structural issues. When a venue is being designed, the architect and structural engineer calculate the effects of additional weight and stress being placed on the venue's roofs, walls, floors, and structural beams. These stresses may include snow load and wind shear tolerances.

Example of Rigging for Lights and Sound

Back-of-House Labor

Virtually all venues use a large number of part-time employees to produce the events. A performing arts theater may have a professional manager and a small, full-time staff responsible for the daily operation of the venue. However, on event days, the number of event staff may increase significantly with the addition of part-time stagehands, **front-of-house** staff, security and parking guards, catering employees, and others. Back-of-house labor, particularly for arenas and theaters, may be divided into five categories: load-in/load-out; set-up/teardown; production labor; clean-up labor; and conversion/changeover labor.

- **Load-in and load-out labor** generally is responsible for organizing and assembling equipment, unpacking equipment prior to the event, dismantling and packing equipment at the end of the performance, and removing equipment from the venue.

- **Set-up and teardown labor** is needed to prepare the venue and its equipment prior to load-in and to return the venue to the same condition after the event has loaded out of the venue.

- **Production labor** is required during the course of the actual event and in many venues is referred to as the **show call**. This type of labor may require the services of employees possessing higher skill levels than normally available from in-house and contracted labor. In such instances, these workers generally belong to an organized labor union and command a higher rate of pay.

- **Clean-up labor** is the staff needed to clean the venue after an event to a standard that is both sanitary and clean. This should be completed to the extent that when guests enter the venue for the next event, it is difficult to tell that another event preceded it.

- **Conversion or changeover staff** is the labor needed to change the configuration of the venue from one event to the next.

Decorators are an event labor category common to certain types of venues, such as convention and conference centers. Within the context of a venue, a **decorator** is an individual or company that provides exhibit booth set-ups and exhibit hall decor for a **trade show** and/or its exhibitors, which may include items such as carpet, tables, chairs, and **pipe and drape**. Some large, busy convention centers have a decorating unit within their organizational structure, with its manager reporting to the venue operations manager.

Labor Unions

Some venues have a working relationship with labor unions to supply various types of skilled and unskilled **back-of-house** event staff. Prior to entering into a relationship and agreement with a union, venue and union representatives negotiate a labor contract. This contract is normally a two-to-three-year agreement and establishes pay rate schedules, employee benefits, minimum crew calls, employee training, work rules and guidelines, and employee supervision.

Some venues may elect, while others are legally obligated, to use the local stagehand employee worker's union for stagehand work. In the United States, the International Alliance of Theatrical and Stage Employees (IATSE) union is capable of meeting most production-related labor requests for **production calls**, while the International Brotherhood of Teamsters (IBT) may coordinate truck loaders for unloading vehicles carrying event equipment including vans and trucks of all sizes. Typically, the union's local business agent (BA) identifies, recruits, and trains potential employees; certifies skills and abilities; negotiates wages and rates of pay; and establishes working rules with the venue management on an annual or biennial basis.

The union will also provide employee oversight in the form of a supervisor or steward. Sometimes, labor requests and requirements for an event scheduled in a union-contracted venue can be submitted directly to the venue's union steward or the local union secretary. The union fills the labor call, and the union bills the event's promoter directly or through the venue. In many instances, all financial activities between the client or promoter and the union might be separate and distinct from those between the venue and the promoter.

Prior to the start of a tour, some shows contract with the international union administration to negotiate stagehand services throughout the tour. Known as **yellow card shows**, these shows are typically theatrical events like Broadway shows or family entertainment such as ice shows. If the venue has booked a yellow card show, they are mandated to follow the national agreement.

Again, the number and type of activities presented, local politics, and the venue's ownership and governance type are usually the prime variables that determine which employee source or combination of sources is used. In some jurisdictions, the law will affect the labor supplier decision. In **right-to-work states**, it is illegal to require an employee or potential employee to hold union membership. In such instances, union members can be employed, but non-union workers cannot be systematically excluded.

Back-of-House Event Equipment

A venue manager is responsible for providing the necessary equipment and supplies to support customers, clients, and events. Depending on the type of venue and the events booked, back-of-house event resources can be divided into two categories: venue event equipment and supplies and client event equipment and supplies. Some of the venue's event equipment and supplies, and, hopefully, all of the client equipment rental and supplies, will be charged back to the event, such as:

- Portable stage with wings, handrails, and stairs
- Portable dance floor
- Tables and chairs
- Dressing room or office furniture
- Pipe and drape
- Carpet
- Utility connections
- House sound system
- Spotlights
- Forklifts
- High lifts/scissor lifts
- Dollies and handcarts
- Crowd control barriers
- Sports floors and surfaces

Marshaling Areas

Marshaling areas are used to manage and regulate incoming load-in traffic for large events. At a convention center, marshaling areas allow for parking and security searches of the large number of trucks arriving with trade show and convention materials. At stadiums and arenas, events such as rodeos, circuses, and large concerts may require significant space dedicated to staging the event or performance and often require access to electrical hookups usually referred to as "shore power." Such areas may be reserved for queuing contestants, herding or sorting of animal acts or rodeo performers, or simply for overnight parking of trucks, buses, and other vehicles and equipment.

The venue may be responsible for managing the staging areas, including developing policies and procedures for load-in and load-out, which must be communicated to appropriate clients and vendors. Providing a centralized process for receiving shipped materials is essential. In some cases, particularly with hazardous materials or under extreme security alerts, separate, even off-site, venues will be dedicated to screening materials destined for the venue.

SUMMARY

The operations department maintains the venue while facilitating essential event functions. The operations department may be organized in different ways in different types of venues, and some services may be provided by union labor, but the basic components remain the same. These functional areas include engineering, maintenance, trades, housekeeping, and event operations and services.

Management must create, implement, and monitor programs designed to train all full-time and part-time operations staff on how to meet and exceed customer and client expectations. The operations department is responsible for delivering services anticipated by the customers and clients. Charged with the care of the physical plant, this department must maintain and plan for replacement of the physical assets of the venue. Risk management and emergency preparedness are important components of this department's mission and are addressed more specifically in chapter 10 under Safety and Security.

It is the responsibility of the operations manager and staff to keep the venue safe, secure, clean, and comfortable. A well-maintained environment is critical to providing a satisfactory atmosphere for guests and clients. Safety must be the first consideration in every decision, as well as providing event-related services with a high level of service.

The role of the operations department is crucial to the delivery of event services that both the customers and clients demand. Customers do not buy tickets to a venue; they purchase tickets to an event with the expectation to be entertained in a clean, safe, secure, and well-maintained environment. Likewise, clients arrive with the anticipation that the venue will be comfortable, set up, and staffed according to their production rider.

CHAPTER 9

EVENT MANAGEMENT AND SERVICES

INTRODUCTION

Long before the doors open, the lights dim, or the curtain rises, the **event management** process has been well under way. Although public assembly venues vary in terms of mission, function, and configuration, they are all designed to produce events. To do so successfully requires extensive planning and attention to detail on the part of the venue's event management staff. This chapter focuses on the **front-of-house**, which refers to areas of the venue typically occupied by the guests in attendance.

Venue personnel must remember that the product, the event itself in this case, is simultaneously produced and consumed (Mullin, et al., 2007). Once the event has taken place, you cannot go back and change the outcome for the client or the experience for the customer. Venues are in the business of "selling experiences" and must strive to provide the highest quality service in a way that enhances the event experience, not detracts from it. If the customer remembers that the concession stand sold out of bottled water, an usher provided incorrect seating information, or the restrooms were not clean, then the venue has negatively impacted both the customer's experience and the venue's public image. Likewise, the client will remember unclean dressing rooms, poorly catered meals, or faulty equipment. If customers or clients have a negative experience, they may not come back and they may share that experience with others.

A successful event is one where the efforts of management and staff are transparent, creating distractions for neither the client nor the customer. The customers expect the event to take place in an environment that will enable them to see and enjoy it. When the customers leave the venue, their memories of the experience centers on the performances by the cast, what they learned from the educational sessions at the conference, or the final score of the game, not the expertise of the venue's employees. Customers do not buy tickets to a venue; they purchase tickets to an event. A venue's poor conditions or lax customer service may be the reason they choose not to purchase tickets there in the future. Customers have many choices when it comes to spending their discretionary money and will not waste it on what they expect to be a negative experience or a poor value.

While the planning process varies from venue to venue, the objective for every event is to plan and prepare in such a way as to enable the customer to focus on the event. When both client and customers deem the event successful, the venue manager's potential to retain or gain future business is enhanced.

EVENT SERVICES DEPARTMENT

The role and responsibility of event management is that of integrating the necessary resources at the right time and location to effectively deliver the event experience. The venue manager is ultimately responsible for fulfilling the obligations outlined in the event contract and rider, regardless of the venue or event type. However, in larger organizations, the venue manager often delegates these responsibilities to an event manager. The formal commitment of the venue's time and space is the beginning of the event management process, which is defined as the communication of pertinent details and the resulting coordination of those obligations.

From a planning standpoint, event management is the process of organizing and coordinating multiple details, some concurrently and others in sequence, to produce a tangible experience for an audience. Typical titles for employees who are the promoter's contact points and handle event-related issues include event manager, event services manager, event supervisor, event coordinator, and production manager. Depending on the type, size, and structure of the venue, these positions may be part of the operations department, or they may constitute a separate department. Regardless of the organizational structure, the role of the individuals in these positions is to facilitate the event planning and implementation processes. These responsibilities may be fulfilled by a single individual or through a collaborative effort, depending on the venue, the number and size of events booked, and the event types.

In the production of every event, venue managers and staff interact with all of the involved parties, such as the tenants, promoters, meeting planners, show managers, sponsors, vendors, exhibitors, and/or contractors. In the final analysis, the venue manager is the central figure charged with balancing the relationships among these parties as they work collectively toward producing the event. In some instances, one or more of these parties may work independently with the venue manager, and only when the event occurs do all of the stakeholders come together at one place and time.

EVENT MANAGER

Regardless of how the responsibilities are delegated, **promoters** expect the role of the event manager to be undertaken by a knowledgeable person or persons employed by the venue. If the venue's size or event volume does not justify assigning a dedicated employee to coordinate event-related information and make appropriate decisions, then others, such as the booking manager, operations manager, or, at times, venue manager, must perform these tasks. In every instance, someone must assume the responsibilities for coordinating activities and disseminating information to the promoter from the venue, as well as coordinating and relaying information from the promoter back to the appropriate venue personnel.

The event manager becomes the central communications point for tenants, promoters, meeting planners, show managers, sponsors, contractors, vendors, exhibitors, and event staff. The primary point of contact with the event itself may be referred to as the promoter, meeting planner, or show manager, depending on the type of event. For example, the event manager would likely be working with the promoter for a national touring concert, a meeting planner for a corporate function, or a show manager for a trade show. For the remainder of the discussion in this chapter, the term "promoter" will refer to whoever is the primary point of contact for the event itself.

Effective event managers must be skilled in time management, organizational skills, customer service, problem–solving, and working with diverse populations. The event manager should make every effort to plan and coordinate as much as possible in advance of the event, which provides an opportunity to identify and address any areas of concern. In addition, effective advance preparation allows time for the event manager to troubleshoot issues during the event. Depending on the event and event requirements, the event manager may be working on an event more than a year in advance and will be responsible for multiple events at the same time. While there is no such thing as a perfect event, the dedicated event manager will always strive for perfection.

EVENT PLANNING PROCESS

Regardless of the type of public assembly venue or the nature of the event, there are similarities in the way venue managers initially approach the event. Once an event is booked, staffing assignments are determined based on factors such as venue type and size, the number of staff available, and the event type. For instance, in a convention center, public consumer shows may be assigned to one event coordinator, while conventions may be assigned to another event coordinator. In an arena, sporting events may be assigned to one individual and concerts assigned to another. Some venues may have staff dedicated to event coordination, while others require certain managerial employees to function as an event coordinator or manager on duty.

Event-day surprises can be frustrating and perplexing. For example, it is not uncommon for there to be minor production changes, such as speakers or video screens unexpectedly blocking sightlines, requiring the relocation of a hundred guests. A concerted effort to minimize problems is the clear objective of effective event management. A thorough planning process reduces the potential for details to fall through the cracks. Experienced event management staff can often anticipate event problems and either prevent them or prepare to address them when and if they arise.

It is the venue manager's responsibility to build a management team, rather than a collection of individuals functioning independently. Left to operate in relative vacuums, individual departments, such as security, operations, ticket office, marketing, and so forth, may adopt objectives beneficial to their particular unit, but detrimental to the overall success of a particular event. They may also fail to disseminate event information critical to the successful operation of the other units. Effective event management requires a cooperative effort and productive communication between all units of the organization.

Event and Production Planning

Event and production planning begins once an event has been booked and contracted. Following booking and after reviewing the event rider, there are critical points where department managers, involved staff members, and promoters need to discuss every aspect of the event in detail. In the course of these discussions, important issues and challenges specific to the event will be identified and addressed. Most problems are easier to deal with if identified early. As a rule, the later a problem is discovered, the harder it may be to resolve. The venue management team has a number of event planning responsibilities, including:

- Providing both market and venue information to the promoter
- Providing a qualified and motivated workforce and required operating equipment
- Providing the promoter with a properly prepared venue as outlined in the rider
- Providing safety and security for the event
- Planning and preparing for all emergency situations
- Development of an event advertising and promotion campaign, when required
- Providing **ancillary services** for guests (i.e., food and beverage and parking)

Before booking an event, the promoter should be provided with information about the venue and market to help determine whether the venue is appropriate for the event. This information may include the following:

- Line drawings of spaces available for rent
- Seating diagrams
- Layout of meeting rooms and breakout spaces
- **Rigging** capabilities and plot diagrams (load limits)
- Fly system (theatrical rigging system)
- Stage size capabilities (wings and thrusts)
- List of house-owned equipment and corresponding rental rates
- List of available labor and corresponding rates
- Loading dock capabilities
- Contact information for service vendors
- Contact information for key venue personnel
- Policies and procedures
    - Catering
    - Merchandise and retail sales
    - Tax collection
    - Business license requirements
    - Fire and safety codes
- Parking arrangements
- List of hotel locations
- Maps of the area

Generally, the venue and market information is readily available on the venue website, though some venues prefer to restrict access through use of a password shared with promoters. For those promoters unfamiliar with a specific venue, reviewing the venue website may substitute for an on-site visit. A creative website can be an effective marketing tool and valuable venue resource. Venue websites may provide links to other sites, such as the convention and visitors bureau (CVB), local hotels, and event calendars. It is important to provide promoters and meeting planners with the ability to download venue floor plans in a variety of formats, including:

- .pdf —Portable document format (probably the most common format, accessible with Adobe Acrobat and other programs)

- .dwg—AutoCAD (used by many entertainment show designers and professional decorating companies)
- .flp—Optimum Settings (used by many meeting planners for room setups)

Overall, the more organized and detailed the planning process, the less likely it is that problems will arise and the more likely successful achievement of objectives for both the venue and the promoter will be. Generally, the events that require the greatest coordination are touring shows, theatrical performances, conventions, and commercial music concerts. On the other hand, banquets, assemblies, and small group meetings may require less staffing,but may also require extensive coordination due to the client's expectations.

From several perspectives, touring theater and concert productions are similar. Both tend to travel between performances, from site to site, using buses for the talent and supporting cast and trucks to haul their equipment and props. They will perform in a number of different venues during the course of their tour, some for one-night stands and others for multiple performances on consecutive days. To maintain consistent performance quality while on the road, the event rider specifies the staffing and equipment requirements for all venues. These standards provide for efficiency in the load-in and load-out process, even though the process takes place in different cities and venues.

Staging a convention, **exhibition**, or large meeting demands much the same effort and coordination as that required for touring theater and concert productions. Convention center events may range from a simple one-day meeting to a multi-day convention complete with a **trade show**, breakout sessions, receptions, and banquets. Convention centers must have established policies and procedures to address the following:

- Convention, exhibition, and meeting setups
- Advance delivery of equipment and materials from the organizers and exhibitors
- Provision of electrical service and audiovisual equipment
- Exhibit booth sizes
- Pipe and draping and furnishings
- Food and beverage service
- Meeting room capacities and configurations
- Exhibit breakdowns
- Movement of materials and equipment for shipping or pickup at the loading dock

Event coordination for the venue's permanent tenants, such as sports teams or **resident companies**, requires the same attention to detail, though the consistency in their event schedule provides an element of continuity in the planning process. The repetition provides the opportunity to continually improve the event coordination process, as well as the guest's event experience.

Most public assembly venue managers will agree that the more difficult events to manage are those produced by less experienced promoters who may not understand the risks involved or the details, intricacies, and necessary planning associated with a well-orchestrated event. Therefore, the venue manager must create policies, procedures, and processes that guide and encourage promoters to collaborate with the venue's department managers in achieving positive event outcomes.

Production Rider

As previously mentioned in chapter 8, a production/performance rider detailing each of the elements required to produce a quality event is provided by the event's producer. This rider is part of the performance contract signed between the promoter and the event producer, performer, or talent agency. By signing it, the promoter is agreeing to provide everything stipulated within the production/performance rider (sample rider can be found in Appendix A 8-1). While most events have production/performance riders, theatrical, touring show, concert production, large sporting events, and convention/exhibit riders are typically more complex.

Once the event is contracted between the producer and the promoter, the promoter becomes responsible for making sure the rider requirements for the event are met. Failure by the promoter to fulfill the requirements of the rider may have serious consequences to the successful completion of the event. Consequently, the promoter should always have knowledge of the rider requirements prior to booking the event. It should be noted that production riders often change. By providing the venue with the most current rider and its requirements, the promoter further assures his ability to comply with the contract-rider expectations.

The promoter often relies on the venue operations staff to fulfill many of the conditions of the rider. Therefore, it is critical for the promoter to confer with venue staff and management to ensure they can fulfill each of the venue-related requirements stipulated in the rider, either independently or with assistance from third-party vendors. Typically, this initial meeting/conference may include the promoter, venue manager, event manager, operations manager, and departmental representatives from security, marketing/promotions, and the business office. A careful review of the rider by venue management should uncover any problems or issues that must be addressed or negotiated before the promoter signs the event contract. It must be clearly understood that unless the contract between the promoter and the venue addresses which requirements of the rider the venue agrees to fulfill, there is no legal obligation for the venue to do so. Anything in the rider the venue does not agree to provide remains the responsibility of the promoter. Most rider requirements have associated costs. The venue manager should be certain these costs are identified and responsibility for each has been correctly assigned. A key issue is clarifying who has the authority to agree to expenses. Once responsibility has been assigned, it should be formalized as an addendum or attachment to the event contract, which allows for a clearer and more efficient operational relationship during the course of the event.

Occasionally, the promoter may want to complete the venue lease agreement and establish an **on-sale date** before the venue manager and/or operations manager has reviewed the production rider. However, venue operating policies should clearly state that tickets will not go on sale before a lease agreement and rider addendum are signed and the venue has received the **certificate of insurance**. The promoter may challenge this position since they ultimately bear the responsibility for all rider requirements. The fallacy of this argument is that there can be instances in which a rider requirement cannot be accomplished. For example, an agreement between the artist and promoter to use **pyrotechnics** during an indoor performance is explicitly prohibited and illegal in some jurisdictions. Therefore, any request to prematurely complete the lease agreement should be denied.

Internal Planning Documents

As stated earlier, while the production rider is generally specific to touring shows, theater, and concert productions, all events have some form of production criteria that the event depends upon, formal or informal, which serves the same purpose. Convention centers generally use a **banquet event order (BEO)** to confirm catering reservations and room set-up diagrams to stipulate necessary seating arrangements, audiovisual equipment, floor plans, show booth locations, and so forth. Every event should have a similar type of document stating exactly what venue management and those producing the event have agreed upon with respect to room arrangements and necessary production equipment, as well as who is responsible for providing each production element. In other types of venues, this document may be referred to as an event guide, event memo, or event resume. Some events are so complicated, lasting over the course of several days, that they may require the event manager to compile an event manual to clearly outline the requirements and expectations for the event. Regardless of the event-planning document used, it is imperative that it be shared with all appropriate personnel.

While **front-of-house** event staff may not need information regarding load-in and backstage catering, they do need event-specific information. Many event managers create a one-page event information sheet that is distributed at event staff check-in. This document may provide information such as expected attendance, **event timeline**, meet-and-greets, concession-stand openings, event-specific policies, and a seating map.

Other internal planning documents may include timelines, equipment lists, staffing estimates, diagram layouts, and floor plans. In addition to the tools used in preparing for an event, other documents are used post-event, including event reports, **incident reports**, and other summary reports. All of the pre-event and post-event documents should be included in the event file.

Event File

The event file is a valuable tool compiled by the event manager to document planning activity and track progress. This file documents the event chronologically, starting with the booking memo and concluding with the post-event reports. The event file may include:

- Event contacts
- Event contract
- Certificates of insurance
- Production rider
- Seating diagrams
- Ticket office statements and attendance reports
- Rigging plot plans
- Settlement sheets
- Event-staffing plans
- Incident reports
- Post-event reports
- Event-related correspondence

These documents provide management with an understanding of the entire event process and factual information needed to respond to any questions. The event file is an important tool when planning future events. After an event, it is advisable to have the following reports prepared for review by the venue manager:

- General incidents report and first-aid logs
- Ticket office statement and settlement
- Event summary/report

The venue manager will then be knowledgeable about anything out of the ordinary and has the resources available to confidently address any inquiries.

Event Timelines

An **event timeline** will assist the event manager with scheduling issues and identifying potential problems. Depending on the specific issues and the size of the event, individuals representing the following areas may provide input:

- Senior venue management
- Event management/coordination
- Ticket office
- Operations
- Parking and traffic
- Housekeeping
- Engineering
- Food and beverage/merchandise
- Event promoter/producer
- Police, fire, and appropriate medical personnel
- Public transportation
- Unions

In a venue with a busy event calendar, a production meeting may serve to outline strategies for multiple events. Small and/or routine events may simply require a phone call or electronic communication between the promoter and a liaison from the venue, who then disseminates the information to others as needed.

As the venue staff reviews the event's schedule on an hour-by-hour basis, issues may arise that require clarification and discussion. Issues such as event staff parking, load-in and load-out schedules, meal schedules, dress and decor, and the event's start, intermission, and ending times all have different implications for the various segments of venue personnel. Bringing the staff together and creating a timeline that accommodates the needs of each area will enable the staff to assess the event comprehensively and efficiently. In essence, the **front-of-house** must relate to the needs of the **back-of-house** and vice versa. Although simple in concept, the feedback gained from a meeting of this nature generally proves very useful in reducing distractions or surprises on the day of the event. Figure 9-1 illustrates a sample event timeline.

EVENT NAME   **June 24, XXXX**
Doors @ 6:00 pm
Event @ 7:30 pm
Ends @ 10:00 pm

WHO	WHAT	WHEN	DETAILS
F	Conversion Completed	6/23	Event floor, all dashers set and removed, plugs in place, per rider requirements
F	Locker, Catering & Production Rooms	6/23	Clean, vacuum, sanitize, set per rider requirements
SH	Stage Set	6/23	Set 60x40 stage per rider
P	Production Set	6/24 @ 7am-11am	Dasher drapes, house curtain, FOH prep
F	Load-in Prep	6/24 @ 7:30 am	Prep forklifts, open elephant door, clear loading dock and path to floor
P-SH-E	Load-in	6/24 @ 8:00 am	Support event needs, electrician available
F	Event Set-up	6/24 @ 1:00 pm	Chair set, set stairs, tighten rails
P-F	Operations Checks	6/24 @ 3:30 pm	Check all technical aspects, bathrooms stocked, merchandise set, floor chairs chalked, floor entry signage set, etc.
ALL	Sound Check	6/24 @ 4:00 pm	Check sound levels and acoustics - No venue personnel in the seating area
ALL	Venue Check	6/24 @ 4:30 pm	Check overall event readiness, signage set, concourses clear, proper lighting, etc.
ES-EM-GM	Event Briefing	6/24 @ 5:30 pm	Cover security requirements, any expected seat relocations, meet-and-greets, trouble areas, last call, etc.
ALL	Doors	6/24 @ 6:00 pm	All staff in position, each dept. confirm readiness, doors to be called by MOD
ALL	Show	6/24 @ 7:30 pm	Maintain FOH area, prep for load-out
ALL	Crowd Load-out	6/24 @ 10:00 pm	Begin by ushers crowd of the floor area
ALL	Load-out	6/24 @ 10:15 pm	Remove entire house set-up except items required for next event
F	Post-event Cleanup	6/24 @ 10:30 pm	Conversion crew reports to restore venue
SH-F	Stage Out	6/25 @ 2:00 am	Stage removed and properly stored

Figure 9-1 : Event Timeline

Particular attention must be paid to timing requirements for live televised events. Whether a convention, trade show, sporting event, banquet, political speech, theatrical performance, Fourth of July celebration, or an awards program, live televised events have particular timing demands. These events must start on time and often must be programmed to conclude at a specified time. If television commercial breaks are involved, they must be accommodated and accounted for within the **event production** timeline. Special effects must be ready for implementation on demand. All personnel associated with the event production must be organized in a manner to ensure the timing requirements are met in order to facilitate a seamless televised presentation.

Equipment

As previously discussed, the rider outlines the specific elements necessary to produce the event. Just as it is not feasible for a traveling attraction to bring enough people to address all of their labor requirements (such as **stagehands**, **riggers**, loaders, drivers, **runners**, and follow-spot operators), it is also not feasible for it to carry all the equipment and supplies needed to produce the event. The production rider should outline in detail the specific equipment to be provided from local sources. Usually, it is the responsibility of the venue's staff to procure that equipment and the necessary operators. Many venues have their own equipment, including:

- Forklifts
- Spotlights
- Tables and chairs
- Crowd control barriers
- Performance stages
- Electrical connections
- Compressed air/water/natural gas lines
- Telephone lines
- Internet connections
- Dressing room furniture

This equipment may be rented to the promoter or may be included in the venue lease agreement. Equipment rental expenses are documented on a separate invoice and included in the event settlement. Special equipment can usually be rented as needed from outside sources if the request is made in a timely manner.

Staffing

While the production rider clearly specifies the number of stagehands, riggers, loaders, equipment operators, and other personnel required by the event, there is no such document that definitively outlines the staffing needs for the front-of-house staff. The promoter does not know the building as well as the event manager, and, therefore relies on venue personnel to staff as needed for their event. However, because venue management is responsible for decisions directly affecting the promoter, it may be advisable to provide the promoter with a pre-event estimate of these associated costs. Figure 9-2 is an example of an event-staffing estimate for a particular event.

EVENT:	Arena Concert		EVENT DATE:		6/24		
DATE COMPILED:	5/15		EXPECTED ATT:		18,000		
DOORS:	6:00 PM	START: 7:30 PM	END:		11:00 PM		

	#	Time In	Time Out	Hours	Total	Rate	Sub. Total	
PARKING								
SUPERVISORS	2	1:00 PM	12:30 AM	11.5	23	$11.75	$270.25	
Parking Attendants	18	3:00 PM	12:00 AM	9	162	$8.75	$1,417.50	
	20							$1,687.75
USHERS								
SUPERVISOR	8	4:45 PM	11:30 PM	6.75	54	$10.50	$567.00	
Entry Level	30	5:15 PM	11:30 PM	6.25	188	$8.25	$1,546.88	
Club Level	26	5:15 PM	11:30 PM	6.25	163	$8.25	$1,340.63	
Upper Level	34	5:15 PM	11:30 PM	6.25	213	$8.25	$1,753.13	
Kill Seats	0	5:15 PM	11:30 PM	6.25	0	$8.25	$0.00	
Elevators	4	5:15 PM	11:30 PM	6.25	25	$9.25	$231.25	
	102							$5,438.89
TICKET TAKERS								
SUPERVISOR	4	4:45 PM	11:30 PM	6.75	27	$10.50	$283.50	
Early Gates	4	2:00 PM	9:00 PM	7	28	$8.25	$231.00	
SE Entrance	4	5:15 PM	9:00 PM	3.75	15	$8.25	$123.75	
SE Entrance (late)	3	5:15 PM	11:30 PM	6.25	18.8	$8.25	$154.69	
NE Entrance	4	5:15 PM	9:00 PM	3.75	15	$8.25	$123.75	
NE Entrance (late)	3	5:15 PM	11:30 PM	6.25	18.8	$8.25	$154.69	
NW Entrance	4	5:15 PM	9:00 PM	3.75	15	$8.25	$123.75	
NW Entrance (late)	3	5:15 PM	11:30 PM	6.25	18.8	$8.25	$154.69	
	29							$1,349.82
SECURITY								
SUPERVISORS	3	3:00 PM	12:30 AM	9.5	28.5	$10.50	$299.25	
Entrances	0	5:15 PM	11:30 PM	6.25	0	$8.25	$0.00	
Stage	6	5:15 PM	12:00 AM	6.75	40.5	$8.25	$334.13	
Floor/Floor Access	22	5:15 PM	11:30 PM	6.25	138	$8.25	$1,134.38	
Backstage	8	5:15 PM	1:00 AM	7.75	62	$8.25	$511.50	
Miscellaneous	3	7:00 AM	6:00 PM	11	33	$8.25	$272.25	
	42							$2,551.51
GUEST SERVICES								
SUPERVISOR	1	4:45 PM	12:00 AM	7.25	7.25	$10.50	$76.13	
Guest Services	4	5:15 PM	12:00 AM	6.75	27	$8.25	$222.75	
	5							$298.88
MISC. POSITIONS								
Early Staff	8	1:00 PM	6:00 PM	5	40	$8.25	$330.00	
Uniform Room	1	2:00 PM	1:00 AM	11	11	$8.25	$90.75	
Sign-In / Office	1	2:00 PM	1:00 AM	11	11	$8.25	$90.75	
Set / Tear-Down	1	2:00 PM	1:00 AM	11	11	$8.25	$90.75	
Dispatch	1	4:00 PM	12:00 AM	8	8	$8.25	$66.00	
	12							$668.25

| **TOTAL STAFF** | 210 | | **TOTAL ESTIMATED BILLING** | | | | $11,995.10 |

Figure 9-2 : Event-Staffing Estimate

Front-of-house personnel (event staff) are present only when there is an event and work in areas directly serving customers. Depending on venue and event type, front-of-house staff may include ushers, ticket takers, security personnel, ticket sellers, parking attendants, and other guest-services personnel. When managed in-house, front-of-house staff is primarily composed of part-time employees who are recruited, trained, employed, and supervised by venue management. It is not unusual for some venues, such as performing arts, university venues, and small auditoriums and civic centers, to use volunteers. As in many other areas in the venue, management has the option to contract out all or part of their event staffing needs. Other front-of-house safety personnel, such as police, EMTs, and fire marshals, are provided by outside sources.

Venue management determines the staffing level necessary to ensure the comfort and safety of guests attending the event. More specifically, the number and composition of the event staffing mix is determined by a number of factors including:

- Projected attendance
- Type of event
- History of the event
- Physical configuration of the venue
- Time of year
- Time of day
- Expected weather conditions
- Community expectations
- Legal regulations

Prior to event day(s), if venue management or the promoter believes the event to be overstaffed, there are ample opportunities to consider adjustments. Staffing and **cost estimates** provide the promoter advance notice regarding one of the larger event expenses. This process conveys vital information to the decision makers at a time and manner that allows them, if deemed necessary, to review, react, and adjust the staffing plan. The reason for engaging in this process is to eliminate event-day issues. Even if the contract is all-in and front-of-house staffing is not being billed back to the event, it is important for venue management to adjust staffing levels when appropriate.

Diagram Layouts and Floor Plans

Once the promoter, event manager, and operations manager have made their initial decisions concerning space accommodations for each aspect of the event (i.e., room sets, equipment needs, and parking), it is the responsibility of the venue operations staff to create a detailed diagram of the contracted spaces, a listing of the equipment provided, and the labor necessary to produce the event (sample diagrams in Figures 9-3 and 9-4). When designing the floor plan, additional factors must be addressed including:

- Occupancy ratings
- Space usage and functionality
- Fire code restrictions
- ADA requirements

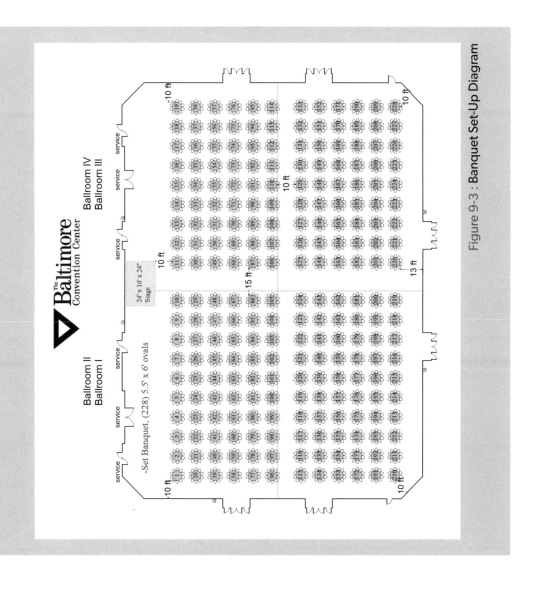

Figure 9-3 : Banquet Set-Up Diagram

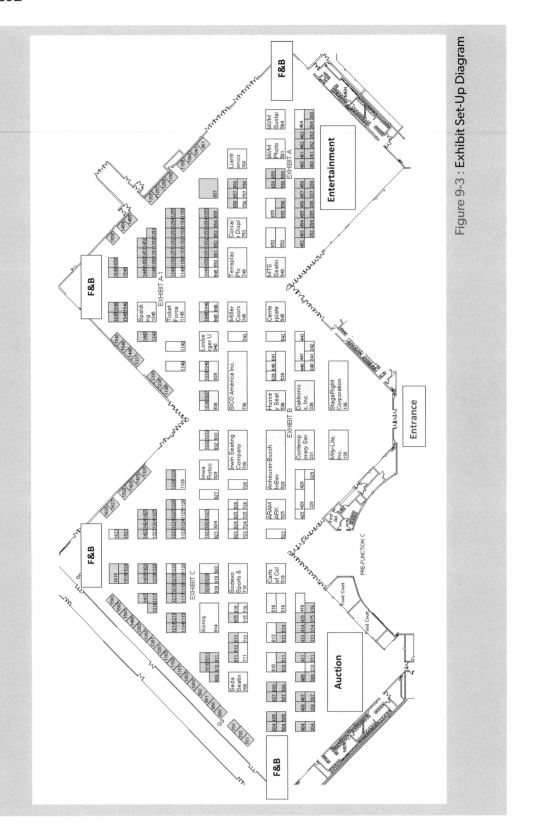

Figure 9-3 : Exhibit Set-Up Diagram

In most communities, the local fire department may assign a fire marshal to review and approve all floor plans for some events, particularly those using **pyrotechnics**. This is done to ensure the aisles are wide enough to handle the anticipated attendance, that exits are kept unlocked and clear of exhibit materials or other barriers, and that other safety issues of this nature are addressed and satisfied. When a fire marshal is assigned to a venue, the venue may be charged for the service. The venue, in turn, may pass along that charge to the event promoter.

Providing the operations staff with detailed space drawings and a list of required equipment and services is essential when setting up for the event. The more events and activities booked in the venue, the greater the need for detailed space drawings and lists. For example, if a venue has multiple events scheduled for the same time or day, precautions must be taken to verify that room times committed to each event do not overlap, that sufficient time is provided in order to change over the space, and that there is sufficient equipment available to cover all simultaneous event requests.

The planning process is critical for identifying potential issues. Before proceeding, the client should be required to approve and sign off on the event diagrams and production requirements. Although this will not eliminate last-minute changes, it provides the venue a level of protection and confirms its right to charge for any additional services requested. If additional equipment or services are provided, the client should be required to approve a written **change order,** and a revised cost estimate should be issued to eliminate any unexpected expenses.

FRONT-OF-HOUSE EVENT MANAGEMENT

Experienced and knowledgeable event managers understand the importance of addressing details associated with the **front-of-house**, which typically includes lobbies and concourses, concession stands, public restrooms, the ticket office, parking lots, and seating and exhibit areas. Significant emphasis should be placed on the training required for the part-time employees who provide services to the venue's guests. Beyond the delivery of those services in the most efficient and effective manner, the venue has a responsibility to ensure the safety and security of every guest. Effectively managing the variables associated with front-of-house operations will help ensure event attendees have a safe and enjoyable event experience and contribute to the venue's overall image in the community. Managing an event from the front-of-house includes responsibilities associated with guest communication, guest services, and event staff training. Front-of-house personnel are also involved in **incident reporting** and responding to emergency situations.

Guest Communication

An important element in making the event experience enjoyable for the guest is communicating to that guest any relevant venue policies that may affect their experience. Most venue policies tend to be consistent from event to event, while some can be influenced or necessitated by the event type. An example of consistent policies would be prohibiting smoking or weapons within the venue, while policies that might vary would be the use of cameras and recording devices or the age limit of children required to have their own ticket. Communicating these policies to guests needs to be effective and clear, especially policies that pertain to **crowd management** or emergency response. In all instances, every effort should be made to inform guests of these policies in a timely manner. This can be accomplished in a variety of ways:

- Standard policies posted on the venue website
- Event-specific policies posted on the event page within the venue website
- Event-specific policies included on the event ticket
- Standard or event-specific policies distributed via social media channels
- Pre-event e-mail alerts to guests who have purchased tickets in advance
- Media alerts
- Venue signage (either permanent or using the scoreboard or other message boards)
- Off-site digital mobile signage
- Event brochures or programs
- Season ticket information
- Public address announcements

When determining what information needs to be communicated and the best methods to do so, venue management should consider the likelihood that expected event attendees have visited the venue previously. For example, season-ticket holders are generally more familiar with the venue and its policies, while guests attending a high school graduation may not have any knowledge of venue policies and procedures.

It is also important for those venue employees who have direct contact with the guests, such as the venue receptionist and ticket office personnel, to be well versed in venue and event-specific policies so they are able to use their contact with guests to effectively and efficiently communicate appropriate information.

Graphics and/or signage are an important element of both the **crowd management** strategy and the communication process. When properly conceived and professionally produced, graphics can be particularly effective in informing guests and may be permanently installed or posted when needed. For example, venues often post visible signage in parking areas or at venue entrances displaying the venue's policy regarding prohibited items. This may save the guest from having those items confiscated at the entrance or save them a trip back to their vehicle and possibly missing a portion of the event.

Public address systems and digital message boards provide excellent means for delivering information to large numbers of guests. The emergency response plan should include pre-recorded messages and instructions for the public address/message board operator to use as directed in the event of an emergency. The same information should be provided to the event receptionist, especially if a situation occurs that necessitates an evacuation of the venue.

In addition, all venue event staff must be aware of these venue- and event-related policies and be able to communicate those policies immediately to the guests when required.

Modern technology has transformed how people communicate with one another, as well as how businesses communicate with customers. Communication technology and social media are powerful tools, which may be used by venues for both marketing and educational purposes. However, they do require that venue management stay abreast of the ever-changing technology and adapt to the most effective means to deliver the information.

Reliant Park Prohibited Items - Houston, TX

Guest Services

In public assembly venues, guest services and crowd management are inseparable. As staff controls **ingress** by taking tickets or checking credentials, checking for prohibited items, and enforcing both venue and event policies, they are, in fact, managing the crowd by providing guest services. Guests are admitted efficiently and effectively, and provided with directions to their seat or other locations and are then able to enjoy their time at the venue in a safe and comfortable environment.

When you consider all the various aspects and logistics of an event, as well as the number of guests involved, it is inevitable that issues will arise. The venue staff handles most issues without guests being aware or distracted, but there may be issues with the potential to negatively impact guests and their event experience. It is important to approach these issues as opportunities rather than problems. As stated earlier, the event experience is a unique process in which, once the event has taken place, you cannot go back and change the outcome for the guest. However, when the event manager or event staff is made aware of an issue, they are being provided with the opportunity, in fact, to change the outcome for guests. Therefore, guest services and addressing guest issues should be viewed as a positive opportunity for venue management.

While it is virtually impossible to develop detailed procedures or policies covering every potential issue event staff may encounter, the event manager should be proactive and have pre-planned responses to predictable and repetitive occurrences. For example, properly trained event staff members should be able to efficiently handle issues such as ticket relocation, a broken seat, a beverage spill, or a lost child. Dedicated event staff members want to assist guests when an issue arises. Unfortunately, without clearly understood procedures, these well-meaning event staff members may initiate an action that does not meet with management approval or resolve the issue. Obviously, inappropriate or ill-advised actions can produce additional concerns that create an even larger issue and one much more difficult to resolve.

Much of the venue's public image results from the guest's interactions with the front-of-house staff, including ushers, ticket takers, greeters, security guards, ticket sellers, concessions personnel, merchandise vendors, and parking attendants. Due to their potential impact on the guests' event experience, it is important that venue management recruit and hire individuals with the skills necessary to deliver outstanding customer service. Management must then provide the tools and information necessary to be effective, which can be accomplished through training programs. Lastly, management must create a supportive environment where the event staff is empowered to provide outstanding guest services.

Ticket Taker Directing Guests
(provided courtesy of Show Pros Entertainment Services, Inc.)

Training

Most venues opt to expose all event staff to a broad-based venue orientation followed by position-specific training, as well as specialized topics such as guest services, alcohol management, crowd management, and emergency procedures. In all aspects of the training program, customer service and guest safety must be emphasized as the primary goals.

For example, newly hired ushers should be required to attend an orientation session, which addresses human resources topics and covers standard venue procedures. The session may also serve to familiarize them with the venue's physical layout and important locations, such as concession stands, restrooms, first-aid stations, and seating sections. They should also be required to attend a session that focuses on their responsibilities in the overall event presentation, including how to resolve seating, ticketing, and security issues. They also need to understand their role in the event of a venue evacuation, and they must be provided guidelines to assist them in determining when to request assistance from a supervisor.

A significant amount of information is provided and reviewed during employee orientation and training sessions. It is unrealistic to expect part-time employees to retain all of this information. Consequently, all employees should be provided with a manual detailing all the information each employee should know, which may be distributed as a hard copy or electronically. The manual may include human resources information regarding uniforms, scheduling, and payroll, but also should address building and event policies and procedures. Topics that may be covered during training and reinforced in the manual may include the following:

- Guest services
- Dealing with difficult guests
- Providing services for guests with disabilities
- Basics of crowd management
- Safety and security procedures
- Emergency planning and preparedness
- Resolving seating and ticketing issues

If the venue does not supply employee manuals to part-time employees, they should receive this information orally from staff supervisors or managers. This information should be reviewed, amended, and discussed on a regular basis. The manual should also address procedures and responsibilities for potential major issues, such as severe weather, bomb threats, fires, and threats of domestic or international terrorism. Special attention should be given to procedures related to the evacuation of guests from the venue and its grounds in emergency situations.

Pre-event briefings present an excellent opportunity to share event-specific information, as well as reinforce training topics. Event briefings may include information regarding expected attendance, whether alcohol is being served, specific security requirements, **meet and greets**, VIP guests, and any identified risks or threats.

A venue may have all the right policies, procedures, technology, and equipment in place, but they are ineffective without properly trained personnel to implement them. Therefore, venue management must create an ongoing training and orientation program that will prepare event staff to handle the challenges of delivering live events while providing an outstanding event experience within a safe environment.

Security Working at a Stage Barricade

Incident Reporting Procedures

The dynamics of public assembly venues include an ever-present potential for incidents to occur. Whenever an incident does occur, front-of-house personnel should record and report all pertinent information relative to the incident through the venue's Incident Report Form (see sample in Appendix A 9-1). Such incidents may include counterfeit ticketing issues, altercations, ejections, and medical issues. When someone is injured, an **incident report** should be completed even if the individual refuses medical or first-aid treatment. While many incidents may seem minor, it is always advisable for venue personnel to document each occurrence.

These reports should be kept on file for no less than the time period allowed by state law (or other legal jurisdictions) for filing a lawsuit by the parties involved in the incident. Only authorized individuals should have access to these reports. Medical information related to those involved must be kept confidential and only shared with individuals or agencies authorized by law and/or those authorized by the specific individual's consent. Staff members should be required to complete these reports following the event before their departure from the venue.

Emergency Procedures and Preparedness

A venue manager's goal is to keep everyone associated with either the event or the venue safe. In order to achieve this goal, venue managers must incorporate complete safety and security planning and programming at all times to guard all assets and personnel and to evaluate the risks and threats associated with venue operations during **event production**. This is an ongoing process within which there is always potential for threats, which may present themselves in many different forms. Individuals assigned to manage the event from the front-of-house play a crucial role in providing a safe and secure environment for guests, clients, and staff. The event manager must have the knowledge and competence to implement emergency responses and manage the response of the event staff, if necessary. chapter 10 will address emergency procedures and preparedness in more detail.

PARKING, TRAFFIC, AND TRANSPORTATION

Parking, traffic, and transportation operations impact nearly all guests whether or not they drive a vehicle to the venue. Guests' interactions with parking, traffic, and transportation personnel may be their first impression of the venue and event. Every effort should be made to make this impression as positive as possible.

Parking

When a venue owns the parking lots, the venue must be equipped to provide efficient traffic operations, as well as assume the liability and risk involved in this operation. It does not matter whether a fee is charged or the parking is free; the venue must provide a safe environment for both guests and their vehicles. To accomplish the goal the parking areas should:

- Have adequate lighting for parking and security
- Keep surfaces free from debris, snow, ice, and other hazards
- Maintain the surface in good repair
- Assign parking and security personnel to be present in the parking areas before, during, and after the event in an effort to deter potential property thefts or physical assaults
- Offer parking lots and garages that provide for the safety of pedestrians leaving and returning to their vehicles
- Provide parking personnel who are properly trained and equipped to handle routine occurrences, such as dead batteries, flat tires, and general requests for information and directions.

In some instances, the venue may not own the parking lots used by their guests during events. They may be privately owned or owned by a municipality. Regardless of ownership, venue management should work with the owners to ensure efficient operations and a positive experience for guests.

Traffic

The design of effective traffic patterns can be a complex issue and often a major source of public criticism for many venues. For both new and existing venues, there are a number of factors which directly impact traffic operations:

- Traffic patterns and signage directing guests from highways and local roads to the venue;
- Location and design of surface parking lots and garages, including available **ingress/egress** points;
- Proper signage directing guests to clearly identified, accessible parking spaces per ADA parking requirements; and,
- Relationships with local law enforcement who work with venue personnel to ensure proper and efficient traffic flow.

In planning for parking, traffic surveys should be designed and conducted. Planners should work closely with the various community services departments, especially the police traffic control department and state department of transportation officials.

Parking lots and garages should be designed to allow for controlled and efficient entry and rapid exit of the vehicles. Sufficient personnel should be available to collect parking fees or check pre-paid passes. In some instances, traffic flow may be expedited when venues opt to include a traffic management fee in the ticket price, which eliminates the need to slow traffic to collect parking fees on site. Entering vehicles should be directed to park in specific areas based on a parking plan. At the conclusion of an event, parking personnel should be available to direct vehicles out of the parking area. As many exits as possible should be opened to facilitate the surge of vehicles departing at the same time.

Local police should be consulted and advised of the anticipated event attendance. Police should be requested to provide sufficient personnel to direct traffic to and from the venue. Usually, the cost for a police detail for parking supervision must be calculated into the event expenses that are charged against the overall parking revenue. Based on previous knowledge, any congested areas should receive special attention from traffic personnel. In certain situations, designating some streets as one-way traffic in and one-way traffic out may prove to facilitate improved traffic flow for the event.

Transportation

Often, sufficient parking is not available in close proximity to the venue. Available solutions generally require the assistance of other agencies. One option is for the venue manager and the local municipal director of public transportation to develop a plan that expands the number of buses or other modes of public transportation that service the venue prior to and following a scheduled event. Management may elect to establish one or more remote parking areas within the community and provide either municipal or private contracted bus service from those sites to the venue. Additional transportation costs may be covered by the parking ticket price, maybe absorbed by the venue as a cost of doing business, or, occasionally, if requested by the promoter, may be considered an event expense.

PUBLIC IMAGE

The effectiveness of event services is an important factor in how the venue is perceived in the community. Many factors impact a venue's public image and may include the following:

- Its success in accommodating community needs through its programming/event calendar;
- The level of maintenance and housekeeping afforded the venue and its adjacent grounds;
- Effectiveness of guest communications and guest services designed to enhance the event experience; and,
- Quality of the interactions between the guests and the front-of-house event staff.

The event staff is primarily composed of part-time employees. They are the face of the organization and represent not only the venue but also the event and the community. Event staff members interact with customers directly, unlike management, which has only infrequent direct contact with guests (Mahoney & Pastore, 2014). Their performance can either enhance or detract from the event experience for guests (Chelladurai & Chang, 2000; Greenwell, Fink & Pastore, 2002). Every day, managers entrust the image of their venue to those employees who could be the least trained, most marginally-supervised, most poorly paid, and least committed to the overall enterprise. For many guests attending an event at a public assembly venue, the annoying parking guard, the stressed ticket seller, the surly ticket taker, or the inattentive usher becomes "the venue." Negative encounters with these individuals may dramatically alter the guest's perception of that venue. The only way to reduce the potential for employees acting in a negative fashion (or not acting at all) is to have a training program that truly emphasizes the need for positive guest relations and that imparts in the employee a sense of ownership in the success of the venue and the event production.

SUMMARY

The event management process begins with the selling of venue time and space and requires the interaction of a variety of people across the venue. Management of the client/tenant relationship is crucial to event management and future business. All public assembly venue managers must assume the responsibility of fostering and maintaining these relationships.

Every effort must be taken to prevent the occurrence of event-day surprises. All anticipated problems and issues should be addressed and resolved prior to event day. This is accomplished through effective planning and preparation, utilizing a variety of resources in an effort to meet the requirements of the production rider, while providing a safe and enjoyable environment for the guests.

Regardless of the venue or event type, management must ensure the venue is properly prepared and the staff is appropriately trained for the variety of challenges they may face. Beyond handling crowd management and safety issues, the event staff represents the face of the organization. They interact with the guests throughout their time in the venue and may have a tremendous impact on the guests' experience. Therefore, it is important that venue management and the event manager provide the training, resources, and support for event staff to take care of the guests.

As discussed previously, the planning process varies from venue to venue, but the goal for every event is to plan and prepare in such a way as to enable the customer and client to focus on the event. When both customers and clients have a positive event experience, the venue manager's potential to retain or gain future business is enhanced.

CHAPTER 10

SAFETY AND SECURITY

INTRODUCTION

One of the greatest, and most important, challenges venue managers face is providing for the safety and security of guests, employees, and venue clients. The excitement generated by a high-energy event can, at the same time, present a variety of safety and security challenges. From severe weather to thousands of pounds of sound and lighting equipment hanging from the ceiling to slippery floors, each event poses unique potential hazards. Guests may not have visited the venue previously and are entering into an unfamiliar environment, which may be noisy, with minimum lighting. The responsibility of the venue manager, as well as all full-time and part-time staff, is to be prepared for any scenario or activity that could threaten a guest's safety or enjoyment of the event.

Proper preparation and communication are the keys to anticipating potential problems, as well as mitigating the effect of those that cannot be avoided. Research is critical when preparing for upcoming events. The venue manager can examine data regarding the event and previous visits to the venue and other venues, as well as other events with a similar profile and attendees. Effective communication, the use of technology, and properly trained staff are also resources necessary for the venue manager to deal proactively with safety and security issues.

This chapter will explore safety and security from both the perspective of the venue and the events they host. Venue safety refers to the overall process of preparing and maintaining a safe environment to host events and includes **risk management**, emergency preparedness, response and recovery procedures, life safety systems, event risk management, event security planning, access management, **crowd management**, safety and security training, and **crisis management**. This chapter is designed to offer a basic understanding of the many challenges venue managers face related to safely and securely preparing for and presenting events.

Modern-day safety and security issues have become more important and more complicated since the events of September 11, 2001, reinforced by the Boston Marathon bombing on April 15, 2013. Prior to 9/11, some venue managers focused only on safety and security concerns within the venue. Since 9/11, most venue managers have expanded their approach to safety and security beyond the entrances to the venue. Measures once considered standard safety and security procedures for protecting guests, employees, and venue clients, have now been significantly expanded. Previous safety and security plans were static, but today's risk environment requires constant updating and training. How this new focus has changed the dynamics of safety and security in the public assembly venue will be included in the information to follow.

VENUE SAFETY AND SECURITY

Governing bodies and owners entrust venue managers and their staffs to protect the substantial investment in public assembly venues. When large numbers of people assemble for a specific purpose, the expectation of those in attendance is that venues be operated in a professional, safe, and secure manner.

Venue safety and security concerns began to increase after the bombing of the Federal Building in Oklahoma City in April 1995. Venue managers, like those responsible for management of any public place, were required to consider how their venue might be at risk for potential attacks. Additionally, since the terrorist attacks on New York in 2001, the focus on these concerns has intensified substantially. The events in Boston reminded more venue managers of the importance of these responsibilities. Terrorists generally seek opportunities to inflict mass casualties, and, therefore, large-scale sporting events provide a potential target for terrorist activity (Hall, Marciani, & Cooper, 2008). As a result, the threat of danger may disrupt normal lifestyle patterns, which may include attendance at events.

A strategic venue safety and security plan addresses not only concerns about potential terrorist threats, but also the general issues that face the venue manager on a day-to-day basis. Safety and security plans must also address such concerns as weather, civil disobedience, improvised explosive devices (IEDs) both vehicle-born and worn by suicide bombers, fire, slippery floors, and loose handrails. All venue managers must address overall venue risk management, emergency preparedness and procedures, life safety systems, and crisis management.

Venue Risk Management

In every activity occurring within a public assembly venue, there is an element of risk (potential for loss/harm) and liability (responsibility). Typically, venue management is involved in monitoring and directly managing the venue's risk management activities. In venue management, risk management includes the following:

- Identification of risk
- Analysis of risk as to its likelihood, frequency, and severity
- Risk reduction/elimination and transfer, to the extent possible, of the remaining risk

(IAVM Glossary, 2010)

The venue management team must understand that risk is constant and liability exists at all times. Therefore, it is imperative that management design a plan for recognizing, managing, and reducing risk and liability.

The public assembly venue manager is responsible for communicating to all employees the importance of understanding that potential risks are associated with every activity held in the venue or on its grounds. They must recognize that every employee is a member of the risk management team and must be constantly vigilant in recognizing, reporting, and minimizing or eliminating potential risks. Risk left unmanaged may become a threat. Therefore, potential risks must be identified as soon as possible and appropriately addressed. Staff members see the issues at ground level on a daily basis and may be particularly helpful when creating solutions.

Whether dealing with an attendee slip-and-fall, a forklift accident, or a catastrophic structural failure, risk and liability are the two most important risk management considerations. For virtually every incident that ends up in litigation, management will be asked the following questions:

1. Were they aware of the issue?
2. Should they have reasonably anticipated a problem?
3. If so, what was done to prevent it?

In other words, what would a reasonably prudent professional have done in this instance? An appropriate venue risk management program will provide venue management with the information required to properly respond to these critical questions.

Regardless of the risk management philosophy, the public assembly venue's plan should address methods of preventing, reducing, and managing anticipated risk. This may be accomplished by understanding the nature of the events on the schedule, anticipated audience, and the venue itself relative to potential accidents. Armed with this knowledge, the venue's risk management team may be able to identify and isolate potential incidents and implement measures to either eliminate them or at least minimize their potential impact.

Venue Risk Assessment

Risk management assessments are the processes undertaken to critically examine risks that may impact property and personnel or subject the venue to liability and/or fines. This process generally includes an assessment of assets, threats, and vulnerabilities, as well as a risk analysis. The information is obtained through a visual inspection of the venue, a review of critical documents, and interviews with appropriate personnel (AVSS, 2009).

In order to accurately identify potential risks, some venue managers use a **risk assessment** model or risk formula. This formula states that **risk** is equal to **vulnerability** times **threat** times **consequences** or:

$$R = V \times T \times C$$

By using this formula, risk managers can understand where to place their efforts. Threats cannot be eliminated, as they are out of the control of the risk manager, and consequences cannot be altered, as they will be what they will be (AVSS, 2009). In order for the manager to accurately determine actual venue risk, assessments must be made regarding assets, threats, vulnerabilities, and risk analysis.

Asset Assessment

An asset assessment involves the identification of those things within an organization that might be the target of a threat. Assets include venue equipment, personnel, venues, confidential data, and events. Key questions that should be asked during the asset assessment may include the following:

- What are the core functions and processes of the venue?
- What are the critical venue elements, including structural and informational?

- What is the value of each asset? (i.e., to what extent would its loss cause a debilitating impact to the venue?)

By identifying the important assets and answering these key questions, an organization takes the first step towards focusing its resources on that which is most important. Asset identification also is important because all additional assessments will flow from it (AVSS, 2009).

Threat Assessment

Webster's Dictionary defines threat as an expression of intention to inflict evil, injury, or damage, or an indication of something impending. To a venue manager, a threat is the negative occurrence that could impact the assets for which the manager is responsible. These threats are generally from external sources and may include acts of terrorism, as well as unsafe conditions or situations that are highly likely to cause an accident. They can be acts of God, such as severe weather, or anything else that might go wrong. When a threat becomes a physical action or situation, it becomes an emergency. At this point, the venue's emergency response plan must be implemented (AVSS, 2009).

Vulnerability Assessment

Vulnerability assessments identify internal organizational weaknesses that could be exploited by a threat. This is also the time to evaluate existing countermeasures or protections and their effectiveness in reducing or eliminating those vulnerabilities. The vulnerability assessment begins by examining the critical infrastructure of the venue, including the building itself, its personnel, and its operational policies and procedures. For example, are all employees required to wear a photo ID when in the venue? The vulnerability assessment also requires venue managers to evaluate the effectiveness of the current level of protection. Management should also consider factors such as the venue's level of visibility in the community, the venue's value to the community, and the potential impact of an attack on the venue (AVSS, 2009).

Risk Analysis

The purpose of this analysis is to establish a level of risk for each asset. During this phase, venue management prioritizes the assets of the venue based upon the potential consequences of loss or damage and establishes the following:

- Degree of impact of such loss relative to each the identified asset
- Likelihood of an attack by a threat
- Likelihood a vulnerability will be exploited
- Relative degree of the risk based upon the countermeasures required

Management must ensure that whatever countermeasures are considered should not introduce an additional hazard to the situation. It does not make sense to reduce or eliminate one risk by replacing it with another.

A simple example may be to consider one possible threat to an outdoor stadium scoreboard. In this instance, a venue manager may apply the assessment process as outlined in Figure 10-1.

Asset Assessment	Stadium scoreboard valued at $3 million.
Threat Assessment	Severe weather occurrence.
Vulnerability Assessment	Wind velocity in excess of rated levels is possible, though unlikely.
Risk Analysis	Damage risk is moderate to low, but has a significantly greater impact during the season. The game could still be played, though sponsor revenue may be lost.

Figure 10-1 : Applied Assessment Process

IAVM's *Best Practices Planning Guides for Safety, Security and Emergency Preparedness* assist the event manager in assessing risk factors and determining threat levels. Once the risk assessment is completed, venue management must determine how to address the identified risks.

Approaches for Dealing with Risk

There are five basic approaches for dealing with risk:

- Risk avoidance
- Risk assumption
- Risk transfer
- Loss prevention
- Loss reduction

Risk Avoidance

Sometimes, the very best method of dealing with an exposure to loss is to try to avoid the loss. Some risks are not avoidable, and, in such cases, the exposure to loss for this type or risk can often be reduced but not entirely eliminated. For other exposures, avoidance is the only reasonable alternative, especially for those risks when the chance of loss is high and loss severity is also high.

As discussed previously, venue managers may decide not to book an event when historical and verified data indicates that the event poses a danger to those in attendance. In such cases, the venue manager may choose to avoid risk by not booking the event. It is not uncommon for venues to avoid activities that have both a high frequency and severity of loss. If venue management chooses not to book an event, they must provide legal justification for their decision and be supported by ownership. A good example might be not booking an event that has a history of violence or one where the artist has failed, on numerous occasions, to appear as scheduled.

Risk Assumption

Risk assumption refers to instances when the loss will be borne by the party exposed to the chance of loss. Often, risk assumption is a deliberated, planned risk management decision. Deliberate risk assumption is a desirable alternative when the maximum severity of loss is relatively low and the chance of loss is also low.

There are some events and activities with such a low risk factor that the venue itself may be willing to assume the associated risk. For example, some venue managers may be willing to rent space for a small meeting or wedding reception without requiring the planner to purchase insurance. However, public assembly venues are less likely to assume risk due to the extremely high number of lawsuits arising out of minor incidents. The litigious nature of society has forced managers to protect their venue and employees at all times.

Risk Transfer

When risk is transferred, the original party exposed to a loss is able to secure another party to bear the risk. Risk transfer is commonly used when the chance of loss is low and the severity of a potential loss is high. The most common form of risk transfer is the purchase of insurance coverage. In addition, when venue managers contract out services like security, guest services, and concessions, they transfer the risks associated with those operations to the contractor.

While management secures insurance coverage for the venue, event promoters are also required to provide coverage for their particular event. In addition, venue user contracts should include an indemnity clause as an additional means to transfer risk to the venue users. Indemnity clauses refer to specific language holding the facility, its manager, employees, agents, and guests harmless from legal action caused by the negligence of the user and may also be referred to as a "hold-harmless" clause (IAVM Glossary, 2010).

Some venues use Tenant Users Liability Insurance Policy (TULIP), a blanket insurance policy held by the venue, wherein the venue obtains coverage for the tenant should the tenant be unable to obtain event insurance. An example of risk transfer would be for the venue to cover a local civic organization's monthly luncheon meeting under its TULIP and simply pass on a charge for the coverage to the organization.

Insurance premiums refer to the cost of insurance coverage as determined by the insurance provider and based upon a number of factors, including level of risk and loss history. Insurance premiums for public assembly venues and events have escalated due to the frequency of incidents, severity of injuries, number of lawsuits, and the high cost of defending and paying claims. The cost of insurance coverage is also dependent upon the desired deductible, which refers to the amount of money the policyholder (i.e., the venue or the insured) must pay before the insurance company becomes responsible. The deductible is established based upon the level of risk the venue is willing to accept.

Loss Prevention

Loss prevention activities are used to lower the chance of loss and to make the occurrence of loss less frequent. Effective loss prevention plans often result in lower insurance costs. Whenever the frequency of loss is high, loss prevention activities should be applied. However, loss prevention is feasible only when benefits are greater than the cost. Examples of loss prevention programs include the installation of reflective, slip-resistant materials and handrails on venue steps, or the installation of a closed-circuit television (CCTV) system.

Loss Reduction

Loss reduction activities are designed to reduce the severity of losses that do occur. Regardless of preventive steps taken, some losses will occur. Loss reduction activities aim at minimizing the impact of the loss. In general, when the severity of loss is great and when the loss cannot be avoided or transferred, loss reduction activities are appropriate, provided the cost of those activities does not exceed the benefits gained. Examples would be the installation of fire walls, silent alarms, or automatic fire sprinkler systems.

In all likelihood, venue managers use all of the above approaches to deal with risk within their venue. Implementation may vary based upon type of venue, events, and perceived or actual risks.

Venue Emergency Management Plan

A venue emergency is an unplanned event that may cause significant injuries, even death, to employees, clients, or the public. It may disrupt operations, shut down the venue, cause physical or environmental damage, or threaten the venue's financial standing or public image (AVSS, 2009).

The ability to respond to an emergency should be a primary goal of the public assembly venue's manager and staff. A venue emergency management plan is an integrated plan that defines and documents the steps and actions to be taken by staff and public safety agencies to minimize or eliminate the potential harm to occupants of the venue and/or lessen damage to the venue. A comprehensive venue emergency plan reduces the exposure and consequences of emergency situations through preparedness, prevention, early detection, communication, evacuation and relocation, damage control, and recovery operations. Every venue and community is unique, and, therefore, each emergency plan must be customized to meet the needs of the venue. Each venue should develop its own emergency plan taking into consideration the venue design, scheduled events, staff resources, public safety agencies, applicable governmental regulations, operational policies and procedures, political environment, and community expectations (AVSS, 2009).

A venue emergency management plan serves six primary functions as outlined below:

1. Provide life safety and protection
2. Minimize or eliminate damage and harm
3. Provide emergency preparedness
4. Prevention
5. Response
6. Recovery

The plan should meet or exceed mandated regulations, provide for clear and explicit internal and external channels of communication, and reduce liabilities and loss. At a minimum, sound and detailed venue emergency planning will accomplish the following requirements:

- Meet professional standards and expectations of providing a safe, non-threatening environment for venue occupants and protect community assets

- Protect the lives and wellbeing of venue employees, clients, and guests as the number-one priority of any and all venue operations

- Provide proper staff training and timely implementation of an established venue emergency plan to greatly reduce the potential damage and loss associated with emergencies

- Meet the legal public safety requirements (fire safety, Americans with Disabilities Act, Occupational Safety and Health Administration, etc.) imposed on public assembly venues by governmental and regulatory policies.

- Provide documentation of the venue emergency planning process and the venue emergency plan, minimizing the liability exposure of the venue, staff, and ownership when an emergency situation develops.

- Minimize the negative media exposure and maintain the venue's positive image and position in the eyes of the community.

- Provide for ongoing productive interface and positive relationships with relevant public safety agencies (e.g., fire, police, and federal authorities) and appropriate government officials.

(AVSS, 2009)

The venue emergency management plan is simply the means to provide comfort, confidence, and credibility. It provides comfort for guests, staff, and clients in knowing that all possible preparations have been made to enable the most rapid and efficient response to a venue emergency. It provides confidence for venue owners and management, who know that the emergency preparations, preventative measures, and responses have been tested, drilled, audited, and updated, and that the responsibilities for both internal and external first responders are clearly outlined. A well-designed plan establishes the venue's credibility in post-emergency recovery and communications and conveys that the emergency preparedness and response did the best job possible to preserve life, property, environment, operations, financial standing, and public image (AVSS, 2009).

Some venues make the mistake of waiting until an emergency occurs to formulate their response, which gives the venue less opportunity to effectively manage the emergency. Likewise, the venue manager should not meet first responders for the first time during an emergency. They should be included in the emergency preparedness process. When creating a venue emergency management plan, the following guidelines should be considered:

- Predict—Identify and anticipate any potential issues
- Prevent—Take preventive measures
- Plan—In the event prevention is not effective, prepare a plan dealing with the emergency
- Evaluate—Review the outcome to determine whether, if a similar emergency occurs, it can be averted or handled in a more efficient manner

Another important element of the venue emergency management plan is a communications plan. In the event of an emergency, the event manager may have a role in managing not only internal communications but also communications with other stakeholders, such as families of injured guests or employees, public officials, venue ownership, vendors, and suppliers, as well as the media. Who is called and in what order those calls are made may be very important to how the emergency is communicated and ultimately concluded. During an emergency when levels of stress are very high, a properly designed and implemented communications plan helps eliminate the possibility of venue management failing to properly advise a key individual or agency.

This process can assist the venue in establishing a venue emergency management plan and keeping it current as the venue's environment changes. In addition to the emergency management plan, each venue should also establish a business continuity plan that lays out the course of action for the venue to continue its core business until the emergency situation has been resolved.

Sound and detailed venue emergency planning, training, and implementation lead to strong execution and positive results in dealing with emergency situations. Managers who believe it will never happen in their venues are putting them in precarious situations, which may lead to disastrous results. A well-designed venue emergency management plan is the cornerstone of an effective response to an unexpected emergency.

Venue Life Safety Systems

All venues have systems, most of them mechanical, that are critical to the safe and efficient operation of the venue. Compromised systems may impact the safety and security of guests and employees and should be part of the risk management program. These systems may include the following:

- Fire suppression systems
- Secondary power source

- Emergency power source
- Emergency lighting system
- Public address system
- Heating, ventilation, and air conditioning (HVAC) systems

Fire Suppression Systems

A fire suppression system, more commonly known as a sprinkler system, is generally required by building codes. Beyond protecting people, suppression systems help control damage and loss to equipment. Common means of detection are through heat/smoke sensors or visual detection. Fire suppression systems in public assembly venues are only designed to provide enough time for evacuation and cannot be relied upon to completely extinguish a fire.

Secondary Power Source

Electrical systems support service to scoreboards, elevators, escalators, CCTV systems, ticketing systems, public address systems, metal detectors, handicapped entrances, lighting, computers, telephones, kitchen and concessions equipment, and many other devices and types of equipment within a venue. A partial or total power failure is a sure interruption of business and operation of a venue. If this power failure occurs during an event, immediate measures must be taken to minimize the negative impact on the event experience and provide for the safety of guests, staff, and clients. As a result, many venues opt to have two main sources of power. For example, if one source is interrupted by a downed tree over the power lines, the system automatically switches to the second power source, which may be an underground system to a separate sub-station. The switch from one system to the other usually takes only seconds and quickly restores the venue to full power.

Emergency Power Source

An emergency power system, usually powered by a gas/diesel generator, is intended to provide sufficient electricity for emergency lighting and communications. These systems provide venue management with the ability to communicate with venue occupants and, when necessary, help expedite safe **egress** from the venue. Local codes require periodic inspection and testing of emergency power systems.

Lighting System

Proper lighting is important to the venue's overall life safety program. Emergency, battery-operated lighting as well as effective security lighting need to be maintained at acceptable levels. Venue management must make sure public spaces, parking facilities, doorways, and areas such as ATMs, pedestrian tunnels, and bus stops are properly lighted and do not pose safety concerns for either guests or employees.

Public Address System

One of the most important life safety systems for a venue is the public address system. In addition to providing information regarding venue policies and procedures, public address systems also provide a crucial means of communication with venue occupants during an emergency situation.

HVAC

Heating, ventilation, and air conditioning (HVAC) refers to how air is circulated, cooled, heated, and moved in or out of a venue. These systems are important to the operation of the venue and can also provide a mechanism for the dispersal of dangerous chemical or biological agents that could cause injury or death to guests or employees in the venue. Venue management must understand how these systems work and what precautions need to be included in their safety and security plan to minimize risks associated with those systems. Most HVAC systems are equipped with an emergency shutoff switch that helps prevent the spread of smoke or other dangerous agents.

In addition to the above-mentioned systems, other devices, such as automatic external defibrillators (AEDs), fire extinguishers, and communication devices, are used in protecting the life safety of guests and employees. Some of these devices may require outside contractors or vendors to service, maintain, or inspect them, and, therefore, should be a part of any established protective procedures.

Portable fire extinguishers should be the first line of defense to fight smaller fires and must be strategically placed throughout the venue. One of the biggest changes in fire extinguishers over the past decade is a computer monitoring system that tracks extinguishers to make sure they are in the proper place, at the right pressure, and that access to them is not blocked by any obstruction. Local ordinances require periodic pressure checks as well as verification of the number required for the venue.

Sudden cardiac arrest strikes more than 350,000 people each year (American Heart Association, 2013). When an automated external defibrillator (AED) is used within the first four to six minutes, there is a better chance of saving the person's life. An automated external defibrillator (AED) is a portable device that checks the heart rhythm and can be used to treat sudden cardiac arrest. In order for AEDs to be effective, they must be placed strategically throughout the venue and staff must be properly trained in their use. AEDs are used as a first response prior to arrival of emergency medical personnel.

Other communication devices are used in communicating with guests and employees and can assist in many life safety situations. Megaphones or bullhorns are used to communicate with smaller groups of individuals or in the unlikely event that the venue's public address system in incapacitated. In addition to mobile phones and other personal communication devices, venue personnel often use handheld radios (i.e., walkie-talkies) to communicate with each other on dedicated radio channels. These devices provide staff with additional capabilities to address venue life safety issues.

As technology continues to advance, venue managers will have additional options for providing improved life safety systems for their venues, guests, clients, and employees. Staying abreast of these new developments is one of the responsibilities of venue management.

EVENT SAFETY AND SECURITY

Public assembly venues exist to host events of many different types. Each event creates a unique set of challenges. Events must be examined to identify potential risks and how they should be addressed. Potential threats may take different forms and are not always easy to recognize. In cooperation with the venue manager and event and operations department, the event manager plays a key role in ensuring that the event is operated in a safe and secure manner. Risk management responsibilities include the effective management of the following:

- Securing event certificate of insurance
- Proper contract administration
- Risk assessment
- Security and crowd management planning
- Emergency and crisis management planning
- Alcohol management
- Fire code and life safety planning
- Staff training for risk management responsibilities

While events that attract large numbers of guests are desirable from a business perspective, they also bring with them an increased degree of responsibility. During all events, venue management essentially holds the safety and well-being of the guests in their hands. Whether guests are attending a small meeting or large sporting event, the responsibilities and need for preparation are the same. The satisfaction, well-being, and safety of guests, employees, performers, contractors, and everyone else depends upon the care taken by the public assembly venue manager and the event management staff. The venue manager must convey this sense of responsibility to each and every employee.

Readiness for dealing with disastrous circumstances during a public event is critical to effective event management. The list of possible problem areas includes:

- Medical emergencies
- Fire/fire alarm
- Bomb threat/explosion
- Mechanical/equipment/structure failure
- Power failure
- Natural disasters/severe weather
- Civil disturbance/riots/criminal acts
- Hazardous material release
- Terrorism
- Ventilation system contamination
- Water supply contamination
- Food poisoning/contamination
- Suspicious mail/packages

A sample **FEMA** bomb threat checklist can be found in Appendix A 10-2.

A manager's goal is to keep all those who use or visit the venue safe. Achieving this goal requires the manager to incorporate safety and security considerations into the planning of each and every event.

Event Risk Management

The venue manager needs to adopt a proactive approach to the well-being of everyone in the venue. A proactive approach entails planning for the myriad of potential negative situations that can occur within the venue and finding ways to prevent them from happening. If they are not preventable, the venue must have a plan to manage the consequences. Risk management is important for both non-event days and event days.

Risk management is very important during non-event days, as well as the time before and after an event when guests are not in the building. It is during those times that the operations department may be addressing general maintenance and repairs, as well as event-related activities including load-in, set-up, teardown, load-out, clean up, and changeovers in preparation for upcoming events. Consequently, with all this activity, a hectic venue atmosphere can become a potentially dangerous working environment.

Event-day risk management refers to the activities centered around providing a safe and secure environment during events. The event risk management plan should consider many factors including the following:

- Event history
- Event day, date, and time
- Expected attendance
- Demographics of attendees
- Whether or not alcohol is being sold
- Expected weather conditions
- **Event production** elements

Event risk management is addressed through a variety of planning processes to address event security, access management, crowd management, emergency planning and crisis communications, and training.

Event Security Planning

Though event security measures have always been present in most venues, they are now significantly more extensive and often more overt in nature. They must repeatedly be reviewed and evaluated based upon situational conditions. Typical enhancements to security include the following:

- Perimeter protection measures, such as installation of bollards and closing of streets

- Heightened admissions control procedures, including the use of metal detectors

- More rigorous employee screening and background checks

- Improved credentialing of employees, contractors, and venue visitors

- More extensive use of "plainclothes" (i.e., undercover) law enforcement officers

- More extensive use of closed circuit television (CCTV) monitoring
- Modification of HVAC air intakes to eliminate the possibility of introduction of biological or chemical agents

Some venues and major events may use sophisticated software programs or consultants to analyze and assess security risks and threats.

Bollards as a Perimeter Protection Measure

Venue Access Management

Venue management is responsible for controlling all access to the venue for guests, employees, clients, and a variety of external groups. This responsibility requires a coordinated plan, which addresses the access needs of all individuals, while at the same time maintaining the integrity of the overall safety and security plan.

Venue access control takes place at all entrances to the venue property, which may include parking lots, loading docks, and guest, employee, media, and security entrances. During events when heightened security is required, a second security perimeter may be established to control access to additional areas surrounding the venue. Venue managers must determine whether sufficient barriers exist to prevent unauthorized entry onto the property. If deficiencies are detected, management must initiate corrective measures. Access controls, search techniques, and other strategies combine to help secure the venue, which may include the following:

- Displaying proper signage to address access policies and list prohibited items
- Inspecting all bags permitted into the venue, including those of guests, media, employees, and vendors
- Requiring a pass list, certified by management, of all working personnel
- Requiring all working personnel to wear proper identification, including venue personnel, media, contractors, exhibitors, and vendors
- Not issuing event credentials to non-essential personnel
- Only permitting authorized personnel and guests in the back-of-house and other restricted areas
- Using metal detectors or pat-down searches when deemed appropriate or required.

Another aspect of venue access management is coordinating guest ingress and egress. In an effort to enhance safety and improve the event experience, management works diligently to provide the most efficient flow of vehicles and people. These efforts are commonly focused on parking lots, venue entrances, vomitories, and concourse flow patterns. Different types of equipment may be used to facilitate ingress, including turnstiles, barricades and portable fences, all of which may need to be removed for safe egress or in an emergency evacuation.

While most venues are designed to facilitate proper ingress and egress, management must often make adjustments based upon event requirements. Therefore, it is important to have experienced individuals involved in the design of any new venues or renovation projects.

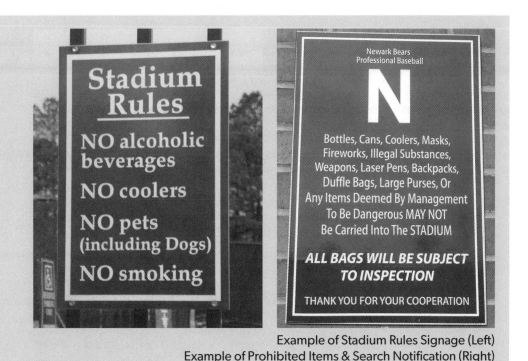

Example of Stadium Rules Signage (Left)
Example of Prohibited Items & Search Notification (Right)

Crowd Management

Each event is unique. Guests attending an alternative rock concert are different from those attending a Broadway show. Fans attending a mid-season sporting event one weekend may be very different from those in attendance for a big rivalry game the following weekend. Every audience is different, and crowd management preparations should reflect those differences.

After watching college football fans rush onto the field following a dramatic ending to a hotly contested game, it is clear that once a large crowd decides to do something, there may be little security can do to stop them. If a fan were to sustain an injury in an incident of this nature, venue management and ownership may be held liable. On the other hand, many crowd management problems may have little or no connection with the event or the venue. The parties involved may have simply decided to confront each other at the venue during that event. Because of liability issues and the desire of the venue to provide a safe and enjoyable event experience, a comprehensive crowd management plan is required.

Crowd management is a proactive organizational strategy which guides venue personnel in providing and maintaining the desired event environment (Siehl, 2013). Crowd management is a component of an event risk management plan. A venue's crowd management plan is created through the analysis of known factors and identification of potential issues. Policies and procedures can then be developed to minimize crowd-related risks (Siehl, 2013). The plan may be created solely by venue personnel or with the assistance of an outside expert.

A comprehensive crowd management strategy impacts management activities before, during, and after the event. Techniques in advance of the event include hiring, training, analyzing, and planning. During events, crowd management is the process of maintaining established policies while executing, communicating, and supervising the crowd management plan. After the event, management should evaluate the effectiveness of the plan and make adjustments as needed (Siehl, 2013).

Crowd control is a reactive measure employed to control crowds through both human and physical elements (Siehl, 2013). Ideally, venue personnel endeavor to manage a crowd, not control it. Their efforts to manage the crowd are intended to provide an enjoyable event experience. Should an incident occur, controlling the crowd should focus on efficiently resolving the issue and re-establishing the desired event environment. As discussed previously, when an incident occurs, venue personnel should document all pertinent information relative to the incident.

A thorough understanding of crowd management can assist the security management team in understanding the differences in crowds and in making appropriate crowd management or crowd control decisions. If it is frequently necessary for security personnel to "control" the crowd, the crowd management plan should be reassessed and updated (see Appendix A 10-2 for detailed information regarding crowd management responsibilities).

Crowd Management Staffing

The exact number of security personnel, especially for the front-of-house, is determined by the event's potential for crowd management challenges. For example, a symphony orchestra performance will require less law enforcement presence than a concert where alcoholic beverages are served. A trade show projected to attract 20,000 attendees over the course of a weekend might require a security director, door guards at each entrance/exit area, and a first-aid team. On the other hand, an electronic dance music (EDM) event projected to attract an audience of 8,000 may require the presence of uniformed police, door guards at each entrance/exit area, several first-aid teams, and large contingent of **peer group security**.

The public assembly venue's event or security manager is generally responsible for assessing each event and recommending the appropriate staffing requirements. The manager assumes the role of liaison between outside law enforcement and the venue's security personnel, including contracted peer security, if used. Strong working relationships with local law enforcement are essential in creating a unified approach to crowd management. Depending on the event, law enforcement may be involved in event planning. They may be able to provide support and resources to facilitate planning, and their knowledge of the event may enable them to respond faster and more effectively if a crisis were to occur.

It may be advisable to gather background about an event and the expected attendees. Information may be obtained from networking with other public assembly venue security managers, following the reports of touring attractions through the trade publications and talking with other public assembly venues' staff where the event is performing, in order to learn more about the expected event attendees. In addition, information may be gleaned from social media, event websites, and media outlets. Each of these information sources is beneficial in keeping the security manager informed and the venue prepared.

Event Staff Conducting Searches at Entry
(provided courtesy of Show Pros Entertainment, Inc.)

SAFETY AND SECURITY TRAINING

Once the plans, processes, and policies are in place, management must disseminate the information and impart the skills necessary to train others who are responsible for executing the plan. Although each component of a safety and security plan is very important, the plan is only effective if it is implemented and executed correctly. In addition, training should be an ongoing process instead of a one-time event (AVSS, 2009).

Just as routine knowledge of a venue is important to ensure guest service, so too is knowledge of each staff member's role in an emergency. Any staff members with direct responsibility for public safety and those who may find themselves dealing with the public in emergency circumstances should receive training in emergency practices. Staff members must have a complete understanding of the procedures to report and respond to such events. All staff members should have a general understanding of emergency procedures even if they are not assigned specific roles or tasks (AVSS, 2009).

Common training techniques may include a classroom review of procedures, tabletop drills, and full-scale exercises. In-depth training exercises may be conducted annually, while refresher training should be incorporated at every opportunity and reinforced on a regular basis. Outside of scheduled training sessions, pre-event staff briefings represent an excellent opportunity to address event-specific issues or a chance to reinforce a particular skill (AVSS, 2009).

ACADEMY FOR VENUE SAFETY AND SECURITY

The Academy for Venue Safety and Security was created in 2004 by the International Association of Venue Managers (IAVM) as an intense training academy in security planning and life safety management for the public assembly industry. The Academy for Venue Safety and Security (AVSS) is an IAVM school designed to teach and promote the best practices of safety and security protocols, methods, and procedures. Venue management professionals are provided information, tools, and methodologies to protect guests, customers, employees, vendors, athletes, and performers, as well as property and assets. This may be accomplished through risk identification, implementation of risk management practices and procedures, emergency planning, preservation of economic viability, and facilitation of recovery. More information about the IAVM Academy for Venue Safety and Security can be found on the IAVM website (www.iavm.org).

SUMMARY

While there are numerous responsibilities that venue management must assume, none is more important than the safety and security of the venue, employees, vendors, and guests. Safety and security have always been a prime concern of the venue manager, but recent acts of global and domestic terrorism have renewed the industry's focus on venue and guest safety. In order to prepare for the possibility of these occurrences, a comprehensive approach to safety and security is essential for all public assembly venues. This approach includes venue risk management, emergency management plan, life safety systems, event risk management, event security planning, venue access management, crowd management, and training.

The successful venue manager and staff must prepare for a wide range of potential safety and security situations. They must effectively handle these situations as expected by the venue owners and governing body, as well as the community. Those who work and attend events in the venue expect to do so in a safe environment, and it is the responsibility of all concerned to take the necessary steps to ensure a safe and enjoyable experience.

Appendix A

Example 2-1 A : Arena Organizational Chart
First Ontario Centre
(Provided by Global Spectrum)

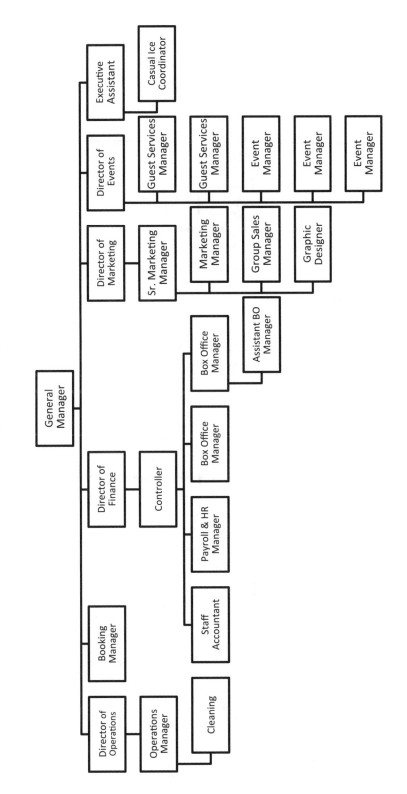

Example 2-1 B : Convention Center Organizational Chart (Medium-Size CC)

Example 2-1 C : **Football Stadium Organizational Chart**
(with professional tenant)

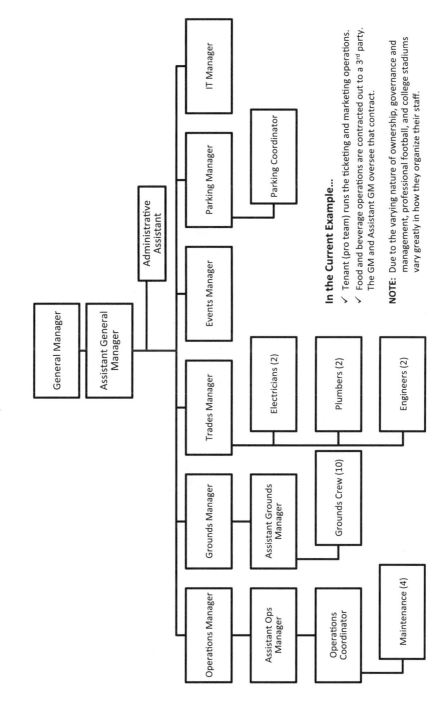

In the Current Example...

✓ Tenant (pro team) runs the ticketing and marketing operations.

✓ Food and beverage operations are contracted out to a 3rd party. The GM and Assistant GM oversee that contract.

NOTE: Due to the varying nature of ownership, governance and management, professional football, and college stadiums vary greatly in how they organize their staff.

Example 2-1 D : Theater Organizational Chart
Township Auditorium - Columbia, SC

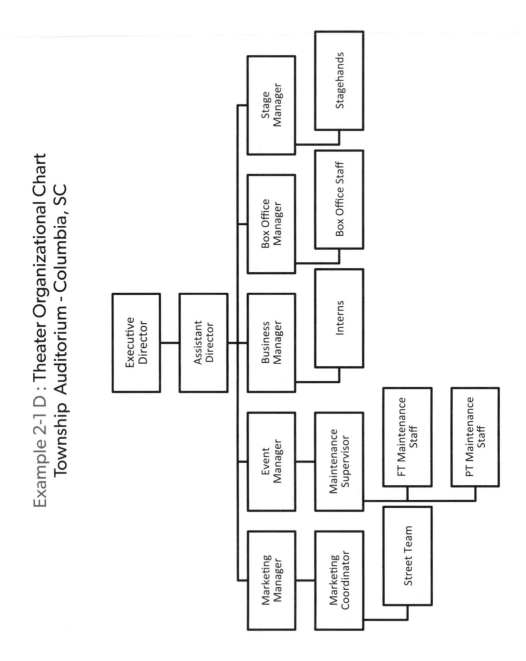

Example 3-1 : Sample Arena Revenue & Expense Categories

REVENUE CATEGORIES

- Rent
- Concessions
- Catering
- Reimbursed Expenses
- Advertising

- Naming Rights / Sponsorships
- Venue Fees & Commissions
- Premium Seating
- Parking
- Event Merchandise

EXPENSE CATEGORIES

Operating Expenses
- Supervision
- Labor
- Building Maintenance
- Equipment Maintenance
- Office Expenses
- Electric
- Water / Sewer / Etc.
- Gas

Concessions
- Supervision
- Labor
- Equipment Maintenance
- Office Expenses
- Food Supplies

Catering
- Supervision
- Labor
- Equipment Maintenance
- Office Expenses
- Food Supplies
- Contracted Services

Administrative
- Supervision
- Labor
- Insurance
- Equipment Maintenance
- Telephone
- Office Expenses
- Travel
- Legal Services
- Misc. Administrative Expenses

Event Operations
- Supervision
- Ushers
- Ticket Takers
- Security
- Stagehands
- Equipment Rentals
- Materials & Supplies

Ticket Office
- Supervision
- Labor
- Outlet Expenses
- Equipment Maintenance
- Office Expenses
- Advertising / Promotion Expenses
- Contract Fees
- Equipment Rental

Accounting
- Supervision
- Labor
- Payroll Services
- Equipment Maintenance
- Office Expenses
- Audit Expenses
- Federal / State Tax Expense

Employee Welfare
- Vacation / Holiday
- Sick Leave
- Unemployment Insurance
- Group Insurance
- FICA
- Workers Compensation
- Professional Development
- Pension / Retirement

Example 3-2 : Financial Statements - Income Statement

IAVM ARENA

INCOME STATEMENT

April 30, 20XX

OPERATING REVENUES	MONTH ENDING	YEAR TO DATE
Rent	$ 60,000	$ 400,000
Reimbursed Expenses	$ 26,000	$ 310,000
Concessions	$ 80,000	$ 520,000
Catering	$ 24,000	$ 280,000
Advertising	$ 10,000	$ 100,000
Commissions	$ 6,000	$ 40,000
Miscellaneous	$ -	$ 5,000
TOTAL OPERATING REVENUES	**$ 206,000**	**$ 1,655,000**
OPERATING EXPENSES		
Event Expenses	$ 75,000	$ 525,000
Building Operations	$ 65,000	$ 475,000
Event Services	$ 12,000	$ 215,000
General and Administrative	$ 20,000	$ 148,000
Marketing and Advertising	$ 5,000	$ 38,000
Ticket Sales and Ticket Office	$ 8,000	$ 84,000
TOTAL OPERATING EXPENSES	**$ 185,000**	**$ 1,485,000**
NET OPERATING PROFIT (LOSS)	**$ 21,000**	**$ 170,000**

NOTE: Some venues may show monthly income from interest, local taxes, and other miscellaneous items. Likewise, there may be additional deductions reflected from debt service or other obligations.

Example 3-3 : Financial Statements - Balance Sheet

IAVM ARENA

BALANCE SHEET

Month Ending April 30, 20XX

ASSETS			LIABILITIES AND EQUITY		
CURRENT ASSETS			**CURRENT LIABILITIES**		
Cash	$	36,000	Accounts Payable	$	164,000
Petty Cash	$	1,000	Notes Payable	$	100,000
Payroll Fund	$	8,000	Loan Payable	$	60,000
Temporary Investment	$	334,000	Consumer Sales Tax	$	4,000
Accounts Receivable	$	128,000	F.I.C.A.	$	2,000
Inventory	$	33,000	Workers Compensation	$	1,000
Pre-Payments	$	20,000	Advance Deposits	$	-
Deposits	$	8,000	**TOTAL CURRENT LIABILITIES**	$	331,000
TOTAL CURRENT ASSETS	$	568,000			
FIXED ASSETS			**EQUITY**		
Building Equipment & Tools	$	214,000	Hotel / Motel Tax	$	2,000,000
Kitchen Equipment	$	218,000	Contributions	$	1,500,000
Concession Equipment	$	132,000	Surplus	$	2,269,000
Box Office Equipment	$	16,000	**TOTAL EQUITY**	$	5,769,000
Office Equipment	$	36,000			
Communications Equipment	$	51,000			
Transportation Equipment	$	64,000			
Building Improvements	$	4,801,000			
TOTAL FIXED ASSETS	$	5,532,000			
			TOTAL CURRENT LIABILITIES		
TOTAL ASSETS	$	6,100,000	**AND EQUITY**	$	6,100,000

Example 3-4 A : Convention Center Example - Public Event

Event Settlement Invoice

ACCOUNT/EVENT
June 7-9, 20XX

Gross Ticket Sales (if applicable):	$140,912.50
Tickets Advanced to Client:	$0.00
Net Ticket Sales (if applicable):	140,912.50

Facility Expenses and Reimbursements:

Rent:	$75,400.00	
Box Office:	$1,330.50	
Stagehands:	0.00	
Event Staffing:	1,230.12	
State Gross Receipts Tax (3%, if applicable):	4,227.38	
Parking:	0.00	
Plumbing:	175.00	
Compressed Air:	0.00	
Equipment Rental: Staging, Chairs, Tables	310.00	
Novelty Fee:	0.00	
Food and Beverage:	1,491.56	
Damages Deposit/Pending Expenses Deposit	0.00	
Contractor Invoices; EMT	690.00	
Contractor Invoices; Decorator	0.00	
Contractor Invoices; Event Staffing/Security	6,782.38	
Total Facility Expenses & Reimbursements:		91,636.94
Deposits Paid in Advance:		75,400.00
Balance Due Facility:		16,236.94
Net Ticket Sales		140,912.50
Balance Due Event (Facility):		

__$124,675.56__

Registered Attendance	
Total Event Attendance	
Peak Day Attendance	

If balance is due, terms are Net 30.
The charges, reimbursements, and payment terms detailed above are acceptable.

_____   _____
For FACILITY   For ACCOUNT/EVENT

Example 3-4 B :
Convention Center Catering Event Detailed Invoice

Invoice

CUSTOMER
INFORMATION

Invoice #:	**16901**
Invoice Date:	XXX
Account:	0004453
Due Date:	XXX
Amount Due:	$0.00

Customer Copy

ACCOUNT/EVENT NAME)	In/Out:	DATES

Departmental Summary

Building Security	**$25.00**
Catering	**$15,877.75**
Facility Services	**$1,160.00**
Space Rental	**$5,500.00**
Utility Services	**$745.00**
Taxes & Gratuity	**$4,715.69**

Order	Description	Units	Rate	Duration	Charges
Building Security					
Green Room (DATE TIMES) - Ballroom Dressing Room					
0161992	Core Lock Change-2 keys	1.00 EA	25.00 / EA		$25.00
Catering					
Luncheon (DATE TIME) - Ballroom CD Zone					
0161968	Napa Valley Salad (Plated)	590.00 PRS	25.95 / EA		$15310.50
	Napa Valley Salad VEGETARIAN	10.00 PRS	16.00 / EA		$160.00
				Total For Luncheon:	**$15470.50**
Coffee Service (DATE TIME) - Ballroom B					
0161969	Coffee (per Gallon)	4.00 GAL	42.00 / EA		$168.00
VIP Area refreshments (DATE TIME) - Ballroom Prefunction 1					
0161970	Infused Water (per 3 Gallons)	2.00 EA	40.00 / EA		$80.00
Continental (DATE TIME) - Ballroom Prefunction 1					
0162592	Continental Breakfast	13.00 PRS	12.25 / EA		$159.25
				Total For Catering:	**$15877.75**
Facility Services					
Lunch Set Up (DATE TIME) - Ballroom CD Zone					
0161979	Stairs	2.00 EA			$0.00
	Blue Fabric Chairs				No Charge
				Total For Lunch Set Up:	**$0.00**
Breakout (DATE TIME) - Ballroom B					
0161984	6' x 30" Rectangle				No Charge
	8' x 30" Rectangle				No Charge
	Blue Fabric Chairs				No Charge
	Stairs	1.00 EA			$0.00
				Total For Breakout:	**$0.00**

Invoice	Account	Charges	Payments	Amount Due	
16901	0004453	$28,023.44	$-28,023.44	DATE	$0.00

CBL100   Page 1 of 2

Example 3-4 B (*continued*)

Invoice

Customer Copy

ACCOUNT/EVENT NAME		In/Out: Start-End:			DATE

Order	Description	Units	Rate	Duration	Charges
acility Services (Continued)					
Silent Auction/Expo Set Up (DATE TIME) (Continued) - Ballroom Prefunction 1					
0161985	6'x30" Table c&s $40	29.00 EA	40.00 / EA		$1160.00
			Total For Facility Services:		$1160.00
Space Rental					
Space Charges & Statistics (DATE TIME) -					
0148020	Ballroom & PF 1-2 Comp	1.00 EA		1.00 Day	$0.00
	Ballroom & PF 1-2 Base Rate	1.00 EA	5,500.00 / DAY	1.00 Day	$5500.00
			Total For Space Charges & Statistics:		$5500.00
			Total For Space Rental:		$5500.00
Utility					**Services**
(DATE TIME) -					
0161977	100 amp 208V 3ph MC Production	1.00 EA	435.00 / EVT		$435.00
	10 amp (1200 Watt) Outlet-Registration	1.00 EA	100.00 / EVT		$100.00
	20 amp (2400 Watt) Outlet- Terrace Prefunction	6.00 EA	35.00 / EVT		$210.00
	20 amp (2400 Watt) Outlet - BallRm C D	2.00 EA	35.00 / EVT		$70.00
	20 AMP (complimentary) Outlet	2.00 EA	-35.00 / EVT		$-70.00
			Total For DATE TIME:		$745.00
			Total For Utility Services:		$745.00
			Total Excluding Taxes:		$23307.75
			Sales Tax, 19,053.30 @ 7.25%		$1,381.36
			Prep Food Tax, 15,877.75 @ 1.00%		$158.78
			Gratuity, 15,877.75 @ 20.00%		$3,175.55
			Total Including Taxes:		$28,023.44

Payments and Adjustments		Reference			Amount
RVCD	Deposit EV-CHK	ACCOUNT NAME- DEPOSIT DATE			USD-5,500.00
RCVD	Payment EV-CHK	ACCOUNT NAME – DEPOSIT DATE			-22,523.44
		Total For Payments and Adjustments:			USD-28,023.44

Invoice Summary		
	Total Excluding Taxes:	$23,307.75
	Total Taxes:	$4,715.69
	Total Invoice Amount:	$28,023.44
	Total Payments:	$-28,023.44
	Total Amount Due:	$0.00

Invoice Remit to: FACILITY

FACILITY ADDRESS

Invoice	Account	Charges	Payments	Amount Due	
16901	0004453	$28,023.44	$-28,023.44	DATE	$0.00

Example 3-4 C :
Convention Center Trade show Detailed Invoice

Invoice

	Invoice #:	**16816**
CUSTOMER	Invoice Date:	XXX
INFORMATION	Account:	0002126
	Due Date:	XXX
	Amount Due:	$0.00

Customer Copy

ACCOUNT/EVENT NAME In/Out: DATE

Departmental Summary

Building Security	**$175.00**
First Aid	**$630.00**
Catering	**$3,658.00**
Concessions	**$305.45**
Facility Services	**$65.00**
Space Rental	**$84,000.00**
Utility Services	**$1,915.00**
Taxes & Gratuity	**$1,086.43**

Order	Description	Units	Rate	Duration	Charges
Building Security					
Exhibit Hall MI (DATE TIME) - Hall AB 101-104					
0160597	Core Lock Change	11.00 EA	25.00 / EA		$275.00
Staff Office (DATE TIME) - VIP Suite 104					
0162066	Core Lock Change	-4.00 EA	25.00 / EA		$-100.00
				Total For Building Security:	**$175.00**
First Aid					
Exhibit Hall MI (DATE TIME) - Hall AB 101-104					
0160594	E.M.T.	21.00 HR	30.00 / EA		$630.00
Catering					
Water Cooler (DATE TIME) - Concourse A					
0160505	Spring Water Station with Cooler	1.00 EA	50.00 / EA		$50.00
Staff Buffet Lunch (DATE TIME) - VIP Suite 104					
0160506	Southern BBQ Buffet	28.00 PRS	26.25 / EA		$735.00
Staff Buffet Lunch (DATE TIME) - VIP Suite 104					
0160507	Mexican Buffet	28.00 PRS	24.25 / EA		$679.00
Water Cooler (DATE TIME) - VIP Suite 103					
0160508	Spring Water Station with Cooler	1.00 EA	50.00 / EA		$50.00
Booth 2146 Water Cooler (DATE TIME) - Hall AB 101-104					
0160509	Spring Water Station with Cooler	1.00 EA	50.00 / EA		$50.00
AM refreshments (DATE TIME) - Hall AB 101-104					
0160510	Coffee (per Gallon)	3.00 GAL	38.00 / EA		$114.00
	Bagels & Cream Cheese (per Dozen)	2.00 DZ	30.00 / EA		$60.00
	Assorted Yogurt	24.00 EA	2.50 / EA		$60.00
				Total For AM refreshments:	**$234.00**

Late Morning Refreshments (DATE TIME) - Hall AB 101-104

Invoice	Account	Charges	Payments	Amount Due	
16816	0002126	$91,834.88	$-91,834.88	DATE	$0.00

Example 3-4 C (*continued*)

Invoice

ACCOUNT/EVENT NAME	In/Out:	DATE

Order	Description	Units	Rate	Duration	Charges
Catering (Continued)					
Late Morning Refreshments (DATE TIME) (Continued) - Hall AB 101-104					
	Coffee (per Gallon)	2.00 GAL	38.00 / EA		$76.00
	Assorted Cookies (per Dozen)	2.00 DZ	32.00 / EA		$64.00
			Total For Late Morning Refreshments:		**$132.00**
PM refreshments (DATE TIME) - Hall AB 101-104					
0160512	Coffee (per Gallon)	1.00 GAL	38.00 / EA		$38.00
	Lemonade (per Gallon)	1.00 GAL	34.00 / EA		$34.00
	Assorted Cookies (per Dozen)	1.00 DZ	32.00 / EA		$32.00
			Total For PM refreshments:		**$104.00**
AM refreshments (DATE TIME) - Hall AB 101-104					
0160513	Coffee (per Gallon)	3.00 GAL	38.00 / EA		$114.00
	Bagels & Cream Cheese (per Dozen)	2.00 DZ	30.00 / EA		$60.00
	Assorted Yogurt	24.00 EA	2.50 / EA		$60.00
			Total For AM refreshments:		**$234.00**
Late Morning Refreshments (DATE TIME) - Hall AB 101-104					
0160514	Lemonade (per Gallon)	2.00 GAL	34.00 / EA		$68.00
	Coffee (per Gallon)	2.00 GAL	38.00 / EA		$76.00
	Assorted Cookies (per Dozen)	2.00 DZ	32.00 / EA		$64.00
			Total For Late Morning Refreshments:		**$208.00**
PM refreshments (DATE TIME) - Hall AB 101-104					
0160515	Lemonade (per Gallon)	1.00 GAL	34.00 / EA		$34.00
	Assorted Cookies (per Dozen)	1.00 DZ	32.00 / EA		$32.00
			Total For PM refreshments:		**$66.00**
Staff Continental (DATE TIME) - VIP Suite 104					
0160563	Coffee (per Gallon)	1.00 GAL	38.00 / EA		$38.00
	Orange Juice (Per Gallon)	1.00 GAL	34.00 / DAY	0.00 Day	$0.00
	Bagels & Cream Cheese (per Dozen)	1.00 DZ	30.00 / EA		$30.00
	Egg, Ham and Cheese Croissant (per Dozen)	1.00 DZ	42.00 / EA		$42.00
	Assorted Yogurt	24.00 EA	2.50 / EA		$60.00
			Total For Staff Continental:		**$170.00**
Tech Theater Coffee (DATE TIME) - Hall AB 101-104					
0161078	Coffee (per Gallon)	3.00 GAL	38.00 / EA		$114.00
Morning Coffee (DATE TIME) - 201AB & 202AB					
0161147	Starbucks Coffee - Regular (per Gallon)	1.00 GAL	46.00 / EA		$46.00
	Starbucks Coffee - Decaffeinated (per Gallon)	1.00 GAL	46.00 / EA		$46.00
	Hot Herbal Tea Selection (per Gallon)	1.00 GAL	34.00 / EA		$34.00
			Total For Morning Coffee:		**$126.00**
2nd AM Coffee (DATE TIME) - 201AB & 202AB					
0161148	Starbucks Coffee - Regular (per Gallon)	1.00 GAL	46.00 / EA		$46.00
	Starbucks Coffee - Decaffeinated (per Gallon)	1.00 GAL	46.00 / EA		$46.00
	Hot Herbal Tea Selection (per Gallon)	1.00 GAL	34.00 / EA		$34.00

Invoice	Account	Charges	Payments	Amount Due	
16816	0002126	$91,834.88	$-91,834.88	DATE	$0.00

Example 3-4 C (*continued*)

Invoice

ACCOUNT/EVENT NAME   In/Out: DATE

Order	Description	Units	Rate	Duration	Charges
Catering (Continued)					
				Total For 2nd AM Coffee:	**$126.00**
3rd Session coffee (DATE TIME) - 201AB & 202AB					
0161149	Starbucks Coffee - Regular (per Gallon)	1.00 GAL	46.00 / EA		$46.00
	Starbucks Coffee - Decaffeinated (per Gallon)	1.00 GAL	46.00 / EA		$46.00
	Hot Herbal Tea Selection (per Gallon)	1.00 GAL	34.00 / EA		$34.00
				Total For 3rd Session coffee:	**$126.00**
1st Session Coffee ((DATE TIME) - 201AB & 202AB					
0161150	Starbucks Coffee - Regular (per Gallon)	1.00 GAL	46.00 / EA		$46.00
	Starbucks Coffee - Decaffeinated (per Gallon)	1.00 GAL	46.00 / EA		$46.00
	Hot Herbal Tea Selection (per Gallon)	1.00 GAL	34.00 / EA		$34.00
				Total For 1st Session Coffee:	**$126.00**
2nd Session Coffee (DATE TIME) - 201AB & 202AB					
0161151	Starbucks Coffee - Regular (per Gallon)	1.00 GAL	46.00 / EA		$46.00
	Starbucks Coffee - Decaffeinated (per Gallon)	1.00 GAL	46.00 / EA		$46.00
	Hot Herbal Tea Selection (per Gallon)	1.00 GAL	34.00 / EA		$34.00
				Total For 2nd Session Coffee:	**$126.00**
3rd Session Coffee (DATE TIME) - 201AB & 202AB					
0161152	Starbucks Coffee - Regular (per Gallon)	1.00 GAL	46.00 / EA		$46.00
	Starbucks Coffee - Decaffeinated (per Gallon)	1.00 GAL	46.00 / EA		$46.00
	Hot Herbal Tea Selection (per Gallon)	1.00 GAL	34.00 / EA		$34.00
				Total For 3rd Session Coffee:	**$126.00**
				Total For Catering:	**$3582.00**
Concessions					
Cash Cards (DATE TIME) -					
0161847	Convention Cash Card Program	1.00 EA			No Charge
	Convention Cash Cards	1.00 EA	277.45 / EA		$277.45
	Cash Card Activation Fee	28.00 EA	1.00 / EA		$28.00
				Total For Cash Cards:	**$305.45**
				Total For Concessions:	**$305.45**
Facility Services					
Exhibit Hall MI (DATE TIME) - Hall AB 101-104					
0160724	Grey Plastic Chairs 50c ea.	50.00 EA	0.50 / EA		$25.00
Exhibit Hall MI (DATE TIME) - Hall AB 101-104					
0160725	6x8 Staging 16",24",32" height	2.00 EA	20.00 / EA		$40.00
Exhibit Hall MI (DATE TIME) - Hall AB 101-104					
0161512	Grey Plastic Chairs 50c ea.	7.00 EA			$0.00
Exhibit Hall MI (DATE TIME) - Hall AB 101-104					
0161511	66" Rounds of 8				No Charge
	Blue Fabric Chairs				No Charge
				Total For Exhibit Hall MI:	**$0.00**

Invoice	Account	Charges	Payments	Amount Due	
16816	**0002126**	**$91,834.88**	**$-91,834.88**	DATE	**$0.00**

Example 3-4 C (*continued*)

Invoice

ACCOUNT/EVENT NAME		In/Out:		DATE	

Order	Description	Units	Rate	Duration	Charges
Facility Services (Continued)					
Exhibit Hall MI (DATE TIME - Hall AB 101-104					
0161545	66" Crescent Rounds of 6				No Charge
	Blue Fabric Chairs				No Charge
				Total For Exhibit Hall MI:	$0.00
UBM Canon Room (DATE TIME) - 201AB & 202AB					
0161573	Blue Fabric Chairs				No Charge
				Total For Facility Services:	$65.00
Space					**Rental**
Space Charges & Statistics (DATE TIME) -					
0140124	Hall AB 101-104 Comp	1.00 EA		2.00 Day	$0.00
	Hall AB 101-104 Move In/Out	1.00 EA	12,000.00 / DAY	2.00 Day	$24000.00
	Hall AB 101-104 Move In/Out	1.00 EA	12,000.00 / DAY	1.00 Day	$12000.00
	Hall AB 101-104 Base Rate	1.00 EA	24,000.00 / DAY	2.00 Day	$48000.00
				Total For Space Charges & Statistics:	$84000.00
Space Charges & Statistics (DATE TIME) -					
0157397	201AB & 202AB Comp	1.00 EA		3.00 Day	$0.00
	204 Comp	1.00 EA		3.00 Day	$0.00
	205 Comp	1.00 EA		7.00 Day	$0.00
				Total For Space Charges & Statistics:	$0.00
Space Charges & Statistics (DATE TIME) -					
0159241	206AB Comp	1.00 EA		1.00 Day	$0.00
				Total For Space Rental:	$84000.00
Utility Services					
Exhibit Hall MI (DATE TIME) - Hall AB 101-104					
0160690	20 amp (2400 Watt) Outlet	2.00 EA	125.00 / EVT		$250.00
Exhibit Hall MI (DATE TIME) - Hall AB 101-104					
0160691	20 amp (2400 Watt) Outlet	2.00 EA	125.00 / EVT		$250.00
Exhibit Hall MI (DATE TIME) - Hall AB 101-104					
0160692	20 amp (2400 Watt) Outlet	7.00 EA	125.00 / EVT		$875.00
Exhibit Hall MI (DATE TIME) - Hall AB 101-104					
0160694	6 outlet power strip	2.00 EA	25.00 / EVT		$50.00
Exhibit Hall MI (DATE TIME) - Hall AB 101-104					
0160695	6 outlet power strip	1.00 EA	25.00 / EVT		$25.00
	20 amp (2400 Watt) Outlet	1.00 EA	125.00 / EVT		$125.00
				Total For Exhibit Hall MI:	$150.00
Exhibit Hall MI (DATE TIME) - Hall AB 101-104					
0160696	20 amp drop cord Production	2.00 EA	35.00 / EVT		$70.00
	10 amp (1200 Watt) Outlet	2.00 EA	100.00 / EVT		$200.00
				Total For Exhibit Hall MI:	$270.00
Exhibit Hall MI (DATE TIME) - Hall AB 101-104					
0160698	20 amp drop cord Production	2.00 EA	35.00 / EVT		$70.00
				Total For Utility Services:	$1915.00

Invoice	Account	Charges	Payments	Amount Due	
16816	0002126	$91,834.88	$-91,834.88	DATE	$0.00

Example 3-4 C (*continued*)

Invoice

ACCOUNT/EVENT NAME	In/Out:	DATE

Total Excluding Taxes:	$90748.45
Sales Tax, 4,389.60 @ 7.25%	$318.25
Prep Food Tax, 3,658.00 @ 1.00%	$36.58
Gratuity, 3,658.00 @ 20.00%	$731.60
Total Including Taxes:	$91,834.88

Payments and Adjustments		Reference	Amount
RCVD	Deposit EV-CHK	ACCOUNT NAME--DATE	USD-21,000.00
RCVD	Deposit EV-CHK	ACCOUNT NAME DATE	-63,000.00
RCVD	Payment EV-CHK	ACCOUNT NAME - DATE	-7,834.88
		Total For Payments and Adjustments:	USD-91,834.88

Invoice Summary	
Total Excluding Taxes:	$90,748.45
Total Taxes:	$1,086.43
Total Invoice Amount:	$91,834.88
Total Payments:	$-91,834.88
Total Amount Due:	$0.00

Invoice Remit to: FACILITY
FACILITY ADDRESS

Invoice	Account	Charges	Payments	Amount Due	
16816	0002126	$91,834.88	$-91,834.88	DATE	$0.00

Example 3-4 D : Arena Rental Settlement

Arena RENTAL Settlement
Peter Parker - August 1st, 20XX

	# of Tickets	$$ Amount
Gross Ticket Sales	14,000	850,000.00
Dress		
Comps	150	
Gross Ticket Sales	14,150	850,000.00
Net Ticket Sales		$ 850,000.00
Concert Expenses:		
Advertising		(1,000.00)
Building Rent		(75,000.00)
Catering		(10,000.00)
Confetti Clean-up		
Gas Rental (Pyro)		(300.00)
Internet		(200.00)
Phones		(100.00)
Plants		(200.00)
Runners		(700.00)
Stagehands		(35,000.00)
Towels		(400.00)
Total Expenses		(122,900.00)
Due to / (from) Promoter		$ 727,100.00
Adjustments to Promoter Share :		
Less Cash Advance		(32,000.00)
Less AEG Consignment		(7,000.00)
Less Band (Peter Parker) Consignment		(3,000.00)
Less Band (Eddie Edwards) Consignment		(500.00)
Less Platinum Tickets		(18,000.00)
Net Due to / (from) Promoter		$ 666,600.00

Promoter Approval:

CASE Representative Approval	Date	
Signature	Date	

Printed

Example 3-4 E : Arena Co-Pro Settlement

ARENA Co-Pro Settlement
Susan Summers - April 1, 20XX

		# of tickets	$$ Amount
Gross Ticket Sales		6,000	350,000.00
Comps		500	-
Total Ticket Sales		6,500	350,000.00
Off The Top Deduction			0.00
Net Ticket Sales			350,000.00

Promoter Expenses	Promoter	Arena	Total
Advertising	8,000.00	20,000.00	28,000.00
Artist Production	5,000.00		5,000.00
ASCAP/BMI	1,000.00		1,000.00
Catering	4,000.00		4,000.00
Catering - AS/BS	800.00		800.00
Credit Card Fees		2,000.00	2,000.00
House Package		60,000.00	60,000.00
Insurance	3,000.00		3,000.00
Internet	-	200.00	200.00
Local Production	3,500.00		3,500.00
Runner		500.00	500.00
Stagehands		9,000.00	9,000.00
Support	8,000.00		8,000.00
Towels		150.00	150.00
SESAC	100.00		100.00
Van Rentals		500.00	500.00
Total Promoter Expenses	33,400.00	92,350.00	**125,750.00**

	Promoter	Arena	
Remaining Ticket Revenue	224,250.00		
Artist Overage	190,612.50		
Promoter Profit	33,637.50		
Venue Contribution			
Venue Rent		32,000.00	
JSC Merchandise Share		3,000.00	
$1 per paid ticket		6,000.00	
	33,637.50	41,000.00	
Total to split	74,637.50		
50% 50%	37,318.75	37,318.75	
Share of Proceeds	37,318.75	37,318.75	
Promoter After co-pro	261,331.25		
Adjustments:			
Less: Cash Advance	(20,000.00)		
Net Due to / (from) Promoter	241,331.25		

_____   _____   _____   _____
Venue Approval   Date   Promoter Approval   Date

Example 4-1 : Rental Application

CONVENTION CENTER RENTAL APPLICATION

The following information is requested to assist in the review and consideration of your request for lease of the venue. The accuracy and completeness of the information provided below are very important insofar as this information will be a critical factor in considering your request. Be as detailed and specific as possible. Until management officially approves this application and a formal agreement is fully executed, there is no legal or binding commitment between the venue and the rental applicant.

EVENT NAME: _____

TYPE OF EVENT: ☐ Consumer Show ☐ Convention
☐ Trade Show ☐ Other (describe below)

EVENT DESCRIPTION: _____
_____

ESTIMATED DAILY ATTENDANCE: _____
SPACE REQUESTED: _____
_____

DATES REQUESTED (specify load-in/load-out and event dates): _____
_____

REQUESTED EVENT AND LOAD-IN/LOAD-OUT TIMES: _____
_____

PAID ADMISSION EVENT: ☐ YES   If yes, state ticket prices:
☐ NO $_____

NAME OF LICENSING ORGAZATION: _____

Address: _____
City: _____ State: _____ Zip: _____
Tax I.D. Number: _____ Or SSN: _____

NAME & TITLE OF PERSON WHO WILL SIGN THE RENTAL AGREEMENT:
_____

HOW DID YOU LEARN OF THE CONVENTION CENTER? _____
_____

BANK & CREDIT REFERENCES:
1. _____
     Name   Phone Number   Account Number
2. _____
     Name   Phone Number   Account Number
3. _____
     Name   Phone Number   Account Number

INDUSTRY REFERENCES:
1. _____
     Name   Company   Phone Number
2. _____
     Name   Company   Phone Number
3. _____
     Name   Company   Phone Number

PREVIOUS EVENTS:
(List event name, event type, date(s) it was held, venue contact name & phone number).
1. _____
_____
2. _____
_____
3. _____
_____

OTHER COMMENTS: _____
_____

SIGNATURE: _____
     Name   Title   Date

Example 5-1 : Run of Schedule

MEDIA		SUN 1	MON 2	TUE 3	WED 4	THU 5	FRI 6	SAT 7	SUN 8	MON 9	TUE 10	WED 11	THU 12	FRI 13	SAT 14	Daypart	Total # Spots	Rate / Unit	Total Gross
KBUL	98.1 FM		5	5	5					5	5	5				ROS	30	$43.00	$1,290
KOH	780 AM		5	5	5					5	5	5				ROS	30	$40.00	$1,200
KRNO	106.9 FM									5	5	5				ROS	15	$42.00	$ 630
KTHX	100.1 FM		5	5	5					5	5	5				ROS	30	$35.00	$1,050
KJZS	92.1 FM		7	7	7					7	7	7				ROS	42	$10.00	$ 420
KOZZ	105.7 FM		5	5	5					5	5					ROS	25	$40.00	$1,000
														TOTAL			172		$5,590

Example 6-1 : Ticket Office Checklist

EVENT:			
EVENT DATE:			
ON-SALE DATE:			
PROMOTER CONTACT:			
ADDRESS:			
OFFICE PHONE:		E-MAIL:	
MOBILE		FAX:	

☐ 1. Notify Ticketing Contractor of event set-up specifics on the ticketing system
☐ 2. Determine venue configuration and potential capacity
☐ 3. Determine event seating chart
☐ 4. Develop manifest and discuss with Operations Manager
☐ 5. Discuss ADA compliance with Operations Manager
☐ 6. Confirm manifest capacity compliance with Operations Manager and Fire Marshal
☐ 7. Check potential on-sale dates with the Promoter
☐ 8. Verify accuracy of ticket text
☐ 9. Verify ticket scale and prices
☐ 10. Verify ticket contractor service and handling charges
☐ 11. Verify mail charges
☐ 12. Verify local and/or state taxes
☐ 13. Confirm ticket text with Promoter
☐ 14. Distribute booking notice to all venue departments
☐ 15. Complete X chart (best available)
☐ 16. Confirm seating holds and kills in writing with Promoter
☐ 17. Confirm ticket transaction limits in writing with Promoter
☐ 18. Determine ticket office on-sale staffing requirements
☐ 19. Determine event on-sale staffing needs with Security
☐ 20. Verification from Booking Manager or Venue Manager that all Promoter requirements have been met and the show is clear to go on sale.
☐ 21. Confirm ticket sale information with Contractor for:
    a. Outlets
    b. Telephone Operators
    c. Internet
    d. Pre-sale holds
☐ 22. Pull hard copy of audit prior to on-sale
☐ 23. Order cash advance (if needed)
☐ 24. Discuss event day set-up with Operations Manager
☐ 25. Specials: _____

Example 6-2 : Ticket Office Statement

Event: _____ Concert _____   Event Date: _____ April 1, 20XX _____

Sale Capacity	Manifest Capacity	Comp Tickets	Passes & G-Type	Special Rates T-Type	TOTAL Not Sold at Full Price	TOTAL Sold	Ticket Price	House Receipts
	1,582	0				1,582	$ 78.00	$ 123,396.00
	3,431	250				2,428	$ 65.00	$ 157,820.00
	2,266	50				1,725	$ 55.00	$ 94,875.00
	5,547	0				2,873	$ 35.00	$ 100,555.00
Total	12,826	300				8,608		

Total House Receipts $ 476,646.00

Net Ticket Price	State Tax	TOT State Tax	City Tax	TOT City Tax
$ 71.76	$ 4.68	$ 7,403.76	$ 1.56	$2,467.92
$ 59.80	$ 3.90	$ 9,469.20	$ 1.30	$3,156.40
$ 50.60	$ 3.30	$ 5,692.50	$ 1.10	$1,897.50
$ 32.20	$ 2.10	$ 6,033.30	$ 0.70	$2,011.10

Less State Amusement Tax $ 28,598.76
Less City Amusement Tax $ 9,532.92

Total Net $ 438,514.32

Weather: Warm / Clear   Temp: 76 degrees

	Number	Dollars
Advance	8,608	$476,646.00
Walk-Up	0	0
Total	8,608	$476,646.00

	Total	Total To Date
Gross Receipts	$ 476,646.00	$ 476,646.00
Less State Amusement Tax	$ (28,598.76)	$ (28,598.76)
Less City Amusement Tax	$ (9,532.92)	$ (9,532.92)
Total Net	$ 438,514.32	$ 438,514.32

Attendance

	Today	To Date
Paid	8,608	8,608
Comp	300	300
Total	8,908	8,908

I certify that I have personally verified the above statement.

_____

Example 6-3 A : Basic End Stage Configuration

BASIC END STAGE

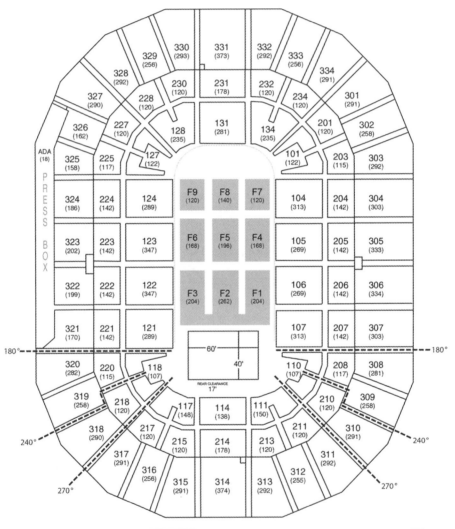

Capacities	Floor	100	200	300	Total
180 deg.	1582	3431	2266	5547	12826
240 deg.	1582	3549	2498	6626	14255
270 deg.	1582	3645	2738	7207	15172
360 deg.	1582	4081	3396	9258	18317

VALUE CITY ARENA
JEROME SCHOTTENSTEIN CENTER™
THE OHIO STATE UNIVERSITY

Example 6-3 B : Basic Center Stage Configuration

BASIC CENTER STAGE

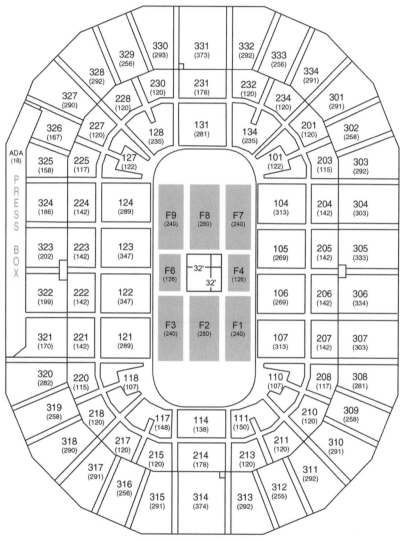

Capacities	Floor	100	200	300	Total
360 deg.	1772	4349	3396	9258	18775

VALUE CITY ARENA
JEROME SCHOTTENSTEIN CENTER™
THE OHIO STATE UNIVERSITY

Example 6-3 C : Basic End Stage Configuration

BASIC HALF HOUSE

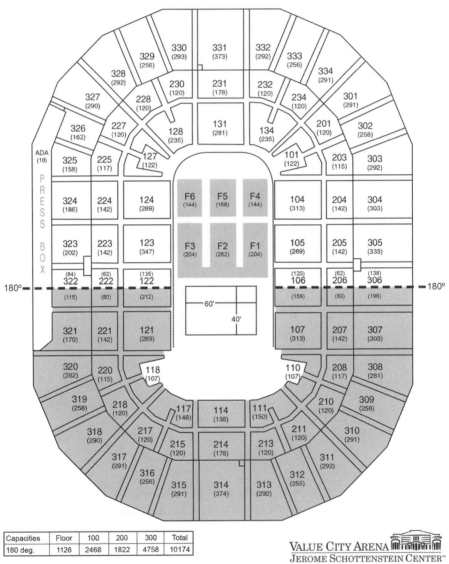

Capacities	Floor	100	200	300	Total
180 deg.	1126	2468	1822	4758	10174

VALUE CITY ARENA
JEROME SCHOTTENSTEIN CENTER™
THE OHIO STATE UNIVERSITY

Example 8-1 : Partial Production Rider

SHOW ADVANCE			
SHOW DATE(S): _____	VENUE: IAVM Arena	CITY: _____	

LABOR CALLS			
LOAD-IN: 9:00 AM	SECOND CALL: _____	SHOW CALL: 6:00 PM	LOAD-OUT: 10:00 PM
STEWARD: 1	STAGEHANDS: _____	STEWARD: _____	STEWARD: 1
HEADS: _____	RUNNERS: _____	DECK HANDS: 6	HEADS: _____
LOADERS: 4	PROD. ASST.: 2	HOUSE SPOTS: 4	LOADERS: 4
STAGEHANDS: 18		ELEC/HSE LTS: 1	STAGEHANDS: 22
UP RIGGERS: 4			UP RIGGERS: 4
DOWN RIGGERS: 1			DOWN RIGGERS: 1
ELECTRICIANS: 1			ELECTRICIANS: 1
FORK OPS: 1			FORK OPS: 1
RUNNERS: 3			

RUNNING TIMES			
SOUND CHECK TECH:	3:00 PM	BAND 1:	7:00 PM - 7:20 PM
SOUND CHECK HEAD:	4:00 PM	BAND 2:	7:40 PM - 8:10 PM
DOORS:	6:00 PM	HEADLINER:	8:45 PM - 10:15 PM
SECURITY MEETING:	4:00 PM	CURFEW:	10:30 PM

STAGE AND FOH RISERS / POWER / SPOTS / BARRICADE			
STAGE SIZE:	60'w x 40'd x 5'h	FOH SOUND POSITION:	16'w x 16'd x 01h
SL WING:	16'w x 24'd x 4'h		on floor at 75' from DS
SR WING:	16'w x 24'd x 5'h		
	wings recessed 4'	FOH LIGHT RISER:	12'w x 8'd x 2'h
			directly behind sound
SPOTS:	Require 4 FOH spots		
		RIGGING POINTS:	14 lights, 6 sound
AUDIO POWER:	200 Amp & 50 Amp	BARRICADE:	tour carrying 120'
LIGHTING POWER:	400 Amp & 200 Amp		will need bike rack for FOH
	120/208 Volt 3Phz, 5 wire		

VEHICLE INFO / PARKING			
PRODUCTION TRUCKS: 4	BAND BUSES: 2	SPONSOR BUSES: 1
MERCH TRUCKS: 2	CREW BUSES: 2	SUPPORT BUSES: 1
SPONS FOH TRUCKS: 2	TRAILER ON BUS: 1	RUNNER VEHICLES: 3
	AND: Van & Trailer	

Example 9-1 : Incident Report

INCIDENT REPORT   THE JEROME SCHOTTENSTEIN CENTER

Type: ☐ Injury ☐ Illness ☐ Damage ☐ Security   Photos: ☐ Yes ☐ No

Date: _____ Time of Report: _____ | **Incident Location:**

Event: _____ | Concourse: _____

Subject/Location Information: | Working Area: _____

Name: _____ DOB: _____ | Exterior: _____

Minor? ☐ Yes ☐ No   If so, Parent's Name: _____ | Parking Lots: _____

Address: _____ | Seating Area: _____

City: _____ State: _____ Zip: _____ | Other: _____

Age: _____ Phone: _____ Ticket: Section- _____ Row- _____ Seat- _____

Subject: ☐ Guest ☐ Employee ☐ Contractor ☐ Tenant   Other: _____

Location Observations:

Area Lighting: ☐ Dark ☐ Dimly Lit ☐ Light   Other Notes: _____

Floor Condition: ☐ Clean/Clear ☐ Debris ☐ Wet ☐ Dry ☐ Obstruction ☐ Even ☐ Uneven ☐ Steps

Notes: _____

Security Information:

Incident Responder: ☐ JSC Staff ☐ OSUPD ☐ Contracted Security ☐ CPD   Other: _____

JSC Staff Responder: _____   Agency Report #: _____

Type: ☐ Disruptive Behavior ☐ Fighting/Assault ☐ Substance Abuse ☐ Trespass   Other: _____

Was Subject Warned About Behavior? ☐ Yes ☐ No   Time: _____ By: _____

Was Subject Ejected? ☐ Yes ☐ No   Ejected By: _____

Was Guest Arrested? ☐ Yes ☐ No   Arrested By: _____

Other Subjects Involved? ☐ Yes ☐ No   *Please note on reverse side their names and involvement*

Medical Information:

Incident Responder: ☐ JSC Staff ☐ ARC ☐ CFD ☐ EMT's ☐ OSUPD   Other: _____

JSC Staff Responder: _____   Agency Report #: _____

Treatment Refused? ☐ Yes ☐ No Refusal by: _____ | **Incident Log:**

Treatment Site: ☐ Main First Aid ☐ Terrace First Aid Other: _____ | Call Received: _____

Complaint: _____ | Medical Staff Called: _____

How was Guest Found? _____ | Medical On Scene: _____

Complaint Prior to Event Arrival? ☐ Yes ☐ No | *Transport Dispatched:* _____

Guest Mobilized? ☐ Wheelchair ☐ C-Collar ☐ Backboard ☐ Stairchair | *Transport Arrival:* _____

Subject Return to Event/Work? ☐ Yes ☐ No Time: _____ | Departure: _____

Guest Transported? ☐ Yes ☐ No Medic #: _____ Hospital: _____

Subject Observations:

Clothing: ☐ Loose Fitting ☐ Form Fitting ☐ Disheveled   Shoe Type: ☐ Tennis Shoe ☐ Boot ☐ Sandal ☐ Heel ☐ Open Toe ☐ Open Heel

Walking Assistance: ☐ Cane ☐ Walker ☐ Wheelchair ☐ Person

Coordination/Behavior: ☐ Unbalanced ☐ Confused ☐ Unconcious ☐ Combative ☐ Unresponsive

Prexisting Impairments:

Visual: ☐ Contacts ☐ Glasses   Hearing: ☐ Hearing Aids

Physical: ☐ Limp ☐ Brace ☐ Cast ☐ Injury Notes: _____

Example 10-1 : Crowd Management Responsibilities

Training
- Knowledge of event and venue
- Perform communications function
- Risk management
- Crowd dynamics management
- Assist guests
- Implement venue/event policies and procedures
- Conflict identification and mitigation
- Major emergency response

Assisting Guests
- Maximize accessibility to guests
- Anticipate guests' needs
- Use good guest service techniques
- Answer questions or assist to find answers
- Provide direction to appropriate locations
- Respond to guest concerns

Implement Venue/Guest Policies and Procedures
- Learn and apply appropriate policies and procedures
- Observe violations of policies and procedures, and report to supervisor
- Inform guests of violations of policies and procedures and ensuing consequences
- Review policies and procedures as appropriate
- Proactively monitor changes to policies and procedures
- Report problems not addressed in policies and procedures to supervisor

Risk Management
- Participate in pre-event orientations
- Conduct pre-event review of assigned work area
- Review checklist of safety hazards
- Identify and mitigate safety hazards, and report to supervisor
- Confirm assigned work area and equipment readiness to supervisor
- Operate and maneuver equipment in safe manner
- Report incidents and property damage to supervisor
- Identify, mitigate, and report medical emergencies to supervisor
- Return assigned equipment in good working order

Crowd Dynamics Management
- Adjust to crowd demographics
- Anticipate crowd activities and behavior
- Maintain the usability of means of egress
- Make guests aware of their responsibilities
- Observe crowd for potential problems, and report to supervisor
- Monitor flow of crowd during duration of event
- Identify changing crowd behavior and demeanor, and report to supervisor

Knowledge of Event and Facilities
- Review schedule of event activities
- Review venue/event diagram
- Review event specific policies and procedures
- Review event specific alcohol policies and procedures
- Review specific event ticketing and credentialing policies
- Familiarize oneself with event seating requirements
- Familiarize oneself with type and activities of the event
- Identify key event/venue personnel
- Maintain control of limited access areas

Example 10-1 (*continued*)

Conflict Identification and Mitigation
- Identify credential/ticketing/seating problems
- React according to policies and procedures regarding problem guests
- Mitigate credential/ticketing/seating problems
- Resolve guest complaints/problems
- Avoid arguments with guests
- Avoid physical contact with guests

Training
- Attend employment orientation
- Fulfill certification as legally required
- Attend venue/event orientation
- Fulfill specific venue training requirements
- Read assigned and posted material
- Attend pre- and post-event briefing sessions
- Participate in job assignment training from supervisor at events
- Maintain focus on role during event
- Share competence with other employees
- Follow chain of command
- Attend continuing education as appropriate
- Participate in on-going training
- Participate in performance evaluations

Perform Communications Function
- Employ good listening skills
- Adapt communication to crowd diversity
- Adhere to proper written and verbal communication channels
- Follow supervisor instruction
- Utilize proper written, verbal, and non-verbal communication techniques
- Report communication breakdowns to supervisor
- Be competent with communication equipment
- Keep communication relevant
- Utilize event/venue terminology
- Communicate with all personnel associated with the event
- Maintain the integrity of confidential information
- Recognize non-verbal crowd communication
- Utilize signage in communication process
- Respond appropriately to all public address announcements
- Complete required written documentation

Minor Emergency Response
- Maintain guest safety as a priority
- Assist guests with special needs
- Follow appropriate instructions applicable to fire, weather, earthquake, crowd incidents, terrorism, hazardous materials, transportation mishaps, or power loss
- Participate in drills
- Report all fires immediately regardless of size
- Permit individual guests to leave if they wish during an emergency
- Execute assigned tasks or responsibilities as provided in event of an emergency
- Provide appropriate information

Example 10-2 : FEMA Bomb Threat Checklist

Date:		Time:	
Time Caller Hung Up:		# Where Call Received:	

Ask Caller:	Exact Words of Threat:
✓ Where is the bomb located (building, floor, room, etc.)? ✓ When will it go off? ✓ What does it look like? ✓ What kind of bomb is it? ✓ What will make it explode? ✓ Did you place the bomb? ✓ Why? ✓ What is your name?	

Information About Caller:

✓ Where is the caller located? (background and level of noise)
✓ Estimated age?
✓ Is voice familiar? If so, who does it sound like?
✓ Other points:

Caller's Voice:		Background Sounds:	Threat Language:
☐ Accent ☐ Angry ☐ Calm ☐ Clearing Throat ☐ Coughing ☐ Cracking voice ☐ Crying ☐ Deep ☐ Deep Breathing ☐ Disguised ☐ Distinct ☐ Excited ☐ **Female**	☐ Laughter ☐ Lisp ☐ Loud ☐ **Male** ☐ Nasal ☐ Normal ☐ Ragged ☐ Rapid ☐ Raspy ☐ Slow ☐ Slurred ☐ Soft ☐ Stutter	☐ Animal noises ☐ House noises ☐ Kitchen noises ☐ Street noises ☐ Booth ☐ PA system ☐ Conversation ☐ Music ☐ Motor ☐ Clear ☐ Static ☐ Office machinery ☐ Factory machinery ☐ Local ☐ Long distance	☐ Incoherent ☐ Message read ☐ Taped ☐ Irrational ☐ Profane ☐ Well-spoken

(Federal Emergency Management Agency, 2014)

Appendix B

CORE COMPETENCIES OF PUBLIC ASSEMBLY FACILITY MANAGERS

Developed by the IAVM Body of Knowledge Task Force

Overview

The Core Competencies of Public Assembly Facility Managers were originally developed in 1999-2000 by the IAVM Body of Knowledge Task Force and updated in 2006. The Core Competencies represent the skills and abilities that managers of public assembly facilities, regardless of facility type, should possess and build upon in order to be judged competent and qualify for the designation of Certified Facilities Executive (CFE).

Functions Common to Public Assembly Facilities

1. Administration (People & Organization)
2. Sales & Marketing (Selling Time & Space, and Event Activity)
3. Fiscal Management (Financial Performance)
4. Facility Services & Operations (Physical Plant & Event Management)
5. Leadership & Management

I. Administration

1. **Capital Improvement**
   Identifying the need
   Forecasting the expense
   Finding the funding
   Budgeting the expense
   Overseeing the project

2. **Construction Management**
   Understanding the bidding process
   Understanding technical specifications
   Reading blueprints and architectural drawings
   Supervision of contractors (both on site and administratively)

3. **Technology**
   Basic understanding of computer systems
   Familiarity with basic terminology
   Ability to identify appropriate technologies
   Ability to evaluate emerging technologies

4. **Insurance/Risk Management**
   Understanding the terminology
   Ability to evaluate risk
   Skilled in risk assessment
   Ability to conduct cost/benefit analysis

5. **Emergency Management**
   Develop communication strategies
   Develop evacuation plans
   Coordinate emergency services with responder agencies (police, fire, etc.)
   Train staff in response preparedness
   Knowledge of emergency equipment
   Develop media relations

6. **Crisis Management**
   Develop response procedures
   > Bomb threat
   > Fire
   > Weather-related incident (hurricane, flood, etc.)
   > Chemical/biological threat
   > Natural disaster (earthquake, tornado, etc.)
   > Terrorist incident
   Staff training and preparedness
   Media relations
   Insurance issues

7. **Human Resources**
   Knowledge of legal and regulatory issues
   Staff training
   Staff retention
   Creating and maintaining workplace morale
   Employee counseling

8. **Contract Management**
   Understanding terminology
   Negotiation skills
   Aware of legal issues

9. **Governance**
   Understanding the operating policies
   Knowledge of the operating environment
   Knowing key persons with authority

10. **Tenant Management**
    Understanding landlord responsibilities
    Understanding tenant's needs

Partnering where mutually beneficial
Creating a happy professional arrangement

11. **Training and Development**
    Needs assessment of staff
    Knowledge of available resources
    Develop meaningful training programs
    Evaluate effectiveness of training programs

12. **Legal Issues**
    Knowledge of laws affecting facility
        Business regulations
        Reporting requirements
        Employment laws

13. **Disability Services**
    Conduct accessibility assessment
    Understand legal responsibilities and requirement
    Staff training

14. **Public and Private Management**
    Understanding the difference

II. Sales & Marketing

1. **Sponsorship**
   Ability to develop partnerships

2. **Perceived Value of Sponsorship to Buyer**
   Understanding the difference between advertising and sponsorship
   Fulfillment of sponsorship contract (promises)
   Value to sponsors' annual report

3. **Community Relations**
   Sensitivity and understanding the community
   Understanding the direct and indirect impact of the facility on the community
   Sensitivity of community standards in programming the facility

4. **Public Relations**
   Understanding the concept of free advertising
   Ability to create a press release and public service announcement (PSA)
   Developing policies for proper use of complimentary tickets
   Understanding the value of facility's website as a public relations tool

5. **Advertising**
   Knowledge of the media (print, radio, television, Internet)
   Ability to develop an effective advertising campaign
   Selling the facility to the industry (i.e., event producers and promoters)
   Selling the facility to the community
   Selling tickets to a specific event

6. **Marketing**
   Creating a demand for the facility
   Understanding the demographics of the market
   Conducting market research and analysis
   Developing a marketing campaign
   Packaging the product (event, facility, sports team, meeting destination)
   Understanding and directing the facility's image

7. **Booking and Scheduling**
   Developing relationships with event producers, event promoters, talent agents, meeting planners, etc.
   Knowledge of event production requirements
   Understanding the facility's capabilities and limitations
   Knowing the competition
   Understanding the concept of yield management

8. **Event Programming**
   Develop a diverse program of events
   Be considerate of the primary tenant(s)
   Develop event acquisition strategies
        Standard rental
        Co-promotion
        In-house promotion/buying and promoting talent
   Develop events through non-profit/community organizations
   Foster sponsorship opportunities through event programming

9. **Fund Raising**
   Balance fund raising with other sources of revenue
   Understand the "not-for-profit" statues of some facilities
   Develop grant-writing skills
   Create events and galas as fund-raising tools

10. **Premium Seating**
    Golden Circle
    Club Seats
    Luxury Suites
    Premium seating add-ons (parking, concierge service, catering, dedicated entrance/exit)

11. **Convention and Visitors Bureau (CVB) Relations**
    Understanding shared marketing responsibilities
    Coordinating joint sales efforts
    Developing booking priorities
    Understanding economic impact studies
    Working with sports commissions in US cities
    Understanding the facility's role in urban/economic development

III. Fiscal Management

1. **Budgeting**
   Developing a budget for the facility
   Ability to monitor and adjust budgets
   Understanding financial statements (income statement, balance sheet, operating statement, profit/loss statement)
   Understanding financial operations (accounts payable, accounts receivable)
   Knowledge of audit controls
       Internal audit
       External audit
       Areas for audit: box office, petty cash, time cards, travel claims, food & beverage commissions, etc.

2. **Inventory Control**
   Supplies
   Equipment

3. **Cost Accounting**
   Identify cost systems
   Allocate expenses
   Understanding fixed and variable costs

4. **Investments**
   Cash flow management
   Investing box office receipts

5. **Capitalization**
   Developing capital improvement budgets
   Understanding bonding capacities

6. **Forecasting**
   Understanding the facility's overall financial performance

IV. Facility Services & Operations

1. **Admission**
    Developing admission control systems
    > Box office operations
    > Credentials

2. **Event Production**
    Developing a thorough understanding of event production elements
    > Stages
    > Sound systems
    > Lighting systems
    > Portable floors
    > Seating configurations
    > Stagehands
    > Television production
    > Power requirements
    > Advancing a show

3. **Rigging**
    Load bearing capacities
    Safety policies
    Rigging maintenance
    Risk management
    Specific trade knowledge

4. **Physical Plant**
    Interior maintenance
    Exterior maintenance
    Grounds keeping
    Heat, ventilation, air conditioning (HVAC)
    Mechanical systems (electrical, plumbing, HVAC)
    Ice making and ice maintenance
    Service contracts with third party specialists

5. **Housekeeping**
    Custodial labor
    Custodial supplies
    Custodial equipment
    Event custodial duties vs. daily custodial duties
    Changeovers
    Inventory control of equipment and supplies
    Trade specific knowledge (carpet care, window washing, floor refinishing, etc.)

6. **Food & Beverage**
    Options: in-house vs. outsource contract
    Concessions and catering

Health department regulations
Alcoholic beverage service regulations and licensing
Products (basic vs. branded)
Sanitation (cleaning & pest control)
Service points-of-sale/staffing
Accounting & cost controls
Auditing (cash & inventory)

7. **Merchandise**
Options: in-house vs. outsource contract
Commission rates
Locations for sale
Staffing
Accounting & cash controls
Auditing (inventory)
Bootleg/counterfeit merchandise

8. **Event Management**
Event labor (hire, train, and supervise)
Ushers, ticket takers, tickets sellers, security, medical, event custodians, parking lot attendants, stagehands
Event briefing
Event incident reports

V. Leadership & Management

1. **Principles of Leadership**
Vision and values
Empowerment of subordinates
Collaboration with colleagues up and down the organizational structure
Risk taking

2. **Use of Power and Authority**
Balance the power
Develop a team

3. **Strategic Planning**
Mission statement
Goals and objectives

4. **Knowing the Ground Rules**
History of the organization
Guiding principles
Policies and procedures

5. **Staff Development**
   Use job descriptions effectively
   Use evaluations as a communication tool
   Provide training and professional development opportunities

6. **Mentoring**
   Provide guidance and learning opportunities
   Impart knowledge and experience
   Instill confidence

7. **Morals and Ethics**
   Maintain highest ethical standards
   Give respect to others
   Lead by example

8. **Motivation**
   Instill enthusiasm in others
   Be accessible to subordinates
   Exercise problem-solving skills

9. **Decision Making**
   Exercise sound judgment
   Consider more than one option before making a decision
   Aim for balanced outcomes

10. **Sense of Humor**
    Maintain a sense of humor
    Be able to laugh at yourself

11. **Communication Skills**
    Be clear and concise
    Never enough communication
    Use different communication tools for different circumstances

12. **Time Management**
    Learn to use time efficiently
    Balance work with leisure time

13. **Crisis Management**
    Understand the leader's role in time of crisis
    Step up to the plate

14. **IAVM Membership and Participation**
    Professional associations
    Networking with colleagues
    Opportunities for service to the industry/profession

Educational opportunities
Certified Facilities Executive (CFE)

Appendix C

CONTRACT COMPONENTS

A tentatively held date becomes a firm commitment when a formal contractual instrument is issued. It becomes a contract when properly signed by all parties. The scope and importance of the event will usually dictate whether any serious negotiating will be required. Many facilities utilize standard form contracts or license agreements with a "fill in the blank" type format. These types of instruments allow the process to be streamlined and somewhat consistent in format.

Negotiated contracts or license agreements require advance preparation. The assistance of an attorney is certainly a must for the original standard facility document. Whether or not an attorney is needed for individual event contracts is a decision to be made by the manager unless there is a policy requiring a sign-off by the facility's attorney. In addition to the "boiler plate" information that usually appears in most documents, several areas must be addressed prior to negotiation. A comprehensive "laundry list" must be developed with major deal points outlined. Armed with the information, the facility negotiator can focus on items such as special terms, condition, and benefits to be obtained by the parties.

Components of a Contract

A contract is defined as an agreement of two or more parties to do or refrain from doing some lawful thing. The agreement must create obligations on the part of all parties. Every contract must meet four basic requirements:

1. Mutual assent of all contracting parties
2. The parties must possess the legal rights and capacity to make the contract.
3. Proper and fair consideration of services or provisions must be received by all contracting parties.
4. Offer of terms of the agreement

The contract must have a lawful objective and a legal method for accomplishing it. In law, a contract is a promissory agreement between two or more parties to establish, change, or rescind a legal relationship. The public assembly facility manager should understand that the prime purpose of a contract is to provide protection to:

1. The owner of the public assembly facility
2. The organization or individual using the facility
3. The patron attending the event (whatever that event might be)

There are some very basic components that should be contained in the facility use contract. These items will, in nearly all cases, be seen as a part of the basic contract form:

1. **Form of Legal Document** - i.e., Is it a contract, license, lease, permit, etc.?

2. **Facility Identification** - Include name, address, city, state, zip code, telephone, and fax number of the facility. Be sure to include legal nomenclature such as Municipal Corporation, Incorporated, Partnership, Joint Venture, etc.

3. **User Identification -** Include business name, address, city, state, zip code, event contact person, telephone number, and fax number of the contracting organization. Be sure to include legal nomenclature such as Corporation, Partnership, Sole Owner, D.B.A., Joint Venture, etc.

4. **Event Identification -** What space is being rented for what purpose and the name of the event?

5. **Event Date(s) -** List date(s) of use, including move-in and move-out

6. **Event Time(s) -** List time(s) of use, including move-in and move-out

7. **Event Schedule -** State what will be going on during specific date/time frames

8. **Venue Identification -** List the exact space(s) that will be rented. This is particularly important when the facility being rented has many spaces. The user must know that he/she is only renting specific areas and not the whole building, unless that is the case. Be sure to also include language which states that the organization will, or will not, also have use of the common public areas for ingress and egress to the event(s).

9. **User Fees and Revenue Sources -** State the specific amount of money that will be paid for rental of the space or a percentage of ticket sales, or even a combination of base rent against a percentage of ticket sales. Other user fees and revenue sources include:

    Equipment use
    Labor charges
    Merchandise
    Parking
    Food/beverage
    Catering
    Flowers, etc.
    Videotaping, etc

10. **Payment Schedule -** State a precise schedule of when payments are due for:

    Advance/contract deposit
    Minimum base rental
    Percentage balance (if appropriate)
    Commission on sales (if appropriate)
    Service/labor costs
    Equipment rental costs
    Other

11. **Insurance Requirements -** Include language to identify the exact type of coverage, limits of liability and scope, and qualified insurance companies required by the facility. Note a Certificate of Insurance will be required by the facility X days prior to the event. Specific wording of any requirement for making the facility or the governing authority an "additionally named insured" should also be included here. Facility

should have right to AUTOMATICALLY provide coverage at user's expense if user fails to provide on time.

12. **Indemnity Clause** - Include specific language holding the facility, its manager, employees, agents, and guests harmless from legal action caused by the acts or omissions of the user.

13. **Cancellation Clause** - Definite and specific language must be in place that spells out the allocation of risk between the parties in the event of cancellation by either party.

14. **Attorney Fees** - Most attorneys will insist on a clause that obligates the payment of attorney fees and court costs by the non-prevailing party to the prevailing party in the event of a lawsuit.

15. **Force Majeure** - This is a clause which states that the facility will not be obligated in any way in the event of an act of God, fire, civil riot, strike, lockout, flood, war, or other situations over which the facility has no control.

16. **No Partnerships** - Unless there is specific language to the contrary, there should be a section that simply states that there is no partnership relationship between the facility and the user.

17. **Obstruction/Alterations** - Include language with regard to the specifics of not blocking, for example, sidewalks, ramps, entries, doors, corridors, passageways, galleries, vestibules, hallways, lobbies, stairways, elevators, aisles, driveways, fire hose cabinets, heating and air conditioning vents, lighting fixtures, and fire prevention water sprinkler systems so as to ensure patron safety. No physical alterations to the facility should be allowed without prior written consent of management.

18. **Signature Lines and the Corporate Seal** - There should be sufficient room at the end of the document to allow for all signatures required by the governing authority in addition to that of the user. If the user is a corporation, a corporate seal may need to be affixed to the document over the signature of the corporate secretary.

19. **Personal Requirements** - A mention should be made with regard to any personnel that are necessary to set up, operate, and tear down the event and who will provide those personnel. Note that worker's compensation law varies from state to state. If union personnel are required, this should be stated.

20. **Basic Services Provided by the Facility** - Reference should be made for the provision of heat, light, air conditioning, cleanliness, water, sewer, and natural gas, if the facility normally supplies these services as a part of the rental agreement. It should be stated whether or not the facility provides these services at a fee, or if it does not provide them at all.

21. **Control of Building** - The building should always be under the ultimate control of the facility manager, and this should be specifically spelled out in the document.

22. **Changes to Agreement** - Changes to the agreement must be in writing and signed by all parties.

This is not meant to be a complete listing of each clause that should be in a facility use contractual document. In addition to the foregoing, each facility manager should regularly seek the counsel and advise of the facility's attorney to be sure that all requirements of federal, state, and local laws are properly covered.

In addition, there are many operating aspects and other items involved in the use of a public assembly facility that need to be addressed, although trying to include them in a contract document may be too complex and cumbersome. Many facilities address this issue by developing "policies and procedure" and/or "rules and regulations" documents which are made a part of the contractual agreement by a statement in that latter document so stating. Some areas that might be addressed in the policies and procedures, if that approach is used, could include, but should not be limited to:

1. *Concessions* - Revenue and expenses connected with food and beverage, merchandise, photography, flowers, etc. would be addressed

2. *Exhibits* - The terms and conditions for exhibits, including storage, freight, locations, local laws, etc.

3. *Alterations/construction* - Requirements for either approval or prohibitions against nails, balloons, adhesives, etc., if applicable

4. *Capacity* - State maximum seating, floor loads, and rigging requirements, among other items

5. *Broadcasting/filming* - Specify who has rights to these, under what conditions, and at what formula for determining costs and revenue distribution

6. *Tickets* - Specify who sells and through what resources, collects money, prints tickets, manifest requirements, box office staffing and statements, seating configurations, complimentary tickets, and trade tickets

7. *Evacuation of facility in case of emergency* - Who controls, diagrams, etc.

Definitions

a. **Contract:** A contract is defined as an agreement upon sufficient consideration to do or refrain from doing some lawful thing. The agreement must create an obligation. Every contract must have at least the following four elements:

1. Mutual assents
2. Parties with the capacity to contract
3. Consideration and valid subject matter
4. Term

b. **Warranties:** Warranties are assurances that are part of a contract.

c. **License:** A license or certificate is a form of written approval to do a lawful thing, often issued by a division of government. Additional elements or provisions are usually added to define the extent and limits of such license. It usually gives the licensee the right to obtain certain space but not possession; therefore, the individual/organization does not become a tenant. To be a tenant, one must have exclusive possession, not mere use alone.

d. **Lease:** A lease is a contract whereby, for a consideration called rent, one party agrees to give possession of premises to another. A lease must contain five essential elements:

   1. Contract
   2. Exclusive possession
   3. Subordinate holding
   4. Reversion in the landlord
   5. Reservations of rent

   Other formal provisions usually found in a lease include the following:

   1. Term of duration
   2. Description of premises
   3. Purpose for which premises may be used
   4. Repairs and improvements
   5. Insurance
   6. Assignment
   7. Security deposit
   8. Default and remedies
   9. Quiet enjoyment

e. **Permit:** A permit is a written acknowledgment of consent to do some lawful thing without command; it grants a liberty and professes to tolerate all legal action.

f. **Agreement:** All contracts are agreements, but all agreements are NOT contracts. Agreements that do not include the essentials of a contract are not enforceable as a contract by law. The use of agreements, therefore, should be for arrangements that are simpler in nature and duration.

g. **Ultimate terms and conditions:** For very large and complex operations, it is advisable to include many more terms and conditions in the contract. The enforcement of certain provisions can become extremely difficult. In all cases, it will require supervision of at least one individual representing the party granting the privilege.

Appendix D

IAVM AND CONTINUING EDUCATION

The International Association of Venue Managers (IAVM) – which can be found at www.iavm.org – provides numerous programs designed to support the ongoing professional development of venue management professionals. These programs provide an expanding bank of industry knowledge along with valuable opportunities to develop a stronger network with colleagues.

Venue Management School

Venue Management School (VMS) and the Graduate Institute (VMS-GI) are considered two of the best professional educational programs available for venue managers. Those new to the industry, or managers looking to expand their overall understanding, will find solid principles and practices for venue management in the VMS program. Venue professionals can further expand their universe of management and leadership skills and understanding by attending the Graduate Institute.

The VMS programs consist of two (2) week-long courses of intensive instruction held over two consecutive years. The VMS curriculum covers topics such as event management, life safety, marketing and advertising, crowd management, and the guest experience. The second year of VMS covers areas such as leadership and image, cost control, risk management and insurance, and strategic business planning.

Venue Management School Graduate Institute

The Venue Management School Graduate Institute (VMS-GI) is held at the Oglebay Resort & Conference Center, in Wheeling, West Virginia. This training program for venue professionals is considered one of IAVM's benchmark programs in venue management.

The Graduate Institute is advanced education for venue professionals covering management theory, professional ethics, leadership, human resource management, problem solving, and decision making. It's goal is to expand an individual's management techniques and leadership skills. The Graduate Institute is more conceptual than VMS, yet not as advanced as IAVM's Senior Executive Symposium.

Senior Executive Symposium

IAVM's Senior Executive Symposium (SES) is a four-day leadership immersion for senior-level venue managers and other individuals on a leadership track inside their organizations. SES curriculum rotates each year through three areas of focus: visionary management, strategic planning, and leadership culture.

Co-developed by IAVM and Cornell University, the course inspires executives to lead their staffs with creativity, collaboration, and a well-rounded management philosophy.

Industry Conferences

IAVM offers various conferences dedicated to topics, issues, and best practices important to the public assembly management industry. In addition to conferences focusing on specific venue types, the VenueConnect Annual Conference & Trade Show is an industry-wide meeting that features recognized speakers, panel discussions, and town halls designed to keep the entire venue management industry connected and informed.

European Academy for Venue Management

IAVM Europe, in conjunction with IAVM and through the support of the IAVM Foundation, opened the European Academy for Venue Management (EAVM). The EAVM is a two-year course, which, upon completion, gives students an internationally recognized certificate of competence. Curriculum at the EAVM is comprehensive and tailored to European venue management practices and procedures.

Venue Management Association (Asia and Pacific)

The Venue Management Association (Asia and Pacific) Limited, which is affiliated with IAVM, provides management practitioners of public venues in Australia, New Zealand, and the Asia Pacific region with an association dedicated to professional development, education, and the growth and success of the venue management industry.

Professional Certifications

IAVM offers the Certified Facilities Executive (CFE) designation and will launch the mid-level Certified Venue Professional (CVP) in 2015. To attain the CFE certification, candidates must complete a personal interview, written essay, and comprehensive written examination. The CFE designation is intended to say three important things about facility executives: they are skilled managers, they are committed to the industry, and they are pledged to continual professional growth and development.

Life Safety & Security

The need for advanced event safety and security training at venues of all types remains one of the top priorities of the venue industry. IAVM's Academy for Venue Safety & Security (AVSS) delivers essential venue safety programs covering best practices on patron safety, crowd management, legal liability, risk management, new technologies, safe sheltering, active shooter preparedness, and other essential concepts that contribute to ensure venues are operating as safely as possible.

Online Education

In addition to the conferences, schools, and programs providing live education, IAVM provides online resources available to members and industry professionals. The Online Learning Center (www.iavm.org) features recorded sessions, webinars, and articles that represent an evolving library of industry knowledge and expertise. A second online resource for IAVM members is VenueNet, an online forum that facilitates diverse discussions around industry-related topics, with the benefit of contributions from venue professionals and vendors from across the entire industry.

Appendix E

ASAE www.asaenet.org
American Society of Association Executives
1575 I St., NW
Washington, DC 20005-1103
Phone: 202/626-2723, Fax: 202/371-8825
E-mail: pr@asaenet.org

APPA www.appa.org
APPA: The Association of Higher Education Facilities Officers
1643 Prince St.
Alexandria, VA 22314-2818
Phone: 703/684-1446, Fax: 703/549-2772

ACOM www.acomonline.org
Association for Convention Operations Management
2965 Flowers Road South, Ste. 105
Atlanta, GA 30341
Phone: 770/454-9411, Fax: 770/458-3314
E-mail: info@acomonline.org

AIPC www.aipc.org
Association Internationale des Palais de Congrès (International Association of Congress Centres)
55 Rue de l'Amazone
1060 Brussels
BELGIUM
Phone: 32-2-534-59-53, Fax: 32-2-534-63-38
E-mail: secretariat@iapc.org

ACCED-I acced-i.org
Association of Collegiate Conference and Event Directors Intl.
Colorado State University, Tiley House
Fort Collins, CO 80523-8037
Phone: 970/491-5151, Fax: 970/491-0667

ALSD www.alsd.com
Association of Luxury Suite Directors
636 Northland Blvd., Ste. 250
Cincinnati, OH 45240
Phone: 513/674-0555, Fax: 513/674-0577

APAP www.apap365.org
Association of Performing Arts Presenters
1112 16th St., NW, Ste. 400
Washington, DC 20036
Phone: 202/833-2787, Fax: 202/833-1543
E-mail: artspres@artspresenters.org

ABRACCEF www.abraccef.org.br
Brazilian Association of Conference Centers (Associacao Brasileira dos Centros de

Convencoes e Feiras)
Rua Barao do Rio Branco 370
 CEP 80010-180 Curitiba, Parana
BRAZIL
Phone: 55-41-322-8955, Fax: 55-41-322-8955
E-mail: abraccef@abraccef.org.br

CEIR www.ceir.org
Center for Exhibition Industry Research
2301 South Lake Shore Dr., Ste. E1002
Chicago, IL 60616
Phone: 312/808-2347, Fax: 312/949-3472
E-mail: ceir@mpea.com

CIC www.conventionindustry.org
Convention Industry Council
8201 Greensboro Dr., Ste. 300
McLean, VA 22102
Phone: 703/610-9030, Fax: 703/610-9005

CMA www.cmaworld.com
Country Music Association
One Music Circle South
Nashville, TN 37203
Phone: 615/244-2840, Fax: 615/726-0314
E-mail: international@CMAworld.com

ESTA www.esta.org
Entertainment Services and Technology Association
875 Sixth Ave., Ste. 1005
New York, NY 10001
Phone: 212/244-1505, Fax: 212/244-1502
E-mail: info@esta.org

EAA www.eaaoffice.org
European Arenas Association
Sarphatikade 12
Amsterdam 1017 WV
THE NETHERLANDS
Phone: 31-20-530-4717, Fax: 31-20-530-4711
E-mail: eaa@eaaoffice.org

EVVC www.evvc.org
European Association of Event Centers
Thueringer avenue 12, House 3, OG
14052 Berlin
GERMANY
Phone: 30-30-38-58-00, Fax: 30-30-38-58-02
E-mail: info@evvc.org

ESMA
European Stadium Managers Association
24 Rue De Commandant Guilbaud
Boulogne 95214
FRANCE
Phone: 33-1-4215-2552, Fax: 33-1-4215-1039

ESCA www.esca.org
Exposition Service Contractors Association
2260 Corporate Circle, Suite 400
Henderson, NV 89074-7701
Phone: 702/319-9561, Fax: 702/450-7732
E-mail: askus@esca.org

IAEE www.iaee.org
International Association for Exposition Management
P O Box 802425
Dallas, TX 75380-2425
Phone: 972/458-8002, Fax: 972/458-8119
E-mail: news@iaem.org

IAAPA www.iaapa.org
International Association of Amusement Parks & Attractions
1448 Duke St.
Alexandria, VA 22314
Phone: 703/836-4800, Fax: 703/836-9678

IAVM www.iavm.org
International Association of Venue Managers
635 Fritz Drive, Suite 100
Coppell, TX 75019
Phone: 972/906-7441, Fax: 972/906-7418

IACC www.iacconline.org
International Association of Conference Centers
243 N. Lindbergh Blvd., Ste. 315
St. Louis, MO 63141
Phone: 314/993-8575, Fax: 314/993-8919
E-mail: info@iacconline.org

IACVB www.iacvb.org
International Association of Convention & Visitor Bureaus
2025 M Street NW, Ste. 500
Washington, DC 20036
Phone: 202/296-7888, Fax: 202/296-7889
E-mail: info@iacvb.org

IAFE www.fairsandexpos.com
International Association of Fairs & Expositions
Box 985

Springfield, MO 65801
Phone: 417/862-5771, Fax: 417/862-0156
E-mail: iafe@fairsandexpos.com

IAPCO www.iapco.org
International Association of Professional Congress Organizers
42 Canham Road
London W3 7SR
UNITED KINGDOM
Phone: 44 20 8749 6171, Fax: 44 20 8740 0241
E-mail: iapco@xs4all.be

ICMA www.icma.org
International City/County Management Association
777 North Capitol St., NE, Ste. 500
Washington, DC 20002
Phone: 202/289-4262, Fax: 202/962-3500

ICCA www.iccaworld.com
International Congress & Convention Association
Entrade 121
NL - 1096 EB Amsterdam
THE NETHERLANDS
Phone: 31-20-398-1919, Fax: 31-20-699-0781
E-mail: icca@icca.nl

IEDC http://www.iedconline.org/index.html
International Economic Development Council
734 15th Street Ste. 900
Washington, DC 20005
Phone: 202/223-7800, Fax: 202/223-4745

IFMA www.ifma.org
International Facility Management Association
1 East Greenway Plaza, Suite 1100
Houston, TX 77046-0194
Phone: 713/623-4362, Fax: 713/623-6124
E-mail: ifmahq@ifma.org

ISPA www.ispa.org
International Society for the Performing Arts
17 Purdy Avenue, P.O. Box 909
Rye, NY 10580
Phone: 914/921-1550, Fax: 914/921-1593
E-mail: info@ispa.org

ISES www.ises.com
International Special Events Society
401 North Michigan Avenue
Chicago, IL 60611-4267
Phone: 312/321-6853, Fax: 312/673-6953
E-mail: info@ises.com

INTIX www.intix.org
International Ticketing Association
250 West 57th St., Ste. 722
New York, NY 10107
Phone: 212/581-0600, Fax: 212/581-0885
E-mail: info@intix.org

IATSE www.iatse.net
International Alliance of Theatrical Stage Employees & Moving Picture Technicians of the US
and Canada
1430 Broadway, 20th Floor
New York, NY 10018
Phone: 212/730-1770, Fax: 212/730-7809

MPI www.mpiweb.org
Meeting Professionals International
4455 LBJ Freeway, Ste. 1200
Dallas, TX 75244-5903
Phone: 972/702-3000, Fax: 972/702-3070
E-mail: confmtgs@mpiweb.org

AMPROFEC www.amprofec.org
Mexican Association of Professionals in Fairs, Exhibitions & Conventions
Ave. Benjamin Frankl0in, Num 166-4
Col. Escandon Mexico, 11800 D. F.
MEXICO
Phone: (55) 5273 1103, Fax: (55) 5273 1103

NAA www.nationalarenasassociation.com
National Arenas Association
27 Friary Avenue
Shirley Solihull, West Midlands B90 4SZ
UNITED KINGDOM
Phone: 44-121-744-2211, Fax: 44-121-774-2211

NACA www.naca.org
National Association for Campus Activities
13 Harbison Way
Columbia, SC 29212-3401
Phone: 803/732-6222, Fax: 803/749-1047

NAAC www.naaconline.org
National Association of Accessibility Consultants
1154 Fort Street Mall, Suite 204
Honolulu, Hi 96813
Phone: 808/523-3344, Fax: 808/523-3008
E-mail: naac@aloha.net

NACDA www.nacda.com
National Association of Collegiate Directors of Athletes
P.O. Box 16428
Cleveland OH 44116
Phone: 440/892-4000, Fax: 440/892-4007

NAC   www.nacoline.org
National Association of Concessionaires
35 E. Wacker Drive
Chicago, IL 60601
Phone: 312/236-3858, Fax: 312/236-7809
E-mail: info@naconline.org

NACS   www.publicshows.com
National Association of Consumer Shows
147 S.E. 102nd Ave.
Portland, OR 97216
Phone: 503/253-0832, Fax: 503/253-9172
E-mail: info@publicshows.com

NAIA   www.naia.org
National Association of Intercollegiate Athletics
23500 W. 105th St., P O Box 1325
Olathe, KS 66051
Phone: 913/791-0044, Fax: 913/791-9555

NAPAMA   www.napama.org
National Association of Performing Arts Managers & Agents
459 Columbus Ave., Ste. 133
New York, NY 10024
Phone: 888/745-8759, Fax: 212/580-5438
E-mail: info@napama.org

NBA   www.nba.com
National Basketball Association
Olympic Tower, 645 Fifth Ave., 15th Fl
New York, NY 10022
Phone: 212/826-7000, Fax: 212/826-0579

NCBMP   www.ncbmp.com
National Coalition of Black Meeting Planners
8630 Fenton St., Ste. 126
Silver Spring, MD 20910
Phone: 202/628-3952, Fax: 301/588-0011

NCAA   www.ncaa.org
National Collegiate Athletic Association
700 W. Washington Avenue
Indianapolis, IN 46206-6222
Phone: 317/917-6222, Fax: 317/917-6888

NFPA   www.nfpa.org
National Fire Protection Association
1 Batterymarch Park, P.O. Box 9101
Quincy, MA 02269-9101
Phone: 617/770-3000, Fax: 617/770-0700
E-mail: public_affairs@nfpa.org

NFL www.nfl.com
National Football League
280 Park Ave., Ste. 12-West
New York, NY 10017
Phone: 212/450-2000, Fax: 212/681-7559

NHL www.nhl.com
National Hockey League
1251 Ave. of the Americas, 47th Fl.
New York, NY 10020
Phone: 212/789-2000, Fax: 212/789-2020

NLC www.nlc.org
National League of Cities
1301 Pennsylvania Ave., NW, Ste. 550
Washington, DC 20004-1763
Phone: 202/626-3000, Fax: 202/626-3043
E-mail: inet@nlc.org

NACPA
North American Concert Promoters Association
P.O. Box 753
McLean, VA 22101
Phone: 703/538-3575, Fax: 703/538-3876
E-mail: necpa@ix.netcom.com

PCMA www.pcma.org
Professional Convention Management Association
2301 South Lake Shore, Ste. 1001
Chicago, IL 60616-1419
Phone: 312/423-7262, Fax: 312/423-7222

PRCA www.prorodeo.com
Professional Rodeo Cowboys Association
101 Prorodeo Drive
Colorado Springs, CO 80919-9989
Phone: 719/593-8840, Fax: 719/548-4876

RCMA www.rcmaweb.org
Religious Conference Management Association
One RCA Dome, Suite 120
Indianapolis, IN 46225
Phone: 317/632-1888, Fax: 317/632-7909
E-mail: rcma@rcmaweb.org

SGMP www.sgmp.org
Society of Government Meeting Planners
908 King Street, Lower Level
Alexandria, VA 22314
Phone: 703/549-0892, Fax: 703/549-0708

SE www.sportengland.org
Sport England
16 Upper Woburn Place
London WC1H 0QP
ENGLAND
Phone: 020 7273 1500, Fax: 020 7383 5740
E-mail: info@sportengland.org

SMA www.stadiummanagers.org
Stadium Managers Association
525 SW 5th St., Ste. A
Des Moines, IA 50309
Phone: 515-282-8192, Fax: 515-282-9117
E-mail: sma@assoc-mgmt.com

LHAT www.lhat.org
The League of Historic American Theatres
616 Water Street, Ste. 320
Baltimore, MD 21202
Phone: 410/659-9533, Fax: 410/837-9664

UFI www.ufinet.org
Union des Foires Internationales
35bis, rue Jouffroy d'Abbans
F-75017 Paris
FRANCE
Phone: (33) 1 42 67 99 12, Fax: (33) 1 42 27 19 29
E-mail: info@ufinet.org

USITT www.usitt.org
USITT: U.S. Institute for Theater Technology
6443 Ridings Road
Syracuse, NY 13206-1111
Phone: 315/463-6463, Fax: 315/463-6525
E-mail: info@office.usitt.org

VMA www.vma.org.au
Venue Management Association
PO Box 1871
Toowong QLD 4066
AUSTRALIA
Phone: 61-7-3780-4777, Fax: 61-7-3780-4666

Glossary

accounts payable	Liability or debt owed to a supplier for the goods or services purchased in the regular course of business that have not been paid for.
accounts receivable	Money owed by customers or clients to the venue in exchange for goods or services that have been delivered or used but not yet paid for.
advertising campaign	A strategic plan for advertising, promotions, and other means by which tickets for events are advertised and promoted in traditional media (radio, television, and print), online, via direct mail, or by other means of general and/or direct contact.
ancillary event revenues	Venue revenue derived from sources other than rent and expense reimbursements. Typical examples of ancillary event revenues include concessions and catering, merchandise, parking, and decorating.
ancillary services	Services such as food and beverage, merchandising and novelty sales, and parking that provide additional sources of revenue for the venue. Additional services might include equipment rental, computer cafes, freight handling (drayage), ticket-office services, and in-house advertising.
avails (available dates)	Venue dates that are available for booking.
back-of-house (BOH)	The areas of the venue where public access is not permitted, usually behind the stage, production area and/or other restricted areas, such as mechanical rooms, dressing rooms, kitchen, etc. Beyond the physical location, this term can be used in conjunction with building functions in those areas.
balance sheet	Statement of the financial position of an economic unit, disclosing assets, liabilities, and the equity of ownership at a given point in time. The traditional and most common form of the balance sheet is the account form, with assets on the left and liabilities and owners' equity on the right.
banquet event order (BEO)	A document generated by the venue that confirms food/beverage service for a specific meeting or event. It may include additional information regarding set-up and other event requirements.
bar-coded tickets	Tickets bearing a series of vertical bars of varying widths conforming to Universal Product Code, used especially

	for computerized inventory control. Bar-coded tickets are now used during the admission process at most venues.
blowout	Common term for the period of time immediately following an event, when the audience is leaving the venue.
branded products	The use of highly recognizable products that enhance the revenue potential in food and beverage or merchandise.
break-even operation	Generally refers to a public assembly venue that does not require an operating subsidy from its owner to cover annual operating expenses. Debt service, capital improvement reserves, and taxes are typically excluded as operating expenses.
building load capacities	The weight the venue's roof truss system can support. A structural engineer usually determines this amount at the time of the building's design. Building load capacities take into consideration rigging weight limitations, as well as possible roof loads in areas that are affected by heavy snows.
capacity rating	The maximum number of people allowed by code in any given venue or area of the venue.
capital expenditures report	An annual report that shows capital improvements made during the year so that stakeholders can see how their money is being used to upgrade and improve the venue, its vehicles, equipment, and other assets.
capital expenditures	Amounts spent for real estate, equipment, furniture and fixtures, and certain major repairs. These funds are not usually included in operating expenses but are shown as separate expenses in the financial statement.
capital improvements	An upgrade, addition, or replacement of a venue asset. These upgrades may be to the venue, its vehicles, equipment, or other assets with a significant dollar value and an extended life cycle.
capital reserve fund	Monies reserved for long-term capital improvement projects or any other large and anticipated expense that will be incurred in the future of the venue. This fund is set aside to ensure the venue has adequate funding to be able to pay, at least in part, for such improvements.
certificate of insurance	Written verification of types, terms, and amounts of insurance carried by the insured entity.

change order	A written, formal acknowledgement of a change made to a Banquet Event Order (BEO) or other previously confirmed event requirements. The change may increase or decrease event expenses. The term may also refer to a request to change some portion of a construction document.
conversion/changeover	The labor and procedures required to change from one venue set-up to another. This may include changing the stage set-up and position, seating configuration, trade show booth arrangement, housekeeping duties, and sports surface type.
co-promotion	Joint participation in the revenues/expenses and profit/loss from an event. Co-promotions often refer to instances when the venue shares the financial risk and reward with an event promoter.
collateral materials	Materials used to support and reinforce a media advertising campaign for a venue or an event. These materials may include brochures, flyers, and booklets, all of which could be either electronic files or printed copies.
collective bargaining agreement	Written agreement between an employer and a union specifying the terms and conditions of employment for workers covered by the contract, the status of the union, and the procedure for settling disputes arising during the contract term. Also known as a labor agreement or union contract.
commissary	A warehouse or food production area for food, beverage, and/or merchandise. The term is also used to describe a vending room that supplies products to the hawkers.
complimentary tickets	Tickets to an event issued at no charge to the recipient. Complimentary tickets have no monetary value and should reflect a $0 value on the ticket.
concessionaire	A person or business that has been given the right to sell food and beverage or merchandise in the venue, the parameters of which may be outlined in a contract.
confirmed date	A specific date or dates for which an agency, meeting planner, tenant, or promoter has acknowledged that a date or dates, on hold for a specific event will, beyond a reasonable doubt, take place. At this point, a contract is negotiated/issued for this date and is awaiting signatures.

contracted date

A specific date or dates for which the venue and the user have signed a formal agreement to hold an event in a designated area, on usually after a binding consideration (deposit) has been made to the venue.

cost accounting

The method of accounting that emphasizes the determination and the control of cost, particularly the costs of production and the final product. It deals with actual costs to be reported on financial statements. One of the principal functions is to assemble and interpret cost data, both actual and prospective, for the use of management in controlling current operations and in planning for the future.

cost allocation

Division of the cost of goods or services over a number of cost centers, such as the ticket office. The purpose is to identify the cost incurred by each cost center in the production of a given product or service.

cost estimate

A written or verbal estimate provided by an organization or individual that may supply products or services to another organization or individual.

crisis management

The plan and process of responding to an emergency situation and minimizing damage to property or injuries to persons once an emergency or crisis has occurred.

crowd control

Crowd control is a reactive measure employed to control crowds through both human and physical elements.

crowd management

Crowd management is a proactive organizational strategy which guides venue personnel in providing and maintaining the desired event environment.

dark day

A day in which the venue does not host a performance or event.

dayparts

The time segments that divide a radio or TV day for advertising scheduling purposes. These segments generally reflect a station's programming patterns. The most common dayparts are prime time, drive time, daytime, late night, early morning, total day, sign-on/sign-off, prime access, and fringe. There is no universal agreement, however, about the exact times for all these dayparts.

deadwood

Unsold event tickets that remain in inventory.

debt service

Scheduled payments on bonds, loans, notes, or capital lease obligations. These payments include interest, principal reductions, or other payments necessary to reduce the level of debt.

decorator
An individual or company who provides booth and hall decorating services for a trade show and/or its exhibitors, which may include the installation and removal of pipe and drape, carpet, and other exhibit requirements.

drop count
The number of tickets scanned or ticket stubs collected for a single event at the entry points of a venue.

dynamic ticket pricing
A method of pricing tickets as their value changes in response to factors including the expected demand for tickets, day of the week, visiting team popularity, or even predicted weather conditions.

egress
The exiting of people or vehicles from designated areas, which may include seating areas, the venue, parking lots, etc.

elephant door
Oversized door through which vehicles or large pieces of equipment can be brought into the venue without disassembly. The name originated from the need for a door literally large enough for elephants to enter the venue.

event operations
The various units needed to operate the event and venue, including, but not limited to, technical staff, sound and lighting operators, laborers, electricians, changeover crews, and maintenance staff.

event production
The process of providing the services and equipment necessary to properly stage an event.

event timeline
An outline or timeline used to help manage an event that lists dates when important event production details are scheduled to occur in the event management process.

exhibition
An event at which products and services are displayed.

feasibility study
An analysis and evaluation of a proposed project to determine if it is technically feasible, can be completed within the estimated cost, and its degree of profitability.

fiscal year
A one-year accounting period that does not necessarily correspond to a calendar year.

front-of-house (FOH)
The areas of a venue to which the public typically has access. FOH usually includes lobbies, concourses, concession stands, public restrooms, ticket office lobby, and seating areas.

fulfillment cost	Fulfillment cost is what it may cost either the venue or the sponsor to provide the benefits conveyed by the sponsorship. For example, a venue may be asked to provide free tickets to an event for the sponsor's staff or customers. The value of those tickets is a fulfillment cost for the venue.
governing body	Typically refers to the highest authority of a venue's ownership level. Examples include city councils, county commissions, university boards of regents, or boards of directors of private corporations.
gross revenue	Total revenue generated before any expenses or taxes are applied or paid.
group ticket sales	The process of selling blocks of tickets to groups. Group tickets are usually offered at a discount for specific events or performances.
hawkers	Individuals who sell selected concession items in the seating areas and concourses.
hotel room nights	Nights in a hotel reserved for and/or actually used by convention or meeting delegates. One room rented for one night is a hotel night or room night. One room rented for three nights by the same person is three hotel room nights.
incident report	Form (pre-printed or electronic) through which venue personnel provide a description of what occurred during a situation and what steps were taken in response.
incremental budgeting	Budgeting method based on slight changes from the preceding period's budgeted results or actual results. This method is often used when venue management does not intend to spend a great deal of time formulating the budget.
ingress	The influx of people or vehicles into designated areas, which may include parking lots, the venue, seating areas, etc.
jurisdiction	The specific tasks which a union claims its members have exclusive authority to perform.
kill seats	Seats designated as "not for sale" due to obstructed view or to accommodate production requirements.
license application	Form completed by potential venue users demonstrating the necessary financial resources, proper insurance

coverage, prior applicable experience, and ability to produce an event.

line item budget A common budgeting method that puts primary emphasis on objects of expenditure for control purposes, such as salaries, travel, services, and equipment, rather than on efficiency and effectiveness of work programs.

market position Market position refers to the ranking or positioning of a given venue relative to that of competing venues within a designated market.

meet and greet Refers to the opportunity for a fan to meet a performer, team member, or other VIP prior to or after an event. Usually some part of a promotion intended to increase ticket sales or sell a ticket at a higher price.

mission statement Brief statement of the purpose for which an organization was created and its philosophy of operation.

mix location The position of the platform set in the audience area for concerts, speeches, or video presentations on which sound and light control boards are set and operated.

naming rights A form of advertising and marketing whereby a business, organization, or individual purchases the right to name a venue for a specific period of time and on agreed financial terms. The arrangement often includes additional commercial rights and benefits.

net income Income minus expenses or costs for a specified accounting period or for a particular activity.

net operating surplus Revenue that is generated and retained in excess of the total operating expenses of a venue.

obstructed view seats Seats in a public assembly venue from which the stage, performance area, or playing field for an event is partially blocked or hidden from sight. Such seats may provide a view of the stage, performance area, or playing field on video screens. Also referred to as limited view seats.

on-sale date The first date an event is placed on sale to the public.

overhead costs Costs necessary to the production of a product or service that are not directly traceable to the product or service. Usually these costs relate to expenditures that are not an integral part of the finished product or service, such as rent, heat, light, supplies, management, and supervision.

peer group security

Part-time event security personnel who assist in crowd management and enforcement of venue policies and procedures. Generally, peer group security personnel mirror the demographics of the event attendees. May be referred to as "T-shirt" security, as they are often given a T-shirt to wear as a uniform.

per caps

Average per person spending at an event or meeting. Arrived at by dividing gross sales by attendance. Per caps may be calculated for food and beverage or merchandise sales.

personal seat license (PSL)

A buyer purchases the rights to a specific seat(s) for the prime tenant's events and then is required to purchase season tickets to maintain their license. PSLs are often used to raise funds prior to construction of a public assembly venue, thereby reducing the amount of public funding necessary. May also be referred to as preferred seat license or a permanent seat license.

physical plant

Refers to the equipment commonly associated with the heating, ventilation, and air conditioning (HVAC) system, electrical distribution system, plumbing/sewage system, etc., within a public assembly venue.

pipe and drape

Pipe material with fabric draped from it to make up side rails and the back wall of a trade show booth or a temporary sightline barrier.

point-of-sale (POS)

The specific location where a customer makes payment in exchange for goods or services.

pouring rights

The award of exclusive soft-drink pouring rights in return for an annual rights payment to the venue. It is against federal law to award exclusive rights to any beer, wine, and/or spirits provider.

premium seating

The sale of individual "club" seats, the cost of which generally include tickets to all prime tenant events. Generally, all other tickets must be purchased on a right of first refusal basis.

private management

An outside operator who specializes in the management, marketing, and operation of public assembly venues who has been contracted by the venue owner to provide day-to-day management of the venue.

production call

A specified list of required personnel, many of whom may be temporary, that are needed to run equipment or perform duties during a specific venue performance or event. May also be referred to as a show call.

production rider

An addendum to the event contract detailing an event's specific requirements in terms of stage location and size, sound and lighting equipment, mix locations, catering requirements, and other pertinent information. May also be referred to as a performance rider.

profit and loss statement (P&L)

Summary of all revenues and costs associated with calculating the net profit or loss for a venue, department, event, or other business unit within the venue.

promoter

Contracted persons or companies responsible for expenses, production, and promotion of an event.

pyrotechnics

Fireworks, explosions, flashes, smoke, or flames, used as special effects in the entertainment industry.

QR codes

Abbreviation of Quick Response code— the trademark for a type of matrix bar code (or two-dimensional bar code). A user scans QR code and is connected to information about the item to which it is attached. In public assembly venues, QR codes can be used on tickets or marketing materials.

rate card

In media-related activities, a document containing the advertising medium rates for time and space.

rate sheet

A document that lists the hourly pay rate for event-related employees.

request for proposal (RFP)

A document that identifies the needs of the issuing entity and the required capabilities, experience, and projected costs necessary to complete a project.

request for qualification (RFQ)

Document often issued prior to a request for proposal (RFP). The purpose is to ascertain that the respondent is qualified in terms of knowledge, experience, and financial capability to provide specified products or services.

resident company

An organization—symphony orchestra, opera, dance, or theatrical company—for which the venue is their primary performance site.

rigging

General term for the rope and pulley system in the ceiling-mounted grid of a theater or the chain motors and wire cables used in an arena or amphitheater to support sound, lighting, scenery, and other production elements.

rigging grid	A structure or system for hanging sound and lighting equipment, banners, or signage from overhead positions. These grids are subject to the maximum weight rating determined by a structural engineer at the time of construction.
rigging plot plan	A schematic layout of the hanging points in a rigging system.
rigging points	The actual position where cables are attached to the rigging grid or truss. Each rigging point has a weight-bearing capacity. There may be any number of rigging points in a venue, though some may not be in position that can help with an event hanging load.
right-to-work state	State in which joining a union cannot be a condition of employment.
risk assessment	The process of evaluating the severity and frequency of loss associated with a particular activity or event.
risk management	The process of identifying risk and the analysis of the likelihood, frequency, and severity of the risk. The risk management process also includes efforts to reduce or eliminate risk, as well as the transfer, to the extent possible, of the remaining risk.
road crew	Staff traveling with a production from venue to venue and often referred to as roadies.
route an event	Planning the most effective route for an event to minimize drive time and expense for performers and equipment.
run of press (ROP)	Publishing of an advertisement at a time left to the discretion of the publisher. Its placement in a particular location or on a specific page usually requires payment of a premium.
run of schedule (ROS)	Broadcast time of a commercial on a radio or TV left to the discretion of the station. Scheduling its broadcast in a specific time slot or during a particular program usually requires payment of a premium.
runner	Individual familiar with the community who is employed locally by the act or promoter to provide a means of transportation for crew members and serve as a "gofer" for the acquisition of various services and sundry items needed during an event's stay in a venue.

scaling the house	The process of assigning pricing levels to different seating areas within a public assembly venue.
secondary market	The ticket market that exists between fans or customers and brokers of event tickets after they have been purchased from a primary ticket market. In some instances, the venues or teams may facilitate the secondary resale market through an authorized broker.
self-sustaining	A public assembly venue that does not require an operating subsidy from its owner to cover annual operating expenses.
settlement sheet	A document that provides a detailed itemization of an event's revenues and expenses, which may include ticket sales, associated production expenses, building rent, ticket office expenses, and other event-related revenues and expenses. The settlement sheet outlines the distribution of monies to the promoter and venue.
show call	A specified list of required personnel, many of whom may be temporary, who are needed to run equipment or perform duties during the actual performance. May also be referred to as a production call.
stagehands	Generic term for backstage production personnel. These personnel are often secured through a local union.
subsidized operation	A venue that has operating expenses greater than the revenue it can generate and which, therefore, requires annual financial assistance (subsidy) from the owner.
tax increment financing districts (TIF)	An area of businesses upon which are levied an additional tax because they benefit directly from the activities of the venue. A TIF may also be used as part of an economic development strategy.
tentative date	A date or group of dates held for the use by an agency, meeting planner, tenant, or promoter on a tentative basis. A held date may have an expiration day, after which the reservation is retracted by the venue.
ticket brokers	An individual or agency who attempts to profit from the sale of event tickets and is generally conducting business from a brick and mortar store or via a website. Ticket brokers often impose service fees to generate additional revenue. These activities are legal in most states.

ticket manifest

A document outlining all tickets potentially available for a specific event or series of events, which may include a seating map.

ticket office advance

Funds advanced to an event promoter from revenue derived from event ticket sales and paid in advance of the event performance or prior to the conclusion of the event.

ticket office statement

An itemized accounting of tickets distributed (sold or complimentary), or unsold and the corresponding monies collected for a specific event.

ticket scalper

An individual who attempts to profit from the sale of previously purchased event tickets, generally conducting business outside the venue prior to an event. This may be illegal in some localities.

trade show

Exposition held for members of a common or related industry, which may not be open to the general public.

trade tickets

Event tickets, which are often complimentary, offered by an event promoter to a vendor or other partner in exchange for event-related goods or services, such as advertising or equipment.

trades

Union workers who provide a specific service to a venue or touring event. They may be electricians, plumbers, carpenters, HVAC mechanics or painters, among other specialties.

transient occupancy tax (TOT)

An additional tax on hotel and motel rooms. Since most occupants of these rooms are out-of-town guests, local citizens rarely contribute to this taxing method. These revenues are usually for the purpose of paying down debt on the venue or providing operating revenues for the venue or marketing efforts.

union shop

A venue that has a contract with a union that states that it may hire any person without regard to union membership, providing that said employee must then join the union within a specified period of time and pay dues.

vomitory

The entrance or exit passages to the seating area in a venue.

walk-up

The guests who purchase their tickets at the venue just prior to the event.

will-call Designated location where tickets reserved by name can be picked up prior to the event. Customers generally must provide proper identification and may have to pay for the tickets if they have not have been paid for in advance.

yellow card An actual yellow piece of card stock upon which the union steward notifies a venue of the crew requirements for that production.

yellow card show Show traveling under the jurisdiction of a contract with IATSE (International Alliance of Theatrical Stage Employees),which sends the yellow card to each venue.

Zamboni Brand name of a vehicle used for preparing or maintaining ice surfaces. Often used generically.

References

Alcohol and Tobacco Tax and Trade Bureau (TTB), U.S. Department of Treasury (2014). *Federal Alcohol Administration Act.* Retrieved from: http://www.ttb.gov/trade_practices/federal_admin_act.shtml

American Heart Association (2013). *Cardiac Arrest Statistics.* Retrieved from http://www.heart.org/HEARTORG/General/Cardiac-Arrest-Statistics_UCM_448311_Article.jsp

Anonymous. (1956, January 20,). World's biggest dome. *Look,* 37.

Beck, B. (2001). *Build it and the crowds will come.* Encino, CA: Cherbo Publishing Group, Inc.

Bigelow, C. (2013). *Foodservice management.* IAVM monograph. Coppell, TX.

Bigelow, C. (2014). Personal communication/interview.

Boone, L. E. & Kurtz, D. L. (2002). *Contemporary marketing.* Orlando, FL: Harcourt, Inc.

Bragg, S. M. (2012). *GAAP: Interpretation and application of generally accepted accounting principles.* Hoboken, NJ: John Wiley & Sons, Inc.

Camp, S. (1990). Managing public facilities by public authority. *Public Management Magazine,* Washington, DC. International City Management Association.

Chelladurai, P. & Chang, K. (2000). Targets and standards of quality in sport services. *Sport Management Review,* 3, 1-22.

Coarelli, F., Gregori, G. L., Lombardi, L., Orlandi, S., Rea, R., & Vismara, C. (2001). *The Colosseum* (M. Becker, Trans.). Milan, Italy: J. Paul Getty Trust (Original work published 2000).

Doupnik, T., & Perera, H. (2009). *International accounting, 5th edition.* New York, NY: McGraw-Hill Irwin.

Greenwell, T. C., Fink, J. S., & Pastore, D. L. (2002). Assessing the influence of the physical sports facility on customer satisfaction within the context of the service experience. *Sport Management Review,* 5, 129-148.

Hales, J. A. (2011). *Accounting and financial management in the hospitality industry.* New York, NY: Prentice Hall.

Hall, S., Marciani, L., & Cooper, W. (2008). Sport venue security: Planning and preparedness for terrorist-related incidents. *The SMART Journal,* 4(1).

IAVM (2006). *2006 IAVM Industry Profile Survey.* Coppell, TX: International Association of Venue Managers.

IAVM (2009). *IAVM Academy for Venue Safety & Security*. Coppell, TX: International Association of Venue Managers.

IAVM (2010). IAVM Glossary. Coppell, TX: International Association of Venue Managers.

Jeter, P. (2013). Personal communication/interview.

Kieso, D. E., Weygandt, J. J., & Warfield, T. D. (2012). *Intermediate accounting, 14th edition*. New York, NY: John Wiley & Sons, Inc.

Kimes, S. E. (1989). The basics of yield management. *Cornell Hotel and Restaurant Administration Quarterly, 30(3)*, 14-19.

Koolbeck (2013). *Marketing, advertising, and public relations*. IAVM Monograph. Coppell, TX: International Association of Venue Managers.

Magruder, D. (2013). *Financial management* I. IAVM Monograph. Coppell, TX: International Association of Venue Managers.

Mahoney, K. L. & Pastore, D. L. (2014). Evaluating the work experience for the paid, part-time event staff at a public assembly facility: A tool to assist facility managers. *International Journal of Sport Management*, 15(4), 1-29.

Marion, M. (2013). *Booking and scheduling*. IAVM Monograph. Coppell, TX: International Association of Venue Managers.

National Travel Association (2003). *A guide to developing crisis management plans*. NTA Market Development Council: Washington, DC.

PCI Compliance Guide (2014). PCI FAQs. Retrieved from http://www.pcicomplianceguide.org/pci-faqs-2/#1

Peters, S. (2013). Personal communication/interview.

Peterson, D. C. (2001). *Developing sports, convention and performing arts centers, Third Edition*. Washington, DC: Urban Land Institute.

Public Relations Society of America (2013). What is public relations? PRSA's widely accepted definition. Retrieved from http://www.prsa.org/aboutprsa/publicrelationsdefined/#.UjyKUWRgbhI

Russo, F. E. Jr. (1990). The case for private management. *Public Management Magazine*. Washington, DC: International City Management Association.

Russo, F. E., Jr. (2008). Event management: Tools of the trade. In G. Lewis and H. Appenzeller (Eds.), *Successful Sport Management*. (191-202). Durham, NC: Carolina Academic Press.

Shank, M. D. (2009). Sports marketing: *A strategic perspective (4ᵗʰ ed.).* Upper Saddle River, NJ: Prentice Hall.

Sharp, L. A., Moorman, A. M., & Claussen, C. L. (2007). *Sport law: A managerial approach.* Scottsdale, AZ: Holcomb Hathaway.

Siehl, J. (2013). *Crowd management.* IAVM Monograph. Coppell, TX: International Association of Venue Managers.

Steinbach, P. (2008, August). Concessions contracts capitalizing on consumers' brand loyalty. *Athletic Business.* Retrieved from http://www.athleticbusiness.com/articles/article.aspx?articleid=1838&zoneid=37

Index

Note:
> Page numbers in *italics* refer to photographs.

N

O